CROSSCURRENTS

CROSSCURRENTS

Transatlantic Perspectives
on Early Modern Hispanic Drama

Edited by
Mindy Badía and
Bonnie L. Gasior

Lewisburg
Bucknell University Press

Associated University Presses
2010 Eastpark Boulevard
Cranbury, NJ 08512

The paper used in this publication meets the requirements of the American National Standard for Permanence of Paper for Printed Library Materials Z39.48-1984.

Library of Congress Cataloging-in-Publication Data

Crosscurrents : transatlantic perspectives on early modern Hispanic drama / edited by Mindy Badía and Bonnie L. Gasior.
    p. cm.
  Includes bibliographical reference and index.
  ISBN 0-8387-5622-0 (alk. paper)
  1. Spanish American drama—To 1800—History and criticism. I. Badía, Mindy, 1968- II. Gasior, Bonnie L., 1971- III. Title.

  PQ7082.D7C76 2006
  862.009'98—dc22

                         2005045681

This book is dedicated to Antonio (meeting you has been my favorite Transatlantic encounter) and to my girls, Emma and Gabriela.
—Mindy E. Badía

This book is dedicated to my best friend, James Gustafson:
"So . . . that's just how I feel . . ."
—Bonnie L. Gasior

Contents

Acknowledgments

THE IDEA FOR THIS BOOK WAS CONCEIVED OVER A DINNER IN MEXICO CITY in 2002. The book itself then developed as an outgrowth of two sessions held at the annual conference of the Association for Hispanic Classical Theater (AHCT) in El Paso, Texas, which took place in March 2003. The editors gratefully acknowledge the support and encouragement received from the AHCT, especially Don Larson, the conference coordinator. We also thank Ben Everhart, our research assistant, for his careful attention to detail and for his patience.

We would like to acknowledge the generous support of our respective universities, Indiana University Southeast and California State University, Long Beach for providing a Summer Faculty Fellowship and money from the Chancellor's Fund (IUS) and a Scholarly and Creative Activities award from the College of Liberal Arts (CSULB) to fund this project. The editors would also like to thank each other ("Y.A.H."), as well as the book's contributors, for their perseverance despite intranational as well as international limitations.

Finally, we extend a warm handshake to the staff at Bucknell University Press and Associated University Presses for making the entire editing process a genuine pleasure, and more importantly, a valuable learning experience. Their help and advice were crucial, especially during the last few months of revisions.

CROSSCURRENTS

Transatlantic Changes and Exchanges: The Permeability of Culture, Identity, and Discourse in Early Modern Hispanic Drama

Mindy E. Badía and Bonnie L. Gasior

THE TERM "CROSSCURRENTS" SEEMS ESPECIALLY FITTING FOR A VOLUME OF essays that explores the cultural exchanges that resulted from the encounter between Spain and the New World. The nautical metaphor alludes to the actual crossing of ships that occurred during the discovery, conquest, and colonization of the Americas by the Spanish as it emphasizes the changes that occurred at these cultural intersections. Mary Louise Pratt describes such places as "contact zones," which she defines as "social spaces where disparate cultures meet, clash, and grapple with each other, often in highly asymmetrical relations of domination and subordination" (*Imperial Eyes,* 4). The reference to water in our title acknowledges and underlines both the force of these currents and, paradoxically, their lack of rigidity. Indeed, our conception of this project contests the notion of cultural fixity by demonstrating that contact between the two continents did not produce a stable cultural product, but rather initiated a process of exchange that continues to this day. "Crosscurrents," as it refers to dissent, underscores the importance of counter-hegemonic discursive tendencies that often surface, implicitly and explicitly, in Hispanic drama of the Early Modern period. The dramatic texts explored in this volume were born of the paradoxical dynamic of both conflict and communion, of *mestizaje* and marked opposition that characterizes sixteenth- and seventeenth-century Hispanic culture. Perhaps for this reason, the essays problematize the polarization of such notions as political/aesthetic, economic/artistic, and text/spectacle by recognizing the complexity of cultural exchange and the scholarly value of balancing inquiry into both text and context.

The book's content reflects this emphasis on such "crossings." We include essays that traverse disciplinary boundaries, featuring contributions from Latin Americanists, Peninsularists, and transatlantic specialists. These contributions are informed by traditional text-centered criticism, as well as by approaches that emphasize performance. Additionally, the essays incorporate recent scholarship from literary studies and other diverse fields, such as anthropology and history. Our title, "Crosscurrents," refers both to this intersection of perspectives and to the back-and-forth trajectory of cultural shifts. What unites these disparate critical angles is an emphasis on the way drama describes and defines the New World and, concomitantly, how contact with the Americas also (re)shaped peninsular Spanish society.

In our understanding of the subject as an *entity in process* (rather than a fixed, stable product), it is important to recognize that the designations on which the dichotomy "Europe/America" rests are fluid, unstable concepts.[1] In the case of Spain, for example, the social realities of the fifteenth and sixteenth centuries belie the notion of a homogenous national identity. Before the merger of Castile and Aragón, what is now Spain existed only as a loose conglomerate of kingdoms with appreciable cultural, religious, geographical, and linguistic differences. Even after the marriage of Fernando and Isabel in 1469, an event that many cite as the birth of the Spanish nation, the Iberian Peninsula remained divided along historically (and geographically) created borders.[2] The Reconquest of Granada in 1492 brought religious unity to the Peninsula, at least officially, but also caused bitter social strife between old and new Christians.[3]

Perhaps for these reasons, preoccupation with inclusion and exclusion dominated Spanish intellectual, religious, and political activities in the sixteenth and seventeenth centuries. As a country, Spain zealously sought both to guard its Iberian borders and to expand them abroad. The Inquisition and the Counter-Reformation attempted to define Spanish culture and nation upon religious or racial terms, granting status to those of "pure" [Christian] blood and relegating others to the margins of society.[4] For slightly more than one hundred years, from 1580–1688, Portugal and Spain were united under a singular crown, erasing the border between the two countries and allowing for complete peninsular unity, at least geographically.[5] As time went on, however, shifting, disappearing, and reappearing topographical (not to mention racial) borders continued to call into question the idea of nationhood and one's relationship to it, making segregation and unification slippery political and social concepts.

Coinciding with Fernando and Isabel's unification/expulsion undertaking, Christopher Columbus's initial, intrepid voyage proved a momentous and defining moment in history for both sides of the Atlantic.[6] Little did Columbus know the resonating effects his discovery would have:[7] "The connection between the Old and New Worlds, which for more than ten millennia had been no more than a tenuous thing of Viking voyages, drifting fishermen, and shadowy contacts via Polynesia, became on the twelfth day of October 1492 a bond as significant as the Bering land bridge had once been. The two worlds, which God had cast asunder, were reunited, and the two worlds, which were so very different, began on that day to become alike" (Crosby, *Columbian Exchange,* 3). Spanish discovery, conquest, and colonization of *terra incognita* questioned old notions of geography, social hierarchy, and the definition of what it meant to be a rational human being.[8] As a result, this sequence of events "produced numerous problems for intellectuals to ponder as well as exchanges between the conquering and vanquished cultures" (Burkholder, *Colonial Latin America,* 60).

Mapping the geographical, political, and human relationships forged during this time of discovery and uncertainty occupies center stage in Spanish literature from the Early Modern period. Many literary texts display this process of self-evaluation (and self-creation) by being paradoxically affirming and subversive of certain social institutions. The development of the picaresque and novels such as *Don Quijote* emphasizes an attempt to transcend the limits of existing social structures and literary genres and to inform readers—sometimes explicitly— of this transcendence. Spanish theater dramatizes a similar testing of literary and cultural boundaries, offering spectators an occasional glimpse, if only briefly, of what the world might look like if the boundaries of gender or class, for example, were erased or expanded. As evidence, one need only remember stock characters such as the *gracioso,* who often proved himself wiser than his master, such as Lope's Mengo in *Fuenteovejuna* ; or the *mujer varonil* (manly woman) or *mujer vestida de hombre* (woman dressed as a man), at times a "better man," in everything from "his" moral codes to physical appearance, than her male counterpart(s) (Ana Caro's Leonor in *Valor, agravio y mujer* comes to mind).[9] Additionally, castigated wives like Mencía from *El médico de su honra* (*The Physician of His Honor*) encourage audiences to cast a critical eye upon the so-called honor code even as they perpetuate certain myths about "appropriate" social roles for men and women.

It is admittedly difficult to undertake a transatlantic study of sixteenth- and seventeenth-century Spanish and Latin American literature without referring to the myriad and sometimes devastating effects of Spanish imperialism in the New World. This holds particularly true of drama from the Early Modern period for two reasons. The first reason is simple happenstance. The historical coincidence of the apogee of Spanish drama and the conquest and colonization of the New World necessarily links the political and the literary in an ongoing, provocative dialogue related to what Bhabha refers to as "the performativity of language" (*Nation and Narration,* 3). To understand six- teenth- and seventeenth-century Spanish theater, it is necessary to understand the cultural context in which it developed, and chief among the many historic events that make up this cultural context is the encounter between Spain and the continent and peoples of the Americas. The second, more deliberate reason is the purposeful use of drama by the Spaniards in the colonial enter- prise, for "all colonial writing had hegemonic and propagandistic intentions" (Jara and Spadaccini, *1492/1992,* 15), particularly if we expand definitions of drama to include religious ritual and political ceremony. Indeed, the connec- tions between spectacle and politics, such as ceremonies for visiting digni- taries, public executions, proclamations, and, of course, theater, reinforced rigid colonial hierarchies. Along with censorship, problems of isolation and a largely illiterate audience (about 10 percent of the population could read and write in Spanish) meant that texts written in Spanish America, their contents rigidly controlled by Spain, enjoyed only limited circulation and readership. Additionally, the use of drama in evangelization efforts, especially by Spanish Jesuit and Franciscan missionaries, brought theater and religion together as a powerful tool of (and justification for) Spanish imperialism.[10]

In spite of drama's function as an arm of empire, one cannot ignore its use as a tool for resistance as well. Statistics such as literacy rates in colonial Latin America, which are often cited in support of the position that Latin American colonial letters were completely dominated by Spain, do not account for Native American literary traditions, both oral and nonverbal graphic, and the widespread influence of performative genres such as music, dance, and drama that may have escaped or circumvented the control mechanisms of imperial power. As the essays by Bradley Nelson and Michael Horswell illustrate, even Sor Juana Inés de la Cruz, who wrote within the boundaries of peninsular *Co- media* convention in many respects, problematizes the very discursive prac- tices that undergird her textual authority.

An important theoretical influence on this volume is postcolonial studies. Postcolonial theoretical perspectives typically emphasize the ways in which nations have attempted to come to terms with their former status as colonies of an imperial power. In work by theorists such as Homi Bhabha, Edward Said and, specific to hispanism, Walter Mignolo, critics examine the ways literature functions to articulate (and disarticulate) hegemonic discursive practices. Though transatlantic scholarship often incorporates postcolonial theories, they do not necessarily insist on a dichotomy of imperial power/

colony. In fact, much of the criticism in the transatlantic field is within the context of the aesthetic relationship between England and the United States and is more comparative than political.[11] This volume attempts to bridge the gap between comparative analyses and postcolonial approaches. While the former have historically ignored the political implications of Western-centered notions of intrinsic literary value and, at least implicitly, have advocated reading "the classics" using methodologies that separate the literary text from its cultural context, the latter, by insisting on Latin America's colonial relationship to Spain as the defining feature of cultural activity in the Americas, leaves little space for exploring New World colonial writers in ways that go beyond issues of political and artistic hegemony. By emphasizing the bidirectional flow of cultural exchange, this volume illustrates what Julio Ortega views as a major contribution of transatlantic studies in the context of the Hispanic world. In the critic's words, transnational approaches have the potential to liberate scholarship "from the disciplinary genealogy and the liberal *parti pris* that condemns the subject to the role of victim—colonial, sexual, imperial, ideological" ("Towards a Map," 10). Though we do not underestimate or downplay the "common negative denominator" (Zavala, "Colonial Subject," 335) ascribed to the colonial other, this collection of scholarship aims to put aside for a moment the constructed binaries and instead focus on the mutuality of the encounter, those points of intersection where the lines between colonizer and colonized are blurred and meaning is negotiated and engendered.

One common, consistent feature of both transatlantic and postcolonial studies is the notion of the discursively constructed reality and, specifically, the idea that America was an "invention" (as Edmundo O'Gorman's well-known thesis asserts). Theorists such as Jacques Lacan and Michel Foucault have helped Hispanists refine their understanding of the notion of a discursively created reality within the context of colonial and postcolonial subjectivities. Lacan's psychoanalytical approach articulates the notion of a linguistically constructed subject based on the principle of lack (or absence), which in the sphere of theater generates what Barbara Freedman terms "an awareness of blindness" (*Staging the Gaze*, 37). Foucault takes the idea of the self as a linguistic construct and places it in a social setting, arguing that reality is created on the basis of power relationships upon which we base notions ("technologies," in Foucault's words) of ourselves. In the context of transatlantic scholarship, the collection of essays *Virtual Americas* makes a similar assertion, explaining that "American Literature" (and by this term the authors mean Anglo-American), in a comparative approach, only exists through its relationship to British literature (something which it is not). What is understood as "American" assert the authors, is only *virtually* American, since its essence is always, necessarily conceived in relation to what is English, a discursively constructed concept as well (Giles, *Virtual Americas,* 1–2). In our book, we acknowledge the idea that the New World was, of course, an "invention." However, just as the New World "other" was discursively created, this "reality of ideas" was one foundation on which Spaniards, by means of contrast, formed notions of themselves, as Bhabha explains: "The 'other' is never outside of beyond us; it emerges forcefully, within cultural discourse, when we *think* we speak most intimately and indigenously 'between ourselves'" ("Mimicry and Man," 4). In this volume, for example, Yolanda Gamboa looks at the way New World chocolate played a role in the construction of identity, particularly gender and class identity, in peninsular Spain and Julio Vélez-Sainz examines the effects of New World capital on the Spanish class system as they are dramatized in literature of the period.

Our approach represents a unique contribution to *Comedia* studies for several reasons. First, we devote the entire book to drama, and we define the term broadly enough to include both traditional dramatic texts and other, less-studied theatrical forms (such as Sor Juana's *Neptuno alegórico* and the *loa* and *sarao* of *Los empeños de una casa*). In our research we have found no book-length study that looks exclusively at Early Modern Hispanic drama from a transatlantic perspective. Because of drama's importance in the colonial project, we believe that theater is a uniquely provocative object of inquiry for transatlantic studies, especially given the obvious relationship between drama and the concept of culture as performative.

Second, we include texts written by both New World and Old World authors, and we feature contributions by both Latin Americanists and Peninsularists. In this fashion, the content of the volume matches our definition of "cross-currents" as an intersection of flowing, diverse ideas. Because Hispanic transatlantic criticism has typically been understood, de facto, as postcolonial studies, few Peninsularists have looked at Spanish drama from this perspective.[12] Additionally, the volume taken as a whole goes beyond traditional postcolonial approaches (which defined colonial Latin American authors in terms of their relationship to Spain) to look at broader issues of discursive power and identity formation in general.

Third, our study includes both canonical and noncanonical texts. For example, though much of what Sor Juana wrote is certainly well-studied, her *Neptuno,* as well as Sigüenza y Góngora's *Teatro de virtudes políticas,* have been less frequently examined. By including essays about these texts, we affirm the relatively recent interest in *géneros menores* within the field of Early Modern Hispanic theater studies and underscore the relationship between the performative and the political (since both Sor Juana's and Sigüenza's pieces were written, ostensibly, to affirm the power of the Spanish monarchs and the representatives of these monarchs in the New World).[13] Finally, we include in the volume analyses of texts that deal explicitly with the European/American encounter (as we see in Gamboa's and Christopher Gascón's essays on *Santa Rosa del Perú* and Eric Kartchner's study of *El rufián dichoso*) along with texts whose implicit references to the New World are skillfully deduced by critics (for example, Vicente Pérez de León's reading of *El viejo celoso*). In doing so, we hope to illustrate the ways authors may have "flowed" with the transatlantic current, even if the texts bear no specific reference to America.

The book is subdivided into four categories, each analyzing a different aspect of the ways Early Modern Spanish and New World playwrights dramatized the literary, social, political, and economic (ex)changes between Spain and the Americas. The first section, *Spectacle, Subversion and Hegemony*, explores the relationship between dramatic and ritual performance and politics. Bradley J. Nelson examines two dramatic pieces, Sor Juana Inés de la Cruz's *Neptuno alegórico* and Sigüenza y Góngora's *Teatro de virtudes políticas*, as examples of the unique contingencies of Baroque and neo-Baroque performative culture. Nelson challenges historicist readings by colonial and postcolonial scholars who view such authors as representative of a *criollo* voice linked to an emerging Latin American national identity. Creating a dialogue between Catherine Bell and Slavoj Žižek, Nelson concludes that whereas Sigüenza's *Teatro* illustrates Bell's notion of "redemptive hegemony," a process involving the (re)appropriation of hegemonic discursive practices in order usurp imperial power, Sor Juana's *Neptuno* deconstructs the very notion of a stable discursive authority.

The second section, *Incorporating America: Commodification and Colonization*, explores the interplay of economics and imperialism manifested in plays by Cervantes and Tirso de Molina. Yolanda Gamboa explores the transatlantic encounter through a study of material culture, examining the history of chocolate in Europe, and especially its consumption in Spain. Gamboa argues that the drink becomes a means for Spanish aristocracy, which had become somewhat displaced due to the social and economic changes that resulted from the encounter between Europe and America, to reaffirm its identity by displaying the wealth and status necessary to consume the expensive concoction. She then moves to an analysis of the references to chocolate in Tirso's *Amazonas en las Indias* and *La lealtad contra la envidia* and

Moreto and Lanini y Sagredo's *Santa Rosa del Perú*. Gamboa concludes that in Tirso's plays, chocolate represents the exoticized Other (Amerindian) and in Moreto's, it is more explicitly associated with women. In both cases, chocolate symbolizes the consumption of the Other implicit in fashioning the Self.

The second study of this section belongs to Julio Vélez-Sainz, who analyzes the interplay between material wealth, greed, and desire that is associated with New World enterprises and its transfer and subsequent implications in Old World society in Tirso de Molina's *La villana de Vallecas*. Velez-Sainz uses Quevedo's poem/protagonist Don Dinero in order to demonstrate his reading that Tirso focuses on the economy of the play in an attempt to criticize New World exploitation and the attitudes born from the superfluous accumulation of riches, including those that result in the commodification of women. The playwright's protagonist, who is an *indiano* (New World entrepreneurs intrinsically linked to the quest for money), embodies the wealth extracted from the New World which then migrated to and circulated in Spain. Tirso's concern with economic issues on both sides of the Atlantic in the seventeenth century reveals how the incessant exchange of money, riches, gems, and precious metals work in materialistic fashion to shape the Renaissance.

Vicente Pérez de León studies Cervantes's *entremés El viejo celoso* as a metaphorical critique of the economic changes brought about as a result of New World commerce. Playing with the linguistic similarity of *celo* (zeal, a characteristic often used to describe Spaniards who went to America) and *celos* (jealousy, the defining feature of the protagonist of *El viejo celoso*), Pérez de León explores the tensions between the New World and the Old World implicitly dramatized in the text through the marriage of Cañizares, an old man, and Lorenza, his young bride. The critic draws parallels between the interlude's plot and characters and the economic situation of Spain in the sixteenth and seventeenth centuries, positing that the relationship between Cañizares and his wife, in which the man's advanced age and extreme jealousy stifles the woman's sexual energy and youthful vigor, symbolically represents an impossible attempt to control the free flow of capital and economic exchange.

Section Three, *Hybridity and Representation*, examines the ambiguous representation of the New World in plays by Sor Juana and Moreto. Michael J. Horswell considers Sor Juana Ines de la Cruz's Baroque "fiesta" *Los empeños de una casa* in the context of postcolonial theories of colonial mimicry and hybridity. He argues that Castaño, the *gracioso*, articulates a new, Creole subjectivity that emphasizes gender, racial, and cultural *mestizaje*. By capitalizing on certain comedia conventions and including subtle and overt references to America, Sor Juana's creation contests the hegemonic power of peninsular

Spain and, paradoxically, works within the systems that perpetuate said power.

Christopher Gascón looks at the transatlantic encounter through an examination of the representation of American "otherness" in Moreto and Lanini y Sagredo's *Santa Rosa del Perú*. Gascón argues that the text represents alterity in three distinct ways. In *Santa Rosa*, asserts the critic, America is usually either represented through "synecdochal exoticism," in that superficial cultural markers are taken to represent the entire civilization, or is rendered as a mirror image of peninsular Spain. Occasionally, however, a hybrid image, one closer to a more authentic Latin American reality, does emerge. Gascón notes this third mode of representation in a scene in which Rosa drinks chocolate and in which the magical, ceremonial properties attributed to the beverage by some Amerindian groups take effect. The critic also cites in the presentation of Rosa and her father Gaspar as examples of an American consciousness, especially in Rosa's rejection of her suitor Don Juan, which could represent Latin American resistance to Spanish control.

The final section, *Morality Plays*, looks at the way the New World is represented as a space in which moral truths are revealed and positive transformation occurs. From this perspective, Eric Kartchner analyzes the role of America in Cervantes's *El rufián dichoso*, in which the protagonist, the delinquent Lugo, retreats to Mexico in the third act of the play. There, Lugo becomes the devout Fray Cruz and is beatified. Kartchner's reading takes into account references to the New World in other Cervantine texts. He asserts, contrary to Glen F. Dille's reading, that Cervantes was, indeed, interested in America and that, based on a careful reading of *El rufián*, may well have viewed the New World as a space in which the decadence of Spanish society could be positively transformed. This transformation occurs as part of a subtle subversive thread in the play, a feature that, as Kartchner points out, appears in many of Cervantes's narrative and dramatic texts.

Taken as a whole, the essays in this volume represent a preliminary step in exploring Hispanic drama of the Early Modern period, mindful of the fact that theater on both sides of the Atlantic was "stimulated by the abundance and wonder of the Americas, and cannot be understood without the gold, silver, chocolate, pineapple, birds, colors and flavors of the laboratory of the New World" (Ortega, "Towards a Map," 9). Our volume successfully encompasses and reflects critically relevant, actual issues of memory, identity, ceremony, and power in an ebb and flow effect from shore to shore, and demonstrates how both the New and Old Worlds were performed, imagined, codified, and allegorized as they were empirically understood.

NOTES

1. Homi Bhabha alludes to the dynamics of this process: "The nation's 'coming into being' as a system of cultural signification, as the representation of social life rather than the discipline of social parity, emphasizes this instability of knowledge" (*Nation and Narration,* 2). Bhabha also uses the term "Janus-faced discourse" (3), a term highly appropriate for our study of theater, which relates to the idea of the construing meaning as *in medias res.*

2. As Ernest Reden explains, the notion of "nation" is a relatively new concept, marked by "an historical result brought about by a series of convergent facts. Sometimes unity has been effected by a dynasty . . . sometimes it has been brought about by the direct will of provinces . . . sometimes it has been the work of a general consciousness" ("What Is a Nation?" 12).

3. Iris M. Zavala points out that *conversos,* like their American counterparts who are marginalized because of their race, can be termed "colonial subjects" ("Represent the Colonial Subject," 328) and as such add fuel to the fire of Spanish imperialism.

4. Reden succinctly sums up why this endeavor, as a result, failed: "Man is a slave neither of his race nor his language, nor of his religion, nor of the course of rivers nor of the direction taken by mountain chains. A large aggregate of men, healthy in mind and warm in heart, creates the kind of moral conscience which we call a nation" ("What Is a Nation?" 20).

5. The irony of this statement is exemplified in the behavior of both Columbus and the Sovereigns. Upon discovering what he thought was Cipango, Columbus becomes tight-lipped about the landmass's coordinates in order "to prevent his own crewmen and subsequent mariners (especially Portuguese) from following his trail to treasure" (Sale, *Conquest of Paradise,* 67). Likewise, when the Santangel letter reaches Fernando and Isabel's hands, notifying them of Columbus's news, they made sure to keep quiet. According to Sale, "they were afraid it might fall within Portugal's sphere of influence" (186).

6. Sale lists four main outcomes of the discovery: the expansion of the European subcontinent; the accumulation of wealth and power; the vast redistribution of life forms; and human achievement in general (ibid., 4). Sale irrefutably highlights this last outcome as the most salient; it is also the one that most concerns this project. We use Columbus here strictly as a starting point in order to identify, trace, and develop the transatlantic connection irreversibly established when the *Pinta* makes landfall in Guanajaní.

7. We are careful to point out that the term "discovery" as a misnomer: "It wasn't so much that Europe discovered America as that it incorporated it and made it part of its own special, long-held and recently ratified, view of nature" (ibid., 75).

8. Sale comments, "The task of achieving this triumph of European rationalism was immense, and it took a whole range of disparate talents—humanist, artisans, painters, surgeons, alchemist—and decades before it was ascendant, centuries before it was commonplace. For there were age-old habits of thought to dispel, fundamentally different modes of perception to supplant" (ibid., 40).

9. Monica Leoni's *Outside, Inside, Aside* is a marvelous study that moves the gracioso from the margin to the center within comedia studies.

10. Linda A. Curcio-Nagy observes that religious celebrations, pageants, and theater pieces—particularly Corpus Christi festivals—were considered such an important means of "symbolically reinforcing the status quo" in colonial Mexico City that by 1618, the cost of Corpus Christi alone accounted for 21 percent of the city's disposable income ("Giants and Gypsys," 3). Additionally, writing on the role of spectacle in colonial and postcolonial

Mexico, the editors of *Rituals of Rule, Rituals of Resistance* observe that public rituals "afford elites an opportunity to reiterate. . . the moral values on which their authority rests." (Beezley et al., xiii)

11. Though comparative approaches are not necessarily apolitical, there has existed, particularly in the field of Latin American studies, a perceived dichotomy between the "traditionalist" or "Eurocentric" emphasis of comparative literature and the politically aware, counter-hegemonic stance of Latin American literary and cultural studies. (See, for example, McClellan, "Comparative Literature.")

12. Ortega laments the fact that many specialists in the Spanish baroque are completely unaware of its American origins. In our own research, we discovered that with the exception of an occasional essay on plays that deal directly with the conquest of the New World (see, for example, essays by Thomas Case and Robert Shannon in Mujica et al., *Looking at the Comedia in the Year of the Quincentennial*) no book-length studies exist that look at peninsular drama from this critical angle.

13. For a detailed study of the *género menor,* see Luciano García-Lorenzo's *El teatro menor en España a partir del siglo XVI.*

WORKS CITED

Arias, Santa, and Mariselle Melendez. *Mapping Colonial Spanish America: Places And Commonplaces of Identity, Culture and Experience.* Lewisburg, Pa.: Bucknell UP, 2002.

Beezley, William, Cheryl English Martin, and William E. French, eds. *Rituals of Rule, Rituals of Resistance: Public Celebrations and Popular Culture in Mexico.* Wilmington, Del.: Scholarly Resources, 1994.

Bhabha, Homi. "Of Mimicry and Man: The Ambivalence of Colonial Discourse," *ScreenOn* 28 (Spring 1984): 360–67.

———. *Nation and Narration.* London: Routledge, 1990.

———. "Signs Taken for Wonders: Questions of Ambivalence and Authority under a Tree Outside Delhi, May 1817." In *Race," Writing and Difference,* edited by Henry Louis Gates, Jr. (Chicago: University of Chicago Press, 1986), 29–35.

Burkholder, Mark A., and Lyman L. Johnson. *Colonial Latin America.* Oxford: Oxford University Press, 1991.

Case, Thomas. "El indio y el moro en las comedias de Lope de Vega." In *Looking at the "Comedia" in the Year of the Quincentennial,* edited by Mujica et. al., 13–21. Lanham, Md.: University Press of America, 1993.

Crosby, Alfred W. The *Columbian Exchange: Biological and Cultural Consequences of 1492.* Westport, Conn.: Greenwood, 1972.

Curcio-Nagy, Linda A. "Giants and Gypsies: Corpus Christi in Colonial Mexico City." In *Rituals of Rule, Rituals of Resistance: Public Celebrations and Popular Culture in Mexico,* edited by William H. Beezley, Cheryl English Martin, and William E. French, 1–26. Wilmington, Del.: Scholarly Resources, 1994.

Foucault, Michel. *Technologies of the Self: A Seminar with Michel Foucault.* Edited by H. Gulinan and P. H. Hutton. Amherst: University of Massachusetts Press, 1988.

Freedman, Barbara. *Staging the Gaze: Postmodernism, Psychoanalysis, and Shakespearean Comedy.* Ithaca, N.Y.: Cornell University Press, 1991.

García-Lorenzo, Luciano. *El teatro menor en España a partir del siglo XVI.* Madrid: Consejo Superior de Invetstigaciones Científicas, 1983.

Giles, Paul. *Virtual Americas: Transnational Fictions and the Transatlantic Imaginary.* Durham, N.C.: Duke University Press, 2002.

Jara, René, and Nicholas Spadaccini. *1492/1992: Re/Discovering the New World. Minneapolis: University of Minnesota Press,* 1989.

Lacan, Jacques. *Écrits: A Selection.* Translated by Alan Sheridan, New York: W.W. Norton and Company, 1977.

Leoni, Monica. *Inside, Outside, Aside: Dialoguing with the Gracioso in Spanish Golden Age Theater.* New Orleans: University Press of the South, 2000.

Luciani, Frederick. "Spanish-American Theater of the Colonial Period." In *The Cambridge History of Latin American Literature,* edited by Roberto González Echevarría and Enrique Pupo-Walker. New York: Cambridge University Press, 1996.

McClennan, Sophia. "Comparative Literature and Latin American Studies: From Disarticulation to Dialogue." In *Comparative Cultural Studies and Latin America,* edited by Sophia A. McClennen and Earl E. Fitz. West Lafayette, Ind.: Purdue University Press, 2002. http://clcwebjournal.lib.purdue.edu/index.html.

Mignolo, Walter D. "Literacy and Colonization: The New World Experience." *1492–1992,* 51–96.

Mujica, Barbara, Sharon Voros, and Matthew Stroud, eds. *Looking at the Comedia in the Year of the Quincentennial.* Lanham, Md., London: University Press of America, 1993.

O'Gorman, Edmundo. *La invención de América: Investigación acerca de la estructura histórica del Nuevo Mundo y del sentido de su devenir.* México City: Fondo de Cultura Económica, 1995.

Ortega, Julio. "Towards a Map of the Current Critical Debate about Latin American Cultural Studies." Translated by Sophia A. McClennan and Corey Shouse. In *Comparative Cultural Studies and Latin America,* edited by Sophia A. McClennen and Earl E. Fitz. West Lafayette, Ind.: Purdue University Press, 2002. http://clcwebjournal.lib.purdue.edu/index.html.

Pratt, Mary Louise. *Imperial Eyes: Travel Writing and Transculturation.* New York: Routledge, 1993.

Reden, Ernest. "What Is a Nation?" In *Nation and Narration,* edited by Homi Bhabha, 8–22. London: Routledge, 1990.

Said, Edward. *Culture and Imperialism.* New York: Vintage Books, 1994.

Sale, Kirkpatrick. *The Conquest of Paradise: Christopher Columbus and the Columbian Legacy.* New York: Plume, 1991.

Shannon, Robert. *Visions of the New World in the drama of Lope de Vega.* New York: Peter Lang, 1989.

Zavala, Iris. "Representing the Colonial Subject." In Jara and Spard accini, *1492/1992,* 323–48.

Consuming the Other, Creating the Self: The Cultural Implications of the Aztecs' Chocolate from Tirso de Molina to Agustín Moreto and Pedro Lanini y Sagredo

Yolanda Gamboa

In the sixteenth- and seventeenth-century Spanish imaginary the Americas were a recurring image of the Other: a place of exotic beings, landscapes, and, moreover, exotic foods such as the chocolate that was to become one of Spain's most important cultural imports from the colonies. Exoticism, "the manifestation of a process by which the [Spaniards] intensify their own sense of Self by exaggerating the distances and differences separating them from their Others," relies on the juxtaposition of essentialized visions of both the indigenous peoples and the colonizers; in this case, of both the producers and consumers of chocolate.[1] From ceremony to banquet, from food of the gods to ornament, chocolate serves to illustrate that the Americas that helped define Spain were not just a product of the imagination but, echoing the late Edward Said's words, "an integral part of [Spain's] *material* civilization and culture."[2]

The food the god Quetzalcoatl gave to humankind and Cortés encountered in Montezuma's court soon became a symbol of splendor in Spain, not only a symbol of power, as it had been for Montezuma, but also a symbol of the consumption of the colonized Self. Even though Columbus was the first to encounter chocolate, Cortés is credited for bringing it to Spain for royal use in 1528.[3] An expensive imported good in the seventeenth century, chocolate constituted one of the "ornaments" of the very wealthy Spaniards. Although chocolate mythology will be created around notions of primitivism, exoticism, and excess, its meaning will slide between its original colonial commodity value to reflect exoticism and attitudes toward women, as will be apparent after observing its original connotation in Tirso de Molina's *Amazonas en las Indias* and *La lealtad contra la envidia*, two works from the Pizarro trilogy, written circa 1630, in contrast with Agustín Moreto and Pedro Lanini y Sagredo's *Santa Rosa del Perú*, written circa 1671.[4]

Approaching literary and historical issues from the perspective of an object is guided by a current trend in Renaissance studies consisting of shifting the focus from the study of the subject to the material world. In a recent collection of essays, Margreta de Grazia, among others, brings objects to the forefront. Problematizing the commonly held Western notion of the predominance of the subject over the object, the collection questions a modernity that is predicated upon presence and upon the narrative of the autonomous early modern subject, a narrative of separation propagated equally by Jacob Burckhardt's *The Civilization of the Renaissance in Italy*, Hegel, or Marx.[5] Reversing the subject-object dialectic, then, may lead to an understanding of their reciprocities and "a sense of how objects have a hold on subjects as well as subjects on objects,"[6] thus allowing for a new understanding of subjectivity from the object.

Bringing chocolate into view may prove particularly useful within transatlantic studies, since it is an element bridging both cultures that, once appropriated, plays a relevant role in the construction of Spanish identity. Foods in general play a dynamic role in the process of dialectic differentiation leading to the construction of cultural identity as they work "on the boundary between self and other."[7] Therefore, along this process of cultural formation foods can become metaphors of the Self as well as stereotypes of the Other. As Terrio notes: "As a cultural commodity whose meanings and associations are produced and reproduced as it is exchanged and consumed, chocolate illuminates shifting cultural ideologies and changing social relations."[8] More particularly, chocolate highlights relationships between the empire and the colony in the process of Spain's cultural formation. In fact, the evolving semantic connotations of chocolate linked to its exotic value provide insight into changing attitudes in Early Modern Spain, to paraphrase Terrio, into the continuities and changing relations between Spanish culture and its others.[9]

An explanation of the tensions between the Spaniards and the Creoles in the eighteenth century may serve as example of the significance and multiple implications of chocolate and particularly of the relevance of food to a group's cultural identity. Rachel Laudan refers to how the Creole population in

Mexico claimed a racial superiority over the natives because of their food habits, particularly wheat and chocolate. Chocolate, therefore, became one of the marks that the Creoles (Spaniards born in the New World) used to distinguish themselves from the Native Americans. Since for the Spaniards food meant "health, status, religion, and race," by the eighteenth century the Mexican Creoles had developed a cuisine, different from the Spanish one, that reflected their identity; significantly, chocolate was the most popular beverage.[10] By their food habits, the Creoles manifest a need to establish their identity in view of their precarious position within their society. The above-mentioned example of food consumption patterns, both in Spain and in the New World, reveals the importance of chocolate as a cultural artifact.

A look into the possible etymology of the word "chocolate" illuminates its long historical trajectory as a series of cultural appropriations.[11] Even though the first piece of archaeological evidence is found in the South coast of Guatemala, Mayan pottery with a hieroglyph reading as "ka-ka-wa," Sophie Coe mentions that the word is not Mayan but comes from the Mixezoquean family, the language of the Olmecs, earlier inhabitants of Mexico, which seems to have contributed to many words in the languages of Meso-America.[12] However, in the *New Survey from the West Indies* (1648) Thomas Gage noted that the name is compounded of "ate" or "attl," a phonetic term describing the sound of water falling, and the also phonetic "choco" from the choco, choco of the stirring.[13] Alternatively, the term could derive from "ate" and "choqui," the phonetic Mayan adjective meaning warm. The most conclusive etymology seems to be "cacahuatl," from the Nahuatl language spoken by the Aztecs, describing the cocoa beans, whereas the beverage would be "chocolatl."[14] Olmec, Mayan, or Nahuatl, a look into the origin of the name reveals the multiple layers of cultural identity. The chocolate encountered by Cortés, and forever linked with the Aztecs, exemplifies the process of cultural formation, since the Aztecs absorbed the cultures that preceded them, among them Mayan mythology and their traditions.

Accounts of Montezuma's court and the Spaniards' encounter with chocolate are found in the second "Letter to Charles V," Carta-relación, from October 30, 1520, by conquistador Hernán Cortés, as well as in Bernal Díaz del Castillo's *Historia verdadera de la conquista de Nueva España*. In his detailed description of the riches of the Aztec court and its cities like Temixtitlan, Cortés notes the importance of cocoa given its value:

> Cacao, que es una fruta como almendras, que ellos venden molida, y tiénenla en tanto, que se trata por moneda en toda la tierra, y con ella se compran todas las cosas necesarias en los mercados y otras partes.

[Cocoa is an almond-like fruit they grind and sell, and they value it so highly that it is used as coin throughout the land, and can buy all necessities in the marketplace and any other location.][15]

(Cortés, *Cartas y documentos*, 65)

In his letter, Cortés also writes "una taza de este precioso brevaje promete un hombre de andar un día entero sin tomar alimento" [a cup of this precious brew allows a man to walk a whole day without any food], meaning that he notes the possible use of the drink in enhancing the productivity of the American workers/slaves.[16] From its origins, chocolate was seen as a consumable commodity, "an edible form of the noble savage."[17]

Bernal Díaz del Castillo, captain and chronicler in Cortés's army, provides a detailed account of Montezuma's court. He pays particular attention to his luxurious banquets and the use of chocolate in chapter 91, and describes a ceremony in Montezuma's lavish court where chocolate was reserved for the highest religious and political uses, given its sacred origin:

Y me parece que sacaban sobre mil platos de aquellos manjares que dicho tengo; pues jarros de cacao con su espuma, como entre mexicanos se hace, más de dos mil, y fruta infinita.

[It seemed to me they brought thousands of those exquisite dishes I mentioned. There were also about two thousand foaming cocoa jars, as is commonly served by Mexicans, as well as infinite amounts of fruit.]

(Díaz del Castillo, *Historia de la conquista de Nueva España,* 168)

In order to convey the idea of luxury and excess, Díaz del Castillo takes care to emphasize the quantity, by pointing numbers, as well as by adding the adjective "infinite" to the appearance of fruit. All in all, it is an exaggerated albeit enticing account of the court intent on promoting the value of the colonial enterprise.

However, for the cultural significance of chocolate for the Aztecs, once other historical records have been eradicated, John West indicates that one has to look into the Codex Mendoza, an artistic Aztec rendition and the only surviving document of the tradition presented to Antonio de Mendoza, Mexico's first Spanish viceroy. According to the Mayan and later Aztec legend, the god Quetzalcoatl gave seeds of the cocoa tree, the food of the gods, to humankind when they were expelled from the Garden of Life. Aside from the above-mentioned social and religious connotations, chocolate was seen to have a practical use. It was "both currency and beverage" and in fact, the beans continued to be used as currency in Latin America even in the eighteenth century.[18]

Even though there is no evidence that the Aztecs viewed the drink as an aphrodisiac, according to Terrio, representations of chocolate consumption at Montezuma's court recall visions of ritualistic excess, of erotic temptation, danger, and sensuous Others.[19] This exoticism was promoted by selective historical accounts of Montezuma's court provided by members of the Cortés entourage, particularly the above-mentioned Bernal Díaz del Castillo.[20] The following excerpt may serve as an example:

> Traían en unas como a manera de copas de oro fino con cierta bebida hecha del mismo cacao; decían que era para tener acceso con mujeres y entonces no mirábamos en ello; mas lo que yo vi que traían sobre ciencuenta jarros grandes, hechos de buen cacao, con su espuma, y de aquello bebía, y las mujeres le servían al beber con gran acato . . . y otros que le cantaban y bailaban, porque Montezuma era aficionado a placeres y cantares.
>
> [They brought some sort of drink made of that same cocoa in fine gold goblets. They said it served to have access to women and we disregarded it. However, I saw what they brought: fifty large jars, with good cocoa, foaming. And he drank from them, and women served him the drink with great respect . . . people danced and sang for him because Montezuma was prone to singing as well as to other life pleasures.]
>   (Díaz del Castillo, *Historia de la conquista de Nueva España,* 167)

As it is apparent in the above-mentioned passage, chocolate helps develop a stereotype of the Other through gender as well as class allusions. It is associated with subservient women—emphasized by "le servían al beber con gran acato," with the respect [acato] in the act of serving him—as well as their accessibility, an effect of the drink, together with music, dancing, and pleasure. Moreover, care is taken to note that Montezuma drank the chocolate beverage from a gold goblet, meaning that the food of the gods was the beverage of the higher classes, not the common man.[21]

Accounts of Montezuma's harem, of his hundred wives, and of his drinking chocolate before the visit to the harem contributed later to ecclesiastical denunciations of "chocolate as a food which leads directly to carnal sin."[22] However, "given its complex trajectory from cultivation and harvest in the third world to processing and consumption in the first world, chocolate is particularly suited to the creation of such mythologies."[23] According to Terrio, exoticism is embedded in the Western accounts of the encounter with the non-West that began in the sixteenth century.[24] Indeed, what is at stake in the exoticism of the cultural Other is the right to consume it, so to speak, and denouncing the Aztecs' behavior justifies their colonization. One should re-

member, however, that Spain's effort to consolidate hegemony over the
colony, over so-called primitive societies, is coupled with its search for clues to
its own identity.

Chocolate's financial potential for a Spain in decline was soon noticed by
the Spaniards: cocoa trees were planted in the overseas possessions and a high
import duty was placed on raw cocoa beans.[25] John West relates that as the
Spaniards extended their rule they took over most of the Mayan agriculture
and trade. "During the sixteenth and early seventeenth centuries, cacao
became the Spaniards' most important export crop, and they controlled its
trade and consumption in Europe as well as in their colonies."[26] Cacao, "on
the boundary between Self and Other" was instrumental in the development
of Spain's cultural identity.[27]

Spain had the monopoly of the chocolate drink, a secret recipe, and of the
cocoa trade from 1519 till 1606 when the secret leaked into Italy, according
to most sources, with Florentine merchant Antonio Carletti.[28] One should
not disregard, however, that it is at the time when Spain's stronghold on the
colonies as well as of the chocolate trade in Europe begins to debilitate, when
the chocolate beverage acquires its cultural and literary representations. It is
not unlike the literary representations of the Moors, centuries after their ex-
pulsion. The seventeenth century in Spain is regarded by Cascardi as a time of
crisis of subjectivity, which originated with the transition from a feudal to a
capitalistic order, a European phenomenon as well, but which had stronger
consequences in Spain due to the resistance to the social values of the bourgeoisie as well as to the culture of modernity.[29] A Spanish aristocracy that is
losing its position amid the social heterogeneity is intent on asserting its frail
subjectivity by means of the external signs of identity. Dress-code prescrip-
tions as well as treatises of behavior proliferate in this century as the aristocracy becomes the role model of "civility," a concept emphasizing the emergence of the early modern subject, a subject defined in relation to its Others.
Therefore, surprising as it may seem, chocolate, a cultural object, is extremely
influential for the definition of the Spanish subject.

The difference between the original, bitter taste of Mexican chocolate and
the popular sweetened European variety, to which sugar and spices were
added by nuns or monks for consumption at court, "to domesticate a bitter,
cold drink," is an example of how foods can work on the boundary between
self and other.[30] It highlights the difference between a primitive Barbaric
product, which stands for the Other, and a refined and "civilized" one, which
stands for the self.

Chocolate became a fashionable upper-class beverage in seventeenth-century Spain, a mark of wealth, a way of showing status. Functioning as a meta-

phor of the self, it continued being the drink of the elite as it had been in Montezuma's court. Served as a hot or a cold drink, it was an expensive imported good and constituted an emblem of the very wealthy Spaniards, the only ones who could afford it.[31] It was an "ornament," to use Patricia Fumerton's term, a peripheral mark of an increasingly trivial nobility whose sense of self is supported by elements of wealth and show. In a sense, it parallels what in Spanish culture is known as "ostentación" [ostentation]. In time, chocolate was also "accompanied by a new and expensive set of utensils," which relates to a later stage in the development of civility.[32] Moreover, since the Spaniards became the European elite, in control of the lucrative trade thanks to their eating habits, it symbolically implied that their cultural identity was asserted by the consumption of the colony.

Eating habits lie at the core of Fumerton's analysis of banqueting in the seventeenth century, a perspective from where she links the development of the early modern subject proposed by Norbert Elias with its growing interest in privatization. When describing the period marked by the crisis of subjectivity, she notes that subjectivity is "unlocatable and itself segmented," and also that "the private self was a sugar-spun identity always on the verge of being consumed by an elusive and feared insubstantiality."[33] The increasingly airy (superfluous) banquets "would seem to argue a mode of self-representation always on the verge of breaking up."[34] I will argue that this fear is what leads to the consumption of the Other.

Ostentation, an excessive display of material goods, distinguishes the aristocracy from the common classes. It is the mark of a group on the wane, fearing its fragile subjectivity in the face of social mobility. However, groups from the lower classes are equally anxious about their position and will also tend to rely on external signs of wealth to assert their subjectivity. The *comedia*, a genre destined for the enjoyment of the masses, deals with issues of interest to society. Thus, the characters of the comedias I will analyze from the perspective of banqueting and chocolate serve as a vehicle for the expression of such contemporary social anxieties.

References to chocolate as a sign of wealth, alluding to the consumption of the colony, appear in several comedias during the seventeenth century including what I believe is a veiled critique against the upper social classes.[35] For example, in the first act of Mexican-born playwright Juan Ruiz de Alarcón's *La verdad sospechosa* (1634), when a description of a banquet that includes chocolate adds to the elaborate lie told by Don García to his audience. Alarcón presents a critique of his contemporary society highlighting the hypocrisy and social falseness he abhors. However, Tirso's more elaborate references in two works from the Pizarro trilogy merit particular attention.

Tirso's *Amazonas en las Indias* and *La lealtad contra la envidia,* written around 1630, are commissioned works for the Pizarro family for the explicit purpose of glorifying the Pizarro brothers in the Incan Court in Peru. Tirso appears to be writing from the center, according to James T. Abraham, although objects like chocolate in my opinion are helpful in supporting Tirso's veiled critique of the Crown. Alongside the representation of the Pizarro brothers, aided by Amazones, in *Amazonas en las Indias,* or saints in *La lealtad contra la envidia,* the references to chocolate are a window into the attitudes of Tirso's Spain. A measure of value, they provide us with an indication about the original connotation of the word for the colonial imagery of the readers in Spain.

Amazonas en las Indias, set in Peru, centers around the figure of Gonzalo de Pizarro. It presents the story of the conquest by means of a quasi-mythical story, with the Spaniards fighting the American Amazones, and long monologues relating the historical events taking place on both sides of the Atlantic. Gonzalo de Pizarro is accompanied by Francisco de Carvajal, not quite a *gracioso,* who introduces a comic double plot and who functions as an alter ego, voicing comments about the conquest and about ruling itself. However, for the purpose of this essay, I will focus on the third *jornada* and on Carvajal's response to Martesia, an Amazon intent on marrying him, just like Amazon Menalipe, who wants to marry Gonzalo Pizarro.

If Gonzalo Pizarro's refusal of his admirer is elegant, Carvajal's is comical. Fearing her and alluding to her as a devil, he assumes she is a prostitute "que todas las de tu especie/en llegando el donativo/vienen para mí *de requiem.*"[36] [All the women of your kind/as soon as they receive a gift/ they come to live forever with me]. He goes on to describe what a potential encounter in Spain with a "medio ojo" [one-eyed] or "tapada" [covered], terms describing street women who were half-covered by a veil to preserve their anonymity, would entail; he describes a street scene in detail, alluding to the carriage, and the buying of colognes, clothes, and chocolate. By contrast, and with the purpose of dissuading her, he says he has nothing to offer her: "pero aquí si no es que pidas/del modo que Eva a la sierpe/o plátanos, o guayabas,/solo tengo que ofrecerte/con bizcochos de estos riscos,/chocolates de estas fuentes." [Here unless you asked me/in the same manner Eve asked the serpent/I can only offer you bananas and guavas/with bizcochos from these cliffs and chocolates from these fountains]. His description of the landscape is symbolic, combining the Spanish imagery with the American natural reality. He imagines "bizcochos" [sponge cake] where there are "riscos" [cliffs], and chocolates where there are "fuentes" [fountains].[37] Of particular interest in this description is the use of chocolate when he fantasizes about what he could offer her in Spain where chocolate is profusely drunk: "pues, después que se conocen/en nuestra nación, se beben/en tres jícaras tres damas/cien escudos en dos meses." [Soon after they meet/in our country three women drink a hundred escudos/ in three jars in two months]. It is to be noted that the quote includes a reference to the high value of chocolate and to the "ostentación" and points to the excesses of the Spanish upper class that is delighted in consuming the colony.

Three women consume "cien escudos" [a hundred escudos] of chocolate in two months. In fact, that is more than sixteen escudos per woman per month, a fair amount of money for a superfluous item, and probably an exaggeration on Tirso's part. Implicit in this passage is that women of the upper class have become the most avid consumers of chocolate in Spain. Thus begins the association between chocolate, economic value, and women, and thus, what was before a critique of the cultural other becomes a critique of the social and generic other.

From a generic point of view Tirso's cultural observation is also highly relevant: seventeenth-century upper-class women are regarded not as producers but as passive consumers, given that they accede to an economically dependent position. In fact "stereotypes of women as passive consumers and men as producers have been historically constructed" and have lasted into the twentieth-century.[38] Even though in seventeenth-century Spain women may already appear to be emblems of consumerism, the implication is that, despite appearances to the contrary, the consumption of the colony is not only, and not even primarily, in the hands of women, contributing thus to what I believe is Tirso's overall critique of his contemporary society.

Tirso's critique of his time is also present in *La lealtad contra la envidia*. The play centers on Fernando Pizarro. It follows the story of his life from his heroic past in Spain in the first act, to his time in Peru in the second act, to be imprisoned in the third act. Even though the presence of Santiago and the Virgin Mary in the second act seems to validate the conquest, figures such as that of Castillo serve to open it for discussion.

In the second act of the play, the gracioso Castillo's desire for riches serves as a comic double plot for the greed of Pizarro's entourage. He captures Guaica, an Indian woman. When she offers him gold for her release, Castillo starts dreaming every Spaniard's dream of wealth, of acquiring land and status: "¿Cien mil pesos? Compro un juro/un mayorazgo opulento/que me ensanche el coranvobis/o para el pobilis vobis,/vita bona, un regimiento." [Ten thousand pesos? I buy property rights/an opulent estate/ to widen my solemn appearance/and for your people,/a good life, and a batallion]. It is important to notice his use of Latin, parodying the style of the learned, the *letrados*, and alluding to the higher classes.[39]

He also thinks about acquiring women, which he will, with a carriage "coche," and chocolate, two items that are sure to attract women: "A cargas el chocolate;/y dos coches echaré/que es el venite post me/de toda dama tomate" (10). [I will carry chocolate/and two carriages with me/'cause coming along with me/is any woman's tomato]. Being with him would then be any woman's "tomato," meaning, any woman's dream, because being a food also imported from the New World, tomato was slower in being adapted and remained a luxurious product into the latter part of the eighteenth century.[40] Notwithstanding, the carriage had become an obsession in seventeenth-century Spain, a place from where to see and be seen, and a mark of social status. It also became a popular location for amorous encounters.[41] Even though in this passage there could be an implicit association of chocolate with women and sex, mediated by the association of chocolate with the "coche," for the most part Tirso gives us an indication of the original meaning of the word chocolate, as a colonial commodity, and of its relevance in the colonial imaginary of Spanish readers. Rather than be motivated by a search for recognition or "fama" [fame], leading the portrayal of Fernando Pizarro, riches are the motivation of the group accompanying the conquistadors and hoping to have an impact when returning to a society easily swayed by material appearances. Unsure of their social position, they count on the external signs to assert their subjectivity.

Even though the explicit purpose of the trilogy may be to glorify the Pizarro brothers, as is apparent, for instance, in Carvajal's long monologues describing the conquest in *Amazonas en las Indias*, Tirso's use of the double plot by means of the *gracioso* together with the allusions to chocolate, serves to highlight cultural tensions and to release the critique of both the colonial enterprise and the progressive idleness and lack of cultural identity of the aristocracy. Castillo's assertion of his dreamt identity by means of external signs (Latin, carriage, and chocolate) is highly relevant and points to the critique of a society questioning its identity and sovereignty. Moreover, as Arturo Pérez-Pisonero has also noted, Carvajal, expressing the sentiment of the soldiers against Gonzalo Pizarro by means of an American political discourse, which is itself a parody of its genre, is instrumental in proposing the critique of the Crown.[42] Focusing on chocolate and the discourse instead of the Pizarro brothers allows for an understanding of the plays from the perspective of the object that ultimately deepens our understanding of the subjects and that calls into question the purpose of Tirso's writing.

A very different representation of chocolate takes place in Agustín de Moreto and Pedro Lanini y Sagredo's *Santa Rosa del Perú*, written toward the end of the seventeenth century (1671). The term chocolate slides from its original connotation as colonial commodity to a more explicit association with women when chocolate serves to cure a woman's ailment.

Otherwise a hagiographic play about beautiful Rosa's triumphs over the flesh, the devil, or war, the inclusion of chocolate serves to provide a humane and comic relief since it demonstrates a moment of weakness in the saint. After fighting stoically throughout the play, in the third act Rosa asks for chocolate as cure for a bodily pain sent by God. While the cure is brought, Bodigo, the gracioso, who calls himself "santo jicarero" (jicara being the goblet where chocolate was served), expresses his commentaries on chocolate, providing an understanding of changing attitudes in Spain.

By saying "lo puede hacer cualquiera que hace vainillas" and playing with the terms "vainilla," (aromatic plant from which the spice added to chocolate is extracted) and alluding to "vainica" (hem sewing), he means [anyone who can make vanilla (or sew vainicas) can do it], in other words, it is so easy that even a woman (or a gracioso), can make a good cup of chocolate. The significance of this passage is that the trade has progressed from its association with riches and sophistication to the domestic sphere. One should remember that, even though it will not be affordable to the popular classes for another century, other Europeans already have access to the recipe. Also, the fact that the chocolate comes served in a "chocolatera," a specific utensil, is indicative of its frequent use. It also signals its quality as an "adornment" of class status. In fact, silversmiths and porcelain makers elaborated chocolate services in France into the following century.[43]

When asking "hay cosa como un licor / tal, que quebranta un dolor, / y no quebranta el ayuno?" [Is there such a liquor/that can break down pain / and does not break one's fasting?], Bodigo alludes to the healing powers of chocolate as well as to the ecclesiastical debate present in books such as *Cuestión moral, si el chocolate quebranta el ayuno* [Moral Question: Whether or not Chocolate Breaks Fasting] written by Leon Pinelo.[44] Sugar and spices were very rare. Since the spices and sugar contained in chocolate were so valuable and rare in Moreto and Lanini y Sagredo's time, they were regarded as healing substances, and so was chocolate. These items that Fumerton regards as ephemeral "were praised in medical treatises for their ability to restore and preserve the body."[45]

Bodigo also marvels at the fact that chocolate may not break the saint's fasting and this alludes ironically to the ecclesiastical debate that started over the pernicious nature of chocolate, and has progressively accepted the drink, to the point that it is not seen to break fasting. Terrio relates that "as a substance surrounded with ambiguous moral and medical notions, chocolate evoked persistent anxieties in its early consumers," which explains the need to make it part of the debate.[46]

Chocolate in this play is regarded as the panacea, capable of curing all of women's ailments, including desire, which, as I said, helps bring the hagiographic play while it reveals Moreto and Lanini y Sagredo's playful tone.

�֍ ✖ ✖ ✖ ✖

A measure of value and wealth earlier in the seventeenth century, the association of chocolate with women became more prominent with the passing of time, as civility became commonplace. From colonial commodity, to the consumption of the colony in the form of a drink, both being references to class, chocolate comes to be associated with women, who soon become chocolate's most avid consumers. Exoticism and power over the unknown underlie that sliding of meanings that takes us from a measure of value in Tirso to a woman's cure in Moreto and the reason for this shift may be found in the initial eroticization of the Aztecs, later transferred onto women.

Chocolate, as a cultural object, was extremely influential in the formation of a class and a national identity in sixteenth-century Spain. It helped Spain stand out in the European scene for a century, until the discovery of the chocolate recipe that parallels the progressive decay of the Spanish Empire. Both a metaphor for the Self [the consumer] and stereotype of the colonized Other [the consumed] chocolate, thus, contributes to the definition of an identity established against the cultural and ethnic Other, the colonial subject, as well as the social Other. Not surprisingly, the exoticized and eroticized Other from the colony slides in the seventeenth century to what is perceived as the problematic Other at home, namely, Woman. Women's association with chocolate in a Spain on the wane, serves to strengthen a cultural identity which is civilized and in control of its Others.

NOTES

1. Terrio, *Crafting the Culture,* 241. The process of subject formation in early Modern Spain, crucial for the formation of the Early Modern State, is characterized, in my opinion, by a series of exclusions and a progressive "mapping," through religion, ethnicity, class, and gender. The colonial Other, focus of this essay, is an example of an ongoing process character-

ized by its exoticism, involving desire and exclusion. I also refer to the colonial other as cultural/ethnic other, not to be confused with the social or generic other within Spain.

2. Said, *Orientalism*, 2.

3. West, "Brief History," 105.

4. Agustín Moreto is known to have written the first and second acts and Pedro Lanini y Sagredo the third one.

5. De Grazia et al., *Subject and Object*, 3.

6. Ibid., 11.

7. Terrio, *Crafting the Culture*, 237.

8. Ibid., 239.

9. Ibid.

10. Laudan and Pilcher, "Chiles, Chocolate, and Race," 61.

11. Susan Terrio notes how most texts written in the 1980s explore chocolate use among the Aztecs and ignore its uses and symbolic meanings for the Olmec and Mayas (Terrio, *Crafting the Culture*, 241).

12. West, "Brief History," 106. Coe, "Cacao," 148.

13. Qtd. in Cook, *Chocolate Production and Use*, 2.

14. Ibid.

15. The translations of the Spanish texts throughout this article are my own.

16. Qtd. in Marcus, *Chocolate Bible*, 29.

17. Lekatsas, "Inside the Pastilles," 99. Note that the descriptive studies of Amerindian foods, already present in Las Casas, with his idealized notion of the "noble savage," has given way to contemporary studies on the consumption of the colony/of the colonized. MLA Conference Panels titles like "Consuming America" organized by Luis Fernando Restrepo (2001), or the influx of publications on the imports of foods from the Americas, particularly in the field of Anthropology (i.e., Cevallos-Candau et al., *Coded Encounters*, and Foster and Cordell, *Chilies to Chocolate*, 1996) seem to attest to this fact.

18. Cook, *Chocolate Production and Use*, 121. West, "Brief History," 108.

19. Terrio, *Crafting the Culture*, 245. Terrio also alludes to Bataille's *Visions of Excess* (1985) and Baudrillard's *For a Critique of the Political Economy of the Sign* (1981) for the French representations of chocolate deriving from Bernal Díaz del Castillo's accounts.

20. The chocolate mythology seems to have been propagated by the critics as well. For example, I have encountered being the same passages from Cortés and Díaz del Castillo extensively quoted by the critics and out of context. Going to the original sources has been invaluable.

21. Lekatsas, "Inside the Pastilles," 100.

22. Terrio, *Crafting the Culture*, 246.

23. Ibid., 240.

24. Ibid.

25. Marcus, *Chocolate Bible*, 29–31.

26. West, "Brief History," 108.

27. Terrio, *Crafting the Culture*, 237.

28. Other sources attribute the loss of the monopoly and secret to European refugees of Jewish origins. See Ullmann, "Location Factors," 190.

29. Cascardi, *Ideologies of History*, 20.

30. Terrio, *Crafting the Culture*, 243.

31. Díaz-Plaja, *La vida cotidiana*, 166.

32. Laudan and Pilcher, "Chiles, Chocolate, and Race," 65.

33. Fumerton, *Cultural Aesthetics: Renaissance Literature and the Practice of Social Ornament*, 128.

33. Ibid., 130, 132.

34. "Chocolate" in the sixteenth and seventeenth centuries becomes a literary allusion for wealth and decadence, and is found also in prose works, like Maria de Zayas's *Novelas amorosas y ejemplares* (1637). It functions similarly to the way references to "el prado" [the garden], will function in the seventeenth century: an allusion to the recently created gardens of "El Retiro" in times of Philip IV, and the meeting place of the idle nobility.

35. Pérez-Pisonero, "Querer ser," 165.

36. "De requiem" is only used in the expression "misa de requiem," Mass for the dead, and therefore the passage alludes to the woman's wish to be with him "until death does us part," given that he has shown to be capable of supporting her.

37. Given that chocolate is allusive to women and bread and their derivatives like "bizcochos" have been associated to female genitals since medieval days, the whole passage may have been highly comical.

38. Horowitz and Mohum, *His and Hers*, 2.

39. The parody of the *letrados* is commonplace in other Golden Age works. See the debate on language and love by the peasants in the first act of Lope de Vega's *Fuenteovejuna*.

40. Davidson, "Europeans' Wary Encounter," 8.

41. Díaz-Plaja, *La vida Cotidiana*, 51–52.

42. Pérez-Pisonero, "Querer ser," 169.

43. Terrio, *Crafting the Culture*, 30–31.

44. Qtd. in Díaz–Plaja, *La vida Cotidiana*, 167.

45. Fumerton, *Cultural Aesthetics*, 134.

46. Terrio, *Crafting the Culture*, 239.

WORKS CITED

Abraham, James T. "The Other Speaks: Tirso de Molina's Amazonas en las Indias." In *El arte nuevo de estudiar comedias: Literary Theory and Spanish Golden Age Drama*, edited by Barbara Simerka, 143–61. Lewisburg, Pa.: Bucknell University Press, 1996.

Cascardi, Anthony. *Ideologies of History in the Spanish Golden Age*. University Park: The Pennsylvania State University Press, 1997.

Cevallos-Candau, Francisco Javier, et al., eds. *Coded Encounters: Writing, Gender, and Ethnicity in Colonial Latin America*. Amherst: University of Massachusets Press, 1994.

Coe, Sophie.D., "Cacao: Gift of the New World." In Szogyi, *Chocolate*, 147–53.

Cook, L. Russell. *Chocolate Production and Universityse*. New York: Harcourt Brace Jovanovich, 1982.

Cortés, Hernán. "Segunda Carta-Relación de Hernán Cortés al Emperador Carlos V, Segura de la Frontera, 30 de octubre de 1520." In *Cartas y documentos*, edited by Mario Hernández Sánchez Barba, 32–115. México City: Porrúa, 1963.

Davidson, Alan. "Europeans' Wary Encounter with Tomatoes, Potatoes, and Other New World Foods." In Forster and Cordell, *Chilies to Chocolate*, 1–14.

De Grazia, Margreta, et al. *Subject and Object in Renaissance Culture*. Cambridge: Cambridge University Press, 1996.

Díaz del Castillo, Bernal. *Historia de la conquista de Nueva España*. Edited by Joaquín Ramírez Cabañas. México City: Porrúa, 1970.

Díaz-Plaja, Fernando. *La vida cotidiana en la España del Siglo de Oro*. Madrid: Edaf, 1994.

Foster, Nelson, and Linda S. Cordell. *Chilies to Chocolate: Food the Americas Gave the World*. Tuscon: University of Arizona Press, 1996.

Fumerton, Patricia. *Cultural Aesthetics: Renaissance Literature and the Practice of Social Ornament*. Chicago: University of Chicago Press, 1991.

Horowitz, Roger, and Arwen Mohun, ed. *His and Hers: Gender, Consumption and Technology*. Charlottesville: University Press of Virginia, 1998.

Laudan, Rachel, and Jeffrey M. Pilcher. "Chiles, Chocolate, and Race in New Spain: Glancing Backward to Spain or Looking Forward to Mexico?" *Eighteenth Century Life* 23, 2 (1999): 59–70.

Lekatsas, Barbara. "Inside the Pastilles of the Marquis de Sade." In Szogyi, *Chocolate*, 99–107.

León Pinelo, Antonio de. *Cuestion moral, si el chocolate quebranta el ayuno eclesiástico*. Edited by Sonia Corcuera. Mexico City: Centro de Estudios de Historia de México Condermex, 1994.

Marcus, Adrianne. *The Chocolate Bible*. New York: G. P. Putnam's Sons, 1979.

Moreto, José Agustín. *Santa Rosa del Perú*. http://www.trinity.edu/org/comedia/moreto/strosa2.html.

Pérez-Pisonero, Arturo. "'Querer ser' y 'deber ser' en *Amazonas en las Indias* de Tirso de Molina." In *Hispanic Essays in Honor of Frank P. Casa*, edited by A. Robert Lauer and Henry W. Sullivan, 165–72. New York: Peter Lang, 1997.

Ruiz de Alarcón, Juan. "La verdad sospechosa." In *Antología del teatro del Siglo de Oro*, edited by Eugenio Suárez-Galbán Guerra, 517–604. Madrid: Orígenes, 1989.

Said, Edward. *Orientalism*. New York: Vintage, 1979.

Szogyi, Alex, ed. *Chocolate: Food of the Gods*. Westport, Conn.: Greenwood, 1997.

Terrio, Susan J. *Crafting the Culture and History of French Chocolate*. Berkeley and Los Angeles: University of California Press, 2000.

Tirso de Molina. *Amazonas en las Indias*. http://wwww.trinity.edu/org/comedia/tirso/amazin2.html.

———. *La lealtad contra la envidia*. http://www.trinity.edu/org/comedia/tirso/lealen3.html.

Ullmann, John E. "Location Factors in Cocoa Growing and the Chocolate Industry." In Szogyi, *Chocolate*, 189–95.

West, John A. "A Brief History and Botany of Cacao." In Forster and Cordell, *Chilies to Chocolate*, 105–21.

Erasure, Exoticism, Hybridity: Cultural Alterity in *Santa Rosa del Perú*

Christopher D. Gascón

Postcolonial theorists seem to be moving away from privileging a given mode of representing cultural alterity toward recognizing that there are a variety of ways of depicting otherness, no one of which can be considered the most enlightened. Against the concept of homogenous national identity and the specter of its worst possible outcome, ethnic cleansing, Homi Bhabha has promoted "a more transnational and translational sense of the hybridity of imagined communities."[1] Demonstrating how such an idea may inform interpretations of contemporary Australian, African, and American theater, Christopher Balme has embraced "theatrical syncretism" which, he maintains, "is one of the most effective means of decolonizing the stage, because it utilizes the performance forms of both European and indigenous cultures in a creative recombination of their respective elements, without slavish adherence to one tradition or the other."[2] On the other hand, revalorizations of Victor Segalen's "Essay on Exoticism" (1904–18), such as that featured in the work of Edouard Glissant, point out the potential of syncretic and hybridizing processes to blur cultural distinctions and ultimately attenuate or silence possible discourses of resistance.[3] Segalen attempts to divest the term "exoticism" of its associations with self-interested oversimplification of the other and reinstate its more general meaning, with emphasis on the prefix "exo," of "everything that lies 'outside' the sum total of our current, conscious everyday events, everything that does not belong to our usual 'Mental Tonality.'"[4] He upholds "diversity" over hybridity: cultures must diverge in order to maintain their purity, but each may be enriched by contemplating irreducible difference, for "it is through Difference and in Diversity that existence is made glorious."[5] Charles Forsdick aligns himself with Roger Célestin and Jean-Marc Moura in negotiating a pluralistic and inclusive compromise to this polarity. He suggests that "exoticism has to be seen as covering a range of representational possibilities and practices," and that, therefore, theorists should think in terms of "postcolonial exoticisms," or a continuum of modes of representation of the cultural other.[6]

This concept is key to the present analysis of Agustín Moreto and Pedro Lanini y Sagredo's *Santa Rosa del Perú*, in which the playwrights use at least three different strategies in representing Latin American otherness. Superficial touches of exoticism evoke the "New World" setting. The dominant mode of representation in this work, however, is that of erasure of otherness: where alterity should be, we find instead a mirror of Spanish peninsular culture. Finally, there are some much more subtle hints of hybridization—moments when Spanish and American cultural texts stand side by side. Before a discussion of each of these, however, some information concerning the historical context and argument of the play is in order.

Pope Clement IX beatified Isabel Flores de Oliva, known as Rosa de Lima, in 1668, and Clement X canonized her in 1671. Scholars generally accept early editor Joseph Fernández de Buendía's explanation that Moreto had written the first two acts of the play when he died on October 8, 1669, and that his protégé, Pedro Francisco de Lanini y Sagredo, penned the final act later for its publication in 1671.[7] Elaborate celebrations of Rosa's beatification took place at the Vatican and in Rome in April of 1668, in Madrid in October of the same year, and in Lima in April of 1669.[8] It is thus possible that Moreto was commissioned to write the play or chose to compose it either on the occasion of Rosa's beatification or in anticipation of her imminent sanctification. Little information on actual productions or the reception of the play is available, though it is known that it was performed three times in Valladolid in 1696.[9]

In the play, the young Rosa is courted by Don Juan, but refuses his hand, much against the wishes of her father, Gaspar de Flores, insisting that she is already enamored of another (the Christian God, of course). The devil, determined to corrupt Rosa, the most virtuous and devout woman in America, uses Don Juan throughout the play as an instrument to tempt and defile Rosa. Rosa resists all of his attempts, expresses her devotion through severe mortifications, and repels the pirate Joris von Spilbergen's attack on Callao harbor through her prayers. Upon her death, she ascends to heaven accompanied by Jesus, the Virgin, Saint Catherine, and a host of angels. Moved by her greatness, a repentant Don Juan swears he will enter the Dominican order.

Most of the miracles dramatized in the play have at least some basis in biographical accounts or popular legends of the saint.[10] At times the dramatists take the liberty of fusing together in a single scene wondrous incidents that are presented as separate anecdotes by her chroniclers.[11] This appears to be an attempt to touch upon as many of the miracles as possible while reducing the tendency toward fragmentation characteristic of hagiographical narrative. The playwrights also leave Rosa's mother completely out of the work while giving a prominent role to her father, Gaspar de Flores. In Pedro de Loayza's version, Gaspar is almost entirely absent while María de Oliva is frequently involved in Rosa's life, often depicted as perplexed by her daughter's behavior and at times abusive.[12] Apparently Moreto and Lanini y Sagredo, like many Golden Age playwrights, saw more utility in a father figure than in a mother figure. Perhaps they felt it appropriate that Rosa's father negotiate her marriage in the first act. The honor dispute in the second act between Don Juan and Gaspar, created through the devil's deception, certainly would not have been possible had the writers followed Loayza; maintaining or avenging family honor was, of course, seen as a male's responsibility.[13] They exercise the most liberty, however, in creating Rosa's servant and the gracioso of the play, Bodigo, her suitor Don Juan, and the devil. This is, of course, hardly an innovation; the gracioso, the suitor, and the devil had become conventional figures in the *comedia de santas* by the middle of the seventeenth century. The former two added profane humor and *capa y espada* action and intrigue to the plot, while the latter enabled the dramatists to make clear distinctions between good and evil, and to account for violence, pride, and temptation without condemning individual characters (in most plays of the genre, all are forgiven at the conclusion). I will discuss later the further aesthetic and political interests the playwrights serve in imitating common comedia de santas conventions.

A clarification of the meaning of cultural alterity within the historical context of the work, as well as an indication of where we might expect to find such otherness in the play, is necessary prior to an analysis of the work's modes of representing difference. The historical context that gives shape to *Santa Rosa del Perú* is obviously that of colonial Lima and imperial Spain from Rosa's lifetime (1586–1617) until Lanini y Sagredo finished the work around 1670. I use "cultural other" in this context to refer to any perspective outside that of the Spanish metropolis, within and for which the Spanish dramatists produced the play.[14] Clearly, most Spaniards would have considered indigenous peoples, Africans, mulattos, and most mestizos (people of mixed ethnicity) as culturally other during this time. If historical and cultural accuracy were to be considered, the character most likely to represent such otherness would be Bodigo. According to a 1614 census of Lima, the population of 25,454 consisted of "9,511 Spaniards, 10,386 blacks, mainly slaves, and an assortment of mulattos and mestizos."[15] It is unlikely that he would be a Spaniard; generally *advenedizos* (upstart newcomers from the peninsula looking to make money in the "New World") from Spain dominated commerce from the top of the field to the bottom and did not work as servants.[16] If, however, we are to take seriously Bodigo's claim in the opening scene that he is descended from a priest,[17] then we may assume that he has at least some Spanish blood, as the clergy was dominated by Creoles (those born in the "New World" but descended from the conquistadores). Nevertheless, most house or convent servants in early seventeenth-century Lima would have been of recognizable African descent.[18] Indeed, Loayza relates that on her death bed, Rosa blesses all the occupants of Don Gonzalo de la Maza's house, where she resided during the final years of her life, calling in turn upon Don Gonzalo and his wife María de Uzátegui, some friends and sisters present, the daughters of the noble couple, and finally, "los negros y negras de la casa" [the black men and women of the house], of whom she begs forgiveness for anything she may have done to annoy them.[19] There is no mention of European or mestizo servants in the household. In sum, the most reasonable expectation would be that Bodigo, as a common house servant in early seventeenth-century Peru, would be of African descent, or at the least, of some degree of mixed ethnicity and recognizably other to the average Spaniard of the day.

Whether Peruvian Creoles like Rosa and her family would be seen by a Spanish audience as other is not quite so clear, however. To begin with, the only thing that all Creoles in Rosa's day had in common besides being born in America was a claim to descent from Spanish conquerors. Since the explorers rarely brought women with them to America, many of their descendants were of course mestizos or mulattos. Thus it is possible that Creoles that appeared Caucasian and claimed pure European descent were not seen by Spaniards as other, while those of noticeably mixed ethnicity were. Furthermore, issues of race aside, there is the problem of defining the relationship that existed between colonial Spaniard and Creole in the first centuries of Spanish colonialism. Recent scholarship on the origins of national identity in Latin American countries maintains that Creoles had begun to see themselves as different from immigrant Spaniards before the middle of the sixteenth century. Elena Altuna, for example, argues that an "awareness of difference" based on feelings of estrangement from Spain, connection with the "New World," and a vindication of the conquerors is evident in Enrique Otte's collected *Cartas privadas de emigrantes a Indias, 1540–1616*.[20] D. A. Brading writes about the growing frustration of Creoles at the beginning of the seventeenth century at

the failure of the Spanish viceroyalty to offer them public offices, and the re-
luctance within the mendicant orders to promote Creole clergy to positions
of power.[21] This suggests that by Rosa's time, Creoles had distanced themselves from Spaniards in the "New World," and that conversely, Spanish immigrants saw Creoles as an inferior other.[22] The more difficult question is
whether Spaniards in the peninsula—for the purposes of this study, Moreto,
Lanini y Sagredo, and their potential audiences—regarded Creoles as culturally other, or as an extension of themselves and the Spanish empire in
America.

According to the dominant mode of representing otherness in *Santa Rosa
del Perú*, the latter is true: in the characters of Rosa and Bodigo, where we
might most expect to see cultural otherness, we find instead a mirror of Spanish society. Allen Carey-Webb notes in Lope de Vega's *El nuevo mundo descubierto por Cristóbal Colón* a "disavowal of difference that most fundamentally
marks the treatment of Native Americans" and the influence of "the cen-
tripetal forces of generic convention" which "pull the Other toward the self."[23]
The same mode of representation is evident in *Santa Rosa del Perú*. The language, actions, and characters of the saint, her servant, and her father suggest
little that is particular to Peru; rather, they are based on character types and
conventions typical of the comedia. In fairness to the playwrights, there is
very little that is place- or culture-specific in the source material on Santa
Rosa. While some saints were public figures actively engaged in their communities and even in international affairs, Santa Rosa's spiritual journey, according to her hagiographers, was primarily inward, centered upon humility,
prayer, fasting, and mortification.[24] Like most Christian ascetics, she strove to
divest herself of the worldly to enter the realm of the divine. Perhaps as a
result of this, her biographies reveal relatively little of her cultural context.
Brading categorizes her hagiography as "vapid," dominated by a "dulcet sen-
timentality," and lacking in "any specifically Peruvian content."[25] Indeed, the
written episodes of her life could have transpired in any number of Christian
countries (a great irony given that Santa Rosa has become the patron saint
and religious symbol of Latin America and the Philippines). Though Santa
Rosa composed poems, letters, prayers, and possibly an autobiography, the
church confiscated many of these materials in 1624, due, according to Kathleen Ann Myers, to their general fear that spiritual writings by laywomen
might be "dangerous to the welfare of both woman and church if they were
made public without the editing (and censorship) of trained church clergy."[26]
The accounts available to the playwrights thus would have contained little of
Rosa's own voice.

Yet Moreto and Lanini y Sagredo must nevertheless make her speak, and we might expect to find in her language some indicators of cultural specificity. Indigenous and African languages contributed greatly to the Latin American Spanish lexicon during colonial times, especially with words related to nature, food, or tools.[27] The dramatists, however, more often than not prefer to use the most general names for things ("árbol," "ave," "flor," "planta" [act 2]) or names of familiar European species. For example, in the second and third acts we find that Santa Rosa's garden apparently contains no native Peruvian flowers, trees, or plants, such as any of a wide variety of native orchids, lobster claws, or cacti; she and Bodigo name, rather, "azucenas," "claveles," "lirios," "rosas," "perales" and "romero"; all common in Spain and Europe.[28] Bodigo furthermore utters two incongruous remarks. His allusion to a tavern in Madrid in act 3 is inexplicable given that, as mentioned, it is unlikely that he could be from Spain or have detailed knowledge of particulars of Madrid. It is also curious that he would refer to Don Juan as a "perulero" in act 1 (Don Gonzalo also calls him an "indiano"). A *perulero* or *indiano* is, of course, what Spaniards called someone returning from America with riches; to use the word in Peru would have been odd. Besides, most *peruleros* would not have voluntarily revealed to permanent inhabitants of the region an intention to make money to take back to Spain. Besides, common terms for one suspected of having such a plan were *advenedizo, gachupín,* or *chapetón* (generally, Spanish immigrant; often used pejoratively to designate one who exploits the region for personal or Spanish profit).

Not only is the lexicon of the play in general and of Rosa and Bodigo in particular decidedly peninsular; their characters too show little difference from established Spanish comedia types. Instead of integrating Creole, mulatto, or mestizo elements into the personas of Rosa, her father Gaspar, or Bodigo, Moreto and Lanini y Sagredo characterize them according to conventions common to the comedia de santas genre. We find a nun confronted with the persistence of one or more suitors in Lope's *La bienaventurada madre Santa Teresa de Jesús* and *Vida y muerte de Santa Teresa de Jesús,* Tirso's *Santa Juana* trilogy, Calderón's *El mágico prodigioso,* and Ángela de Azevedo's *La margarita del Tajo que dio nombre a Santarén,* to name a few.[29] With regard to Gaspar, the father as blocking figure is a staple of innumerable comedias of all types, while the father figure who wants his daughter to marry instead of becoming a nun is especially common in the comedia de santas.[30] Elma Dassbach affirms that the majority of graciosos in comedias de santos enact humorous and often parodic imitations of their saintly masters, as does Bodigo.[31] Even particular moments in the text seem to have been drawn from established precedents. In the third act, as Don Juan is about to kill Gaspar, Rosa enters carrying a cross and falls before him, "para que vos no caigáis / en un error sin disculpa" (act 3) [that you may not fall / into inexcusable error]. This parallels similar interventions on the part of the saint to prevent violence in, for example, Tirso's *Santa Juana, segunda parte* and Azevedo's *Dicha y desdicha del juego y devoción de la Virgen*. Calderón's famous *La devoción de la cruz* features the theme of the cross as salvation, while *Caer para levantar*, by Moreto and various collaborators, and Tirso's *Quien no cae no se levanta* center on the metaphor of falling in order to rise. On two occasions, Rosa rejects the fleeting, superficial beauty of flowers, in favor of "aquella Rosa interior" (act 1) [that interior Rose], divine virtue, since "sombras son las que ayer / fueron en el suelo estrellas" (act 3) [those that yesterday were stars on earth are now shadows]. We see this classical appropriation of typical carpe diem imagery in order to express the theme of *contemptus mundi* also in Sor Juana Inés de la Cruz's sonnet "Rosa divina que en gentil cultura" (which could well be seen as an ascetic response to Garcilaso de la Vega's sonnet 23, "En tanto que de rosa y d'azucena").

In synthesis, what we see here is symptomatic of a phenomenon Stephen Greenblatt has noted: the transparency of cultural otherness for the European; the inability, or unwillingness, to see another culture as substantial, valid, opaque. Greenblatt maintains that "in the eyes of the Europeans, the Indians were culturally naked. This illusion that the inhabitants of the 'New World' are essentially without a culture of their own is both early and remarkably persistent, even in the face of overwhelming contradictory evidence."[32] Europeans of the early modern period (Greenblatt includes several Spaniards as examples) demonstrate a "conviction that reality was one and universal, constituted identically for all men at all times and in all places."[33] This is precisely what we detect in *Santa Rosa del Perú*. In the lexicon, poetic language, and characters of the figures in whom we might expect to see some degree of alterity, we see peninsular forms and conventions. Otherness disappears; the inhabitants of colonial Lima are for the most part representatives or extensions of Spanish customs and values.

Yet, for all of this, our playwrights are aware that Spanish audiences expect to see, if not meaningful difference, at least some hints of the exotic in a play set in America. Another way in which the dramatists represent cultural alterity in *Santa Rosa del Perú* is through what I will call synecdochal exoticism. According to Deborah Root, "exoticism. . . works through a process of dismemberment and fragmentation in which objects stand for images that stand for a culture or a sensibility as a whole. Exoticism is synecdochal, and fragments of culture work to exemplify a larger whole."[34] Using Yuri Lotman's conception of a "cultural text" as "any carrier of integral ('textual') meaning including ceremonies, works of art, as well as 'genres' such as 'prayer', 'law', 'novel', etc.," Balme echoes Root in distinguishing the syncretic theater he studies from theatrical exoticism: "Exoticism involves the use of indigenous cultural texts purely for their surface appeal, but with no regard to their original cultural semantics. They mean little else than their alterity; they are no longer texts in the semiotic sense, but merely signs, floating signifiers of otherness."[35]

We find just such synecdochal signifiers sprinkled throughout *Santa Rosa del Perú*: often Lima is rendered superficially, through references to things Spaniards of the era might easily associate with the "New World." As the play opens, for example, some musicians enter singing that just as "la plata" [silver] has made Peru rich, so too has Rosa made it more beautiful and virtuous (act 1). Often compared to the biblical city of Ophir, source of Solomon's Gold, Peru was virtually synonymous with riches for Spaniards of the time.[36] Peru meant silver in the popular imagination, and silver evoked Peru. Foods are also used to suggest a "New World" setting. In the final act, Bodigo dreams of eating "pepitoria de pavo" [turkey stew]. Turkey, defined briefly as "gallo de las Indias" [rooster of the indies] by Sebastián de Covarrubias, is native to the Americas and was first brought from Mexico to Spain in the early sixteenth century.[37] There is nothing particularly Peruvian about the stew Bodigo mentions, however; Spaniards commonly prepared poultry in a "pepitoria," a stew made from the necks and wings of the bird.[38] Thus a native element is used, but in a familiar European context: no American "cultural text" is included with the superficial symbol.

Chocolate, another important product of Latin American origin, also appears in the third act. Bodigo, however, assesses its utility according to European beliefs when he claims it is a "sánalo todo" (act 3) [cure-all]. The medicinal qualities of chocolate had been praised since the late sixteenth century by Spanish physicians and naturalists such as Francisco Hernández (Philip II's doctor) and Juan de Cárdenas, who, following Galenic theory in categorizing cacao as generally cold and humid in character, recommended chocolate as a remedy for fevers or overheating.[39] Aztec society did not, however, regard chocolate in the same way. Chocolate had many uses for the Aztecs, but they certainly did not consider it a cure-all that generally promoted good health; on the contrary, Aztec authorities often preached temperance in the imbibing of chocolate, as it was believed by some to have a hallucinatory or narcotic effect, and according to at least one legend, is blamed for ruining the health of the entire race of Aztecs. [40]

European concerns are further reflected in Bodigo's rhetorical question, "¿Hay cosa como un licor tal, que quebranta un dolor, y no quebranta el ayuno?" (act 3) [Is there anything quite like this drink which relieves pain, but doesn't break a fast?]. At the time of the publication of the work, a debate in the area of ecclesiastical law had ensued concerning whether or not chocolate should be regarded as a food and thus be forbidden during church fasts. Some argued that not only was chocolate substantial enough to be considered a food, it was furthermore an aphrodisiac, thus should clearly be prohibited at fasts. With Bodigo's comment, Lanini y Sagredo seems to weigh in on the issue, against prohibition. Economically there was much at stake in the decision; a censuring of chocolate by the church would certainly affect the cacao trade, which generally benefited Spanish immigrant merchants and traders more than it did Creoles. This episode in Rosa's life was actually used in the debate to argue that chocolate was a sacred and virtuous drink. In 1680, Giovanni Batista Gudenfridi argues against his antichocolate adversary Francesco Felini, facetiously asking, "Does he think, if chocolate merits the name of a diabolical liquid, that God would command, or permit, that by the hand of his Angels such a drink be given to one of his Brides?"[41] The drink was of course approved by the church and the cacao trade remained strong. Thus, although chocolate is used to suggest a "New World" setting, Bodigo's comments foreground only European uses and interests in the beverage. Later, I will show that if we look beyond the gracioso's remarks, we may find subtle connections to indigenous culture. It remains clear however, that Bodigo attaches European rather than American "cultural texts" to the signifier "chocolate."

We see another, if not synecdochal, equally reductive deformation of Latin America in the first act when the devil rages that "esta tierra, que era siempre mía, donde siempre reinó mi idolatría, no sólo se la quita a mi desvelo, sino que quiere Dios hacerla Cielo" [this land, which has always been mine, where my idolatry has always reigned, is not only being taken from my watch, but further, God wants to turn it into heaven]. Moreto and Lanini y Sagredo place the inhabitants of America at extremes: they were pagan idolaters condemned to hell, but now show the potential in the devotion to Catholicism to make Peru a heaven on earth. In this, the dramatists follow a long succession of chroniclers of America and Peru who had used this binary opposition—"New World" as utopia/dystopia—with varying emphases and toward different ends.[42] By 1670, a richer understanding of native character was possible, but the authors revert to the distortions of Peruvian spirituality which persisted at that time in the Spanish imagination.

A third mode of representation, however, exists simultaneously with those of erasure and exoticism. At certain moments in the play we may detect an American cultural text superimposed upon a peninsular configuration, thereby effecting a subtle, perhaps even unintentional hybridization. The concept of "mimicry" is key to Bhabha's idea of hybridity in representations of culture. He notes two processes that occur in some works of colonial and post-colonial literature. One, mimesis, is akin to the erasure of difference I have already described: colonial subjects are made over in the likeness of their colonizers. Graham Huggan labels this part of Bhabha's theory the "metro-politan mimetic imperative."[43] At the same time, mimicry, or as Huggan explains, "mischievous imitation—the kind of imitation that pays ironic homage to its object" may be at work in the text.[44] Bhabha tends to use the term "mimicry" to refer to both processes working simultaneously: "Mimicry is thus the sign of a double articulation; a complex strategy of reform, regulation and discipline, which 'appropriates' the Other as it visualizes power. Mimicry is also the sign of the inappropriate, however, a difference of recalcitrance which coheres the dominant strategic function of colonial power, in-tensifies surveillance, and poses an immanent threat to both 'normalized' knowledges and disciplinary powers."[45] Writers literally make the other appropriate for their metropolitan audiences, but they also reveal aspects of difference that cannot be appropriated, cannot be brought under the empire's control, and thus constitute a threat to imperial dominance.

We see this phenomenon at work in Moreto and Lanini y Sagredo's depiction of the relationship between Don Juan on the one hand and Rosa and her father Gaspar on the other. The play seems to use the common comedia de santas convention of the noble suitor who, despite his elevated social status, wishes to marry the humble, devout future saint. We see this, for example, in Tirso's *La Santa Juana, primera parte*, Calderón's *El condenado por desconfiado*, Azevedo's *Dicha y desdicha* and *La margarita del Tajo*, and Lope's *Santa Teresa de Jesús*. This topos seems to serve to instruct young bachelors to seek in a wife not necessarily riches, but above all, virtue, modesty, and beauty. Indeed, in this play, Don Gonzalo advises Don Juan not to marry for wealth, but to choose a woman who is "pobre, honesta y bien nacida" (act 1) [poor, honest, and well born].

Yet class differences in this play could well be interpreted in terms of the tension in colonial Lima between immigrant Spaniards and Peruvian Creoles. Some Spanish immigrants felt superior to Creoles, who they believed were unfit for public office because many of the conquerors were artisans or peasants, not nobles, and many of their descendants, as mentioned, were mestizos or mulattos. In the play, we are continually reminded of the social distance between Rosa's father and Juan, as the latter always calls him by his name only, despite his hidalgo status, while Gaspar never omits the title "don" in addressing Juan. We see further evidence of an attitude of superiority when the devil exploits differences in social standing to turn Don Juan against Gaspar, citing the Creole's "arrojo de atreverse / a un caballero tan grande / como tú" (act 3) [boldness in daring to offend a gentleman as great as you]. For their part, Creoles, by the 1600s, felt their true oppressors were not the Crown, the viceroyalty, missionaries, or conquerors, but Spanish *chapetones* or *gachupines* who, as noted, deprived them of opportunity and wealth by taking public offices they felt should be theirs, by taking workers away from Creole landowners, and by taking profits from trade back to the peninsula.[46] Since Don Juan is an entirely fictitious character, the playwrights could have made him anything—a Creole, like Rosa, for example—or they could have left the matter of his wealth ambiguous. Instead, they choose to make him a Spaniard from Toledo, and, as has been indicated, to identify him as an *indiano/perulero* (act 1). He is furthermore literally demonized: under the devil's influence he becomes the villain of the play, pressuring Rosa to marry him, threatening to kill her lover, then trying to violate her and kill her father. All of this could be read in terms of Bhabha's "mimicry": Don Juan is, to use Huggan's term, a "mischievous imitation" of the violent and oppressive forces of colonization which attempt to control Creoles and satisfy selfish interests through any means at their disposal. Rosa and Gaspar embody Peruvian, as distinct from Spanish, identity: Rosa's insistence on choosing her own vocation despite Don Juan's entreaties symbolizes Latin American resistance to Spanish control.

There is also a different way of interpreting the chocolate episode of the third act discussed earlier which foregrounds indigenous issues. I have discussed how the scene initially appears to be informed by European interests and concerns. If, however, we consider some of the Amerindian "cultural texts" of chocolate, we begin to see elements of hybridity in this moment. Chocolate of course had many uses in Mayan and Aztec ritual. Mayans anointed boys and girls with chocolate during a ritual resembling the Christian baptism.[47] Though Rosa is not literally baptized in the scene in question, she could be compared to the subject of a rite of passage: God tests her fortitude by making her endure pain but helps her in her change of status from the human to the divine by giving her chocolate. Mayans also used grains of cacao as a symbol of betrothal in marriage ceremonies.[48] The idea of marriage is present in this scene: Jesus has appeared to Rosa, who addresses him as her "dulce Esposo" [sweet husband], to bring her the ecstatic pain which, according to the mystics, characterizes the union, often presented metaphorically as matrimony, with the divine. In Aztec culture, there was a strong association between cacao and the human heart and blood. Aztecs used the words for heart and blood, *yollotl* and *eztli*, together as a metaphor for chocolate.[49] In sacrificial rituals, the cacao pod sometimes symbolized the heart, whether because they had similar shapes or were both associated with vital fluids, chocolate and blood.[50] In the play, Rosa's pain seems to emanate from the heart: at one moment, she cries, "¡Ay, que en el pecho amoroso / me revienta el corazón!" (act 3) [Oh, in my loving breast / my heart is bursting!] Chocolate, symbol of the heart, quells the pain in Rosa's heart. More importantly, the ritual associations between cacao, the heart, and sacrifice remind us that this episode is a precursor to Rosa's eventual self-sacrifice in the name of God. Indeed, in another Azetc ritual chocolate is used to fortify emotionally and physically one who is to be sacrificed. Fray Diego Durán explains how Aztecs dealt with prisoners to be sacrificed if, after being warned of their fate, they became despondent:

> They went immediately to procure sacrificial knives, washed off the human blood adhering to them . . . and with that filthy water prepared a gourd of chocolate, giving it to him to drink. It is said that the draught had this effect upon him: he became almost unconscious and forgot what he had been told. Then he returned to his usual cheerfulness and dance. . . . It is believed that he offered himself for death with great joy and gladness, bewitched by the beverage. This drink was called *itzpacalatl*, which means "water from the washing of obsidian blades." They gave him this beverage because if a man became sorrowful owing to the warning it was held as an evil omen or sign prognosticating some future disaster.[51]

These indigenous cultural texts are present simultaneously with the European concerns discussed earlier. No single perspective gains exclusive possession of the representative space; all coexist in something akin to what Greenblatt has described as "the inbetween, the zone of intersection in which all culturally determinate significations are called into question by an unresolved and unresolvable hybridity."[52]

Some readers may question the notion that three different and at times opposed modes of representation should operate within the same text. Bakhtin has argued, however, through his theory of "heteroglossia," that a single consciousness can produce a multiplicity of voices. As Michael Holquist explains, Bakhtin's theory suggests that "all transcription systems—including the speaking voice in a living utterance—are inadequate to the multiplicity of the meanings they seek to convey. My voice gives the illusion of unity to what I say; I am, in fact, constantly expressing a plenitude of meanings, some intended, others of which I am unaware."[53] Of course *Santa Rosa del Perú* is the product of at least two such perspectives, those of Moreto and Lanini y Sagredo. Both authors, in addition, had to negotiate a great number of sources, including written hagiographies, popular legends, and comedias about saints and of other genres. Like all Golden Age playwrights, they had to take into account the audience's foreknowledge of the events to be dramatized and their expectation to be entertained. They also had to be wary of the whims of censors and of any royal decrees affecting the theater.[54] It was in the best interest of the playwright who hoped to have his work performed to maintain general propriety and defend Counter-Reformation ideals. Finally, a dramatic script is written in the knowledge that ultimately the performance will be a greatly collaborative effort, a product of the interaction between director, script, actors, the context of the performance, props, effects, and costumes. In summary, Golden Age comedias in general, and *Santa Rosa del Perú* in particular, are highly polyvocal works which must satisfy many other interests besides those of the playwrights and, therefore, may even express competing, contradictory ideas or meanings the writers may not have consciously intended. Both Roland Barthes's characterization of a text as "a tissue of quotations drawn from innumerable centres of culture" and Michel Foucault's contention that writing is about "creating a space into which the writing subject constantly disappears" resonate profoundly in the case of the play in question.[55]

We may further inquire, however, precisely what competing agendas are satisfied by *Santa Rosa del Perú*. I have called the various modes of representation "strategies" because each one serves the interest of one or more of the forces invested in the production of the work. Although it is beyond the scope of this study to evidence thoroughly the motives behind each representational strategy, it is nonetheless possible to discuss some conceivable agendas.

First, in the play's recognition of differences between Creoles and Spaniards, we have at least some degree of affirmation of Creole identity, and with it, some present-day historians might argue, the beginnings of Peruvian nationalism. Historian Teodoro Hampe Martínez maintains that the first American saint was canonized in 1671 largely due to the efforts of the Creole community of Lima to promote her case rather than those of other non-Creole candidates.[56] Peruvian Creoles had, by Rosa's time, reached economic, social, and political preeminence. Yet, as José Antonio Mazzotti maintains,

they longed for "cultural icons which would support their self-accorded prestige."[57] Thus, two Peruvian Creoles were presented as candidates for sainthood in the seventeenth century, Francisco de Solano and Isabel Flores de
Oliva. Brading accredits Flores' relatively precipitated canonization (Solano
was sainted in 1726) to the strength of Marianism at the time.[58] Hampe
Martínez holds that Creoles sought "the recognition of the Church's highest
authorities in order to consolidate their socio-economic prestige."[59] Benedict
Anderson's assertion that nationalism often emerges out of or against dominant cultural systems such as religion lends support to this thesis.[60] If such an
agenda was behind the movement for Rosa's sanctification, then it must also
have been operant in any celebration of her canonization, such as that constituted by *Santa Rosa del Perú.*[61]

Yet while Creoles may have assumed that recognition of their religious
virtue as a class would translate automatically into increased political and economic power, Spaniards forwarding Rosa's cause and celebrating her canonization might have reasoned differently. As mentioned, Rosa was, unlike her
heroine Saint Catherine, an apolitical figure. As a role model, she promotes
devotion to God and the church, a striving for inner spiritual perfection, and
avoidance of the worldliness of politics, economics, and power. It is plausible
that some may have supported her cause in an effort not to forward but to
contain Creole aspirations to power and wealth. Creoles, after all, made up
the largest part of the mendicant orders and were considered best suited for
religious vocations.[62] Rosa may have been seen as the perfect role model to encourage Creoles to "stay in their place" rather than competing with Spanish
nobles for public offices and other positions of power outside the church.

The purpose of the synecdochal exoticism evident in the work in the references to *chocolate, pavo, plata,* and *idolatría* is easily understood and has already been touched upon: the audience would have expected to see signs and
symbols of America in a play set in Perú. Innovation and accuracy in the presentation and contextualization of such emblems would have been of little importance, and might even be antithetical to the purpose of entertaining the
audience. Any signs of the "New World" that did not jibe with the common
associations that existed in the imaginations of Spanish theatergoers might be
questioned or met with disapproval; better, then, from a playwright's view, to
leave them out, sketch in the setting as might best meet the audience's expectations, and get on with the more central task of dramatizing the saint's virtues
and miracles. The decision to draw from earlier successful comedia models for
character types and subplots rather than to adhere strictly to the biographers'
accounts or create innovative modifications would have been equally instinc-

tive for the playwrights toward the same end of finding the best way to enter-
tain the audience. Frank Casa expresses what many Moreto scholars have observed; that he "was not a creator of original plots; he used what was available
to him, and he owes a great deal to his predecessors."[63] Comedia de santos
conventions were well established by the 1670s; the public would no doubt
have been quite disappointed had there been no gracioso, no *galán*, and no
capa y espada jealousy and intrigue in *Santa Rosa del Perú*. Golden Age playwrights, again, collaborated most graciously with their audiences; to this we
owe the exoticism and imitation of previous works, reductionist and fictitious
as they may be.[64]

Finally, the erasure of authentic signs of otherness in Rosa, Gaspar, and
Bodigo in favor of depicting them as, for all intents and purposes, Spaniards,
appears purposeful as well. It is in the best interest of the dramatists and the
Spanish authorities that Rosa be celebrated not as a triumph particularly
for the "New World" but as an affirmation of the virtue of Spain and Catholicism in general, to justify the colonial project in Latin America and with it,
ultimately, empire. From a peninsular perspective, Rosa represents Spain's
presence in the "New World" and the virtue of its evangelical mission of con-
verting the indigenous peoples to Christianity: the fact that Spain has produced a saint in America confirms that the Christian God approves and
blesses its project there. When the devil threatens an angel in act 1 saying "Yo
voy a hacer todo [este] Imperio mío" [I'm going to make this entire empire
mine], he issues a challenge not only to Rosa but to all of Spain and its aspirations of religious and political dominance in America. The success of Rosa
and of Catholicism in Latin America justifies Spain's desire for empire; it vin-
dicates the conquest and all its violence, for in the eyes of Spanish missionaries and the church, countless souls have been and are being won for Christ.

Rosa furthermore symbolizes Spain's triumph in preventing the spread of
Protestantism in America. When the Dutch pirate Spilbergen invades Callao
harbor in the third act, the dramatists depict him as a representative of Protestantism. Gaspar refers to him simply as "la herejía" [heresy] who arrives in an
"armada soberbia" [arrogant fleet]. Rosa prays to the Virgin:

> No permitas que la furia
> de aquesta gente perversa,
> enemigos de la fe
> con la ponzoñosa soberbia
> de sus ritos, inficionen
> esta católica tierra.
> (act 2)

[Do not allow the fury
of this perverse people,
enemies of the faith,
with the poisonous arrogance
or their rituals, to infect
this Catholic land.]

She condemns Protestantism as a "monstruo racional" [rational monster], an "hidra de sectas diversas" [hydra of diverse sects], guilty of "blasfemia" [blasphemy] (act 2). Here Moreto and Lanini y Sagredo follow the example of a good many comedias de santos, which, according to Manuel Cañete, constituted "the trusty arm of the Catholic that fired eternal truths at heresy and the errors of Protestantism."[65] They may have used Tirso in particular as their model. At the beginning of *La Santa Juana, segunda parte,* an angel appears to discuss the threat of Protestantism with Juana:

Llorando estabas el estrago horrible
que al mundo anuncia confusión y espanto
por la ponzoña del dragón terrible
de las siete cabezas que en Sajonia
niega la ley católica infalible.
Llorabas que con falsa ceremonia
y hipócrita apariencia el vil Lutero
imitase a Nembrot en Babilonia,
y que el rebaño del Pastor cordero,
este lobo, en oveja disfrazado,
despedazase con estrago fiero.[66]

[You were weeping ofr the horrible devastation
which cries confusion and fear to the world
wreaked by the venom of the terrible seven-headed dragon
that rejects the infallible Catholic law in Saxony.
You wept to see vile Luther
with false ceremony and hypocritical appearance
imitate Nemrod in Babylon
like a wolf in sheep's clothing
tearing apart the gentle Shepard's flock
with fierce devastation.]

Tirso's angel then tells Juana not to fear, however, and shows her a vision of "el fértil fruto / que en las Indias España al Cielo ha dado" [the fertile fruit of the

Indies that Spain has given to heaven], and praises Cortés for conquering America for Catholicism.[67] Like Tirso, Moreto and Lanini y Sagredo present America as a new frontier for the faith that compensates the growth of Protestantism in Europe which so disturbed Counter-Reformation Spain. Within this scheme, they wish to present Rosa not as a cultural other, but as Spain's crusader in the "New World," defending Catholicism from the threat of Protestantism: through her prayers, the invaders are repelled.

Santa Rosa del Perú is certainly neither Moreto's greatest nor best-known work. The playwright's final effort is, however, interesting to consider as a site of contention over which disparate cultural, textual, and authorial forces clash. Ultimately no single voice, consciousness, or ideology gains exclusive control of the work. The resulting lack of coherence is perhaps both the play's greatest defect and most interesting virtue. That James Castañeda should find the play flamboyant and "desultory" is hardly surprising given, as we have seen, the variety of competing interests, contrasting cultural texts, and conflicting voices prevailing upon the text.[68] This discussion has focused merely on the script or literary text of the play; one can only imagine how the pressures on the work would be multiplied in any performance by the perspectives and idiosyncrasies of director, actors, costumer, and crew. It can only be hoped that a contemporary company might undertake the play and explore the great potential for ironic subversion of imperialist ideology I have attempted to evidence. In the hands of an imaginative director and cast interested in restoring to the play's cultural texts the precise meanings overlooked or ignored by the playwrights, the written script might well be transformed, if not into the type of syncretic theater studied by Balme, perhaps into "presyncretic" drama: a work conceived from the point of view of the colonizer, but appropriated and refracted ironically by contemporary voices speaking in sympathy with the transparent, exoticized, or placated colonial other.

NOTES

1. Bhabha, *Location of Culture*, 5.
2. Balme, *Decolonizing the Stage*, 2.
3. Forsdick, "Travelling Concepts."
4. Segalen, *Essay on Exoticism*, 16.
5. Ibid., 61.
6. Forsdick, "Travelling Concepts," 25–26.
7. Castañeda, *Agustín Moreto*, 48.

8. Hampe Martínez, *Santidad,* 65–68.

9. Morrison, *Lope de Vega,* 27.

10. Since word-of-mouth legends and numerous written versions of Rosa's life were highly circulated throughout the 1600s in Spain and Latin America, it is difficult to determine the exact sources from which the authors drew. Most Spanish playwrights who wrote comedias de santos consulted what scholars consider the two most widely read Spanish-language hagiographical accounts of the time, the *Flos Sanctorum* of Alonso de Villegas (1565) and that of Pedro de Ribadaneyra (1599). See Caro Baroja, *Las formas complejas,* 79; McKendrick, "Calderón's Justina," 2; and Sánchez Lora, *Mujeres,* 374. Although most of Rosa's life (1586–1617) postdates their first publication, the dramatists still may have been able to find entries for her, since in later editions of both works, clergy of the order continued to add vitae. Ribadaneyra's 1761 edition, for example, contains Rosa's life. See Pedro de Ribadeneyra, *Flos Sanctorum,* 641. It is likely that such versions would have been based on the work of others, however, such as Pedro de Loayza's 1619 biography of Rosa (one of the earliest accounts of her life by one of her confessors, written in *castellano*) and/or the latin *Vita* written by Leonardus Hansen and published in 1664 (in Europe, the most widely read and translated biography of the saint). See Hampe Martínez, *Santidad,* 82, 63.

11. Pedro de Loayza, for example, describes Rosa's throwing flowers into the air to form a suspended cross and her saving Callao from Dutch invaders through prayer as two nonrelated incidents, while Lanini y Sagredo links both miracles in the same scene in the third act. See Loayza, *Vida de Santa Rosa,* 25, 59.

12. Ibid., 85.

13. Studies on the exclusion of the mother in Golden Age literature are numerous. For discussion of the topic with regard to Spanish literature of the age in general, see Bergmann, "Exclusion of the Feminine," 123–36; and Cruz, "Search for the M/Other." For discussion of omission of the mother in the Golden Age *comedia* specifically, see Díez Borque, *Sociología,* 86; and Strother, *Family Matters,* 142–43.

14. This is certainly not to suggest that there was no cultural alterity within Spain itself; the proliferation in recent decades of studies of the subcultures of women, homosexuals, and Jewish, Arabic, and African peoples in Spanish society and literature attests to the existence of otherness within the metropolis. My purpose here, however, is to discern where we may most likely discover alterity in *Santa Rosa del Perú.*

15. Brading, *First America,* 320. By Rosa's lifetime, the indigenous population around Lima had dwindled. Many either lived outside of the cities in small communities forced to pay tribute to the Crown or worked in the mines, according to the *mita,* the system of compulsory wage labor instituted by the viceroyalty and dating back to the administration of Francisco de Toledo (1569–81). See Ibid., 131, 133, 137, 318.

16. Ibid., 317.

17. Moreto and Sagredo, *Santa Rosa del Perú,* act 1. This electronic version of *Santa Rosa del Perú* was prepared by Ricardo Castells and Vern Williamsen for the Web site of the Association of Hispanic Classical Theater in 1999–2000. As it does not include line or page numbers, I will hereafter cite the source in the text with reference only to the act in which the quotation appears.

18. Brading, *First America,* 321–22. Brading cites as evidence of the presence of African slaves in Peru a report in Fray Buenaventura de Salinas y Córdova's *Memorial de las historias del*

Nuevo Mundo, Pirú (1630) that maintains that Lima's six great convents housed 1,366 nuns and 899 slaves.

19. Loayza, *Vida de Santa Rosa*, 100. Unless otherwise noted, all translations are my own.

20. Altuna, "Imágenes del Perú," 220–23.

21. Brading, *First America*, 296–98.

22. Brading reports, for example, that in 1612, the Dominican friar Juan de la Puente published a note declaring that Spaniards born and raised in America are prone toward the vices of the natives—inconstancy, lasciviousness, lying—due to the balmy climate. Ibid., 298.

23. Carey-Webb, "Other-Fashioning," 428–29.

24. Saint Catherine of Siena was, for example, an active mediator of conflicts in the Catholic Church: she negotiated the return of the papacy from Avignon to Rome in 1377, and maintained influential correspondences with various heads of state and prominent figures of the church. Rosa took Catherine as her role model. Accordingly, Moreto and Lanini y Sagredo have her appear in various scenes with several of the same iconographic elements with which Catherine is traditionally associated, such as the cross, the lily, the infant Christ, and the crown of thorns. See Hall, *Dictionary of Subjects and Symbols in Art*, 59–60. According to most accounts, however, Rosa imitated primarily Catherine's alleged violent mortifications and interior, spiritual transformation rather then her sociopolitical activism. Kathleen Ann Myers observes that Rosa's biographers systematically downplay her notable learning and writing in favor of a focus on her ascetic practices and implies that inquisitional censorship may have prompted such an emphasis. See Myers, "Redeemer of America," 264–65.

25. Brading, *First America*, 338–39.

26. Iwasaki Cauti, "Mujeres," 594–95. Myers, "Redeemer of America," 270. See also 274, notes 46–47, for a discussion of the post-Tridentine church's need to control the writings and influence of laypeople and religious women in particular, and bibliographical information on where one may find Santa Rosa's letters, collages, poetry, and prayers as well as references she and others made to the notebooks which may have contained her autobiographical writings.

27. See Lapesa, *Historia de la lengua española*, 556–63. Lapesa points out, for example, that as early as the mid 1500s historian and naturalist Gonzalo Fernández de Oviedo used over five hundred *americanismos*, most related to "New World" flora, fauna, and ethnography, in his *Historia General de las Indias* (1535).

28. The *azucena* [lily], or *lilium candidum*, is native to the Balkans and perhaps Israel, Lebanon, and Greece, and is among the earliest flowers to be domesticated (in Crete around 1500 BC) and grown all over Europe. The attribute of the Greek goddess Hera, the Virgin Mary, and numerous saints, it has long symbolized purity and chastity (as Rosa explains in the third act: "De las vírgenes sagradas / esta cándida azucena / es símbolo, pues haciendo / claustro de sus hojas mesmas, / encierra en su castidad / el oro de su pureza" [This candid lily is the symbol of the sacred virgins, as, cloistering itself in its own leaves, it chastely conceals its golden purity]). See Felter and Lloyd, *King's American Dispensatory;* Finch and Parsons, "Lily of the Garden"; Lineberger, "Easter Lily." Bodigo craves pears from a pear tree in the garden in the second act, although such trees were not native to Peru, but to Europe and Asia, and were transplanted to North America by Dutch colonists. Pear trees are easily domesticated, yet even if there were such trees in Lima at the time, the pear is certainly not emblematic of Latin America but is commonly associated with Europe, particularly Greece and the Roman Empire. See Weishan, "Pick a Pear"; and the California Pear Advisory Board, "History of California Pears."

29. For arguments concerning Lope's authorship of *Vida y muerte de Santa Teresa de Jesús*, see Aragone Terni, *Vida y muerte,* 20–39. Robert Morrison remains unconvinced that the play was the work of Lope alone. See Morrison, *Lope de Vega,* 112.

30. Notable examples are Don Alonso of Lope's *La bienaventurada madre Santa Teresa de Jesús,* Juan Vásquez of Tirso de Molina's *La Santa Juana, primera parte,* Cleandro of his *Quien no cae no se levanta,* and various male figures including the pope in his *La joya de las montañas.*

31. As Dassbach observes, we find examples of this type of gracioso in Tirso's *Santo y sastre, Quien no cae no se levanta,* and *El árbol del mejor fruto,* Lope's *La vida de San Pedro Nolasco,* and Calderón's *El José de las mujeres* and *El mágico prodigioso.* See Dassbach, *La comedia hagiográfica,* 146–50, 153.

32. Greenblatt, *Learning to Curse,* 17.

33. Ibid., 28. Greenblatt focuses primarily on what he calls "linguistic colonialism," the colonizer's disregard for native tongues and imposition of his own language on the colonized. He distinguishes British attitudes toward conquest from those of Spain in that Britons, such as his opening example, Samuel Daniel, see expansion of their language as an objective of empire, while Spanish missionaries consider language as an instrument toward their ultimate goal of evangelization. See 16. The language problem he discusses is a manifestation of the larger problem toward which he moves, that of the erasure or silencing of cultural otherness, which I believe to be operant, to varying degrees, in Spanish and colonial literature of the period.

34. Root, *Cannibal Culture,* 42.

35. Lotman, "Theses on the Semiotic Study of Cultures, 6. Balme, *Decolonizing the Stage,* 5.

36. Brading, *First America,* 314.

37. Covarrubias, *Tesoro,* 857. University of Illinois Extension College, "Turkey History and Lore."

38. Covarrubias, *Tesoro,* 862.

39. Coe and Coe, *True History,* 122–23.

40. Ibid., 79–80. Fray Diego Durán reports that the Emperor Motecuhzoma sent an expedition of sorcerers to find Aztlan, their mythical homeland. They found the island, where they were met by a servant of the goddess Coatlicue. He led them up the hill of Colhuacan to see her. Seeing that the Aztecs struggled to climb the hill, he told them that the chocolate and other foods of their lands had made them heavy and would bring them death. Upon meeting the goddess, the Aztecs offered her a gift of chocolate. She told them the chocolate had burdened them. On the way back down the hill, her servant admonished them again, saying that the chocolate had made them old, tired, and weak; in short, it had ruined them.

41. Quoted in ibid., 154.

42. We first see this polarizing tendency used in Cristobal Colón's "Carta a los Reyes" to imply that the peaceful natives of "Española" would be accepting of Spain's evangelizing mission while the natives of "Caribo" deserved to be enslaved for their cannibalism and tyranny over the others. See Colón, *Textos y documentos,* 231, 234. José de Acosta (*Historia natural y moral de las Indias,* 1590) and Bernabé Cobo (*Historia del Nuevo Mundo,* 1653) both condemned the Incas as subjects of the devil. Even El Inca Garcilaso maintained that the pre-Incan inhabitants of Peru were uncivilized pagans in his *Comentarios reales de los Incas* (1609).

43. Huggan, "(Post)Colonialism," 95.

44. Ibid., 94.

45. Bhabha, *Location of Culture,* 86.

46. Brading, *First America,* 293.

47. Coe and Coe, *True History*, 62.

48. Ibid., 63.

49. Ibid., 101.

50. Ibid.

51. Durán, *Book of the Gods*, 132.

52. Greenblatt, *Marvelous Possessions*, 4.

53. Holquist, Introduction, xx.

54. For a summary of royal decrees reported by Rennert, Shergold, and Varey, see Morrison, *Lope de Vega*, 30–31.

55. Barthes, "Death of the Author," 146. Foucault, "What is an Author?" 102.

56. Hampe Martínez, *Santidad*, 115–16.

57. Mazzotti, "Garcilaso," 93.

58. Brading, *First America*, 338.

59. Hampe Martínez, *Santidad*, 9.

60. Anderson, *Imagined Communities*, 12.

61. For a brief summary and bibliography of other theories that explore the causes of Rosa's canonization, see Myers, "Redeemer of America," 252–53 and 272, note 6.

62. Brading, *First America*, 295, 320–21.

63 Casa, *Dramatic Craftsmanship of Moreto*, 5.

64. For a recent synthesis of this commonly remarked notion, see Morrison, *Lope de Vega*, 26–31.

65. Cañete, "Sobre el drama religioso español," 401.

66. Molina, *La Santa Juana*, 825, lines 8–18.

67. Ibid., 826, lines 70–92.

68. Castañeda, *Agustín Moreto*, 49.

WORKS CITED

Altuna, Elena. "Imágenes del Perú y protocriollismo en las cartas privadas de los inmigrantes." *Revista de crítica literaria latinoamericana* 52 (2000): 215–25.

Anderson, Benedict. *Imagined Communities: Reflections on the Origin and Spread of Nationalism*. London: Verso, 1983.

Aragone Terni, Elisa, ed. *Vida y muerte de Santa Teresa de Jesús*. By Lope de Vega. Florence, Italy: Casa Editrice D'Anna, 1970.

Balme, Christopher. *Decolonizing the Stage: Theatrical Syncretism and Post-Colonial Drama*. Oxford: Clarendon Press, 1999.

Barthes, Roland. "The Death of the Author." Translated by Stephen Heath. In *Image, Music, Text*, edited by Stephen Heath, 142–48. New York: Hill and Wang, 1977.

Bergmann, Emilie. "The Exclusion of the Feminine in the Cultural Discourse of the Golden Age: Juan Luis Vives and Fray Luis de León." In *Religion, Body and Gender in Early Modern Spain*, edited by Alain Saint-Saëns, 123–36. San Francisco: Mellen, 1991.

Bhabha, Homi K. *The Location of Culture*. London: Routledge, 1994.

Brading, David A. *The First America: The Spanish Monarchy, Creole Patriots, and the Liberal State, 1492–1867.* Cambridge: Cambridge University Press, 1991.

California Pear Advisory Board. "History of California Pears." *California Pears.* http://www.calpear.com/cns_hist.cfm.

Cañete, Manuel. "Sobre el drama religioso español, antes y después de Lope de Vega." *Memorias de la Academia Española 1* (1870): 368–412.

Carey-Webb, Allen. "Other-Fashioning: The Discourse of Empire and Nation in Lope de Vega's *El nuevo mundo descubierto por Cristóbal Colón.*" In *Amerindian Images and the Legacy of Columbus,* edited by René Jara and Nicholas Spadaccini, 425–51. Minneapolis: University of Minnesota Press, 1992.

Caro Baroja, Julio. *Las formas complejas de la vida religiosa; religión, sociedad y carácter in la España de los siglos XVI y XVII.* Madrid: Akal, 1978.

Casa, Frank P. *The Dramatic Craftsmanship of Moreto.* Cambridge, Mass.: Harvard University Press, 1966.

Castañeda, James A. *Agustín Moreto.* New York: Twayne, 1974.

Coe, Sophie D., and Michael D. Coe. *The True History of Chocolate.* London: Thames and Hudson, 1996.

Colón, Cristóbal. *Textos y documentos completos.* Edited by Consuelo Varela y Juan Gil. Madrid: Alianza, 1992.

Covarrubias, Sebastián de. *Tesoro de la lengua castellana o española.* Edited by Martín de Riquer. Barcelona: Alta Fulla, 1998.

Cruz, Anne J. "The Search for the M/Other in Early Modern Spain." *Indiana Journal of Hispanic Literatures* 8 (1996): 31–54.

Dassbach, Elma. *La comedia hagiográfica del Siglo de Oro español.* New York: Peter Lang, 1997.

Díez Borque, José María. *Sociología de la comedia española del siglo XVII.* Madrid: Cátedra, 1976.

Durán, Fray Diego. *Book of the Gods and Rites and the Ancient Calendar.* Translated by Fernando Horcasitas and Doris Heyden. Norman: University of Oklahoma Press, 1971.

Felter, Harvey Wickes, M.D., and John Uri Lloyd, Phr. M., Ph. D. *King's American Dispensatory, 1898.* Henriette's Herbal Homepage. http://www.ibiblio.org/ herbmed/eclectic/kings/lilium-cand.html.

Finch, Calvin, and Jerry Parsons. "The Lily of the Garden: the Bright and Morning Star." Texas Cooperative Extension Horticulture, The Texas A&M University System. http://www.plantanswers.com/arcadia_pages/lilum%20formosanum.htm.

Forsdick, Charles. "Travelling Concepts: Postcolonial Approaches to Exoticism." *Paragraph: A Journal of Modern Critical Theory* 24, no. 3 (2001): 12–29.

Foucault, Michel. "What is an Author?" Translated by Josué V. Harari. In *The Foucault Reader,* edited by Paul Rabinow, 101–20. New York: Pantheon, 1984.

Glissant, Edouard. *Introduction a une poétique de divers.* Paris: Gallimard, 1996.

Greenblatt, Stephen. *Learning to Curse: Essays in Early Modern Culture.* New York: Routledge, 1990.

————. *Marvelous Possessions: The Wonder of the "New World."* Chicago: University Press of Chicago,1991.

Hall, James. *Dictionary of Subjects and Symbols in Art.* New York: Harper and Row, 1973.

Hampe Martínez, Teodoro. *Santidad e identidad criolla.* Cuzco, Peru: Centro de Estudios Regionales Andinos "Bartolomé de las Casas," 1998.

Holquist, Michael. Introduction to *The Dialogic Imagination*, by M. M. Bakhtin, xv–xxxiii. Austin: University of Texas Press, 1981.

Huggan, Graham. "(Post)Colonialism, Anthropology, and the Magic of Mimesis." *Cultural Critique* 38 (1998): 91–106.

Iwasaki Cauti, Fernando. "Mujeres al borde de la perfección: Rosa de Santa María y las alumbradas de Lima." *Hispanic American Historical Review* 73, no. 4 (1993): 581–613.

Lapesa, Rafael. *Historia de la lengua española.* Madrid: Gredos, 1991.

Lineberger, Daniel. "Easter Lily." *Aggie Horticulture.* Texas A&M University, College Station. http://aggie-horticulture.tamu.edu/plantanswers/publications/lily/lily. html.

Loayza, Fray Pedro de. *Vida de Santa Rosa de Lima.* Lima: Iberia, 1965.

Lotman, Yuri. "Theses on the Semiotic Study of Cultures (as Applied to Slavic Texts)." In *Structure of Texts and Semiotics of Culture*, edited by Jan van der Eng and Mojiír Grygar, 1–28. The Hague: Mouton, 1973.

Mazzotti, José Antonio. "Garcilaso and the Origins of Garcilacism: The Role of the *Royal Commentaries* in the Development of a Peruvian National *Imaginaire.*" In *Garcilaso Inca de la Vega: An American Humanist, a Tribute to José Durand*, edited by José Anadón, 90–109. Notre Dame, Ind.: University of Notre Dame Press, 1998.

McKendrick, Melveena. "Calderón's Justina: The Assumption of Selfhood." In *Feminist Readings on Spanish and Latin-American Literature*, edited by L. P. Condé and S. M. Hart, 1–11. Lewiston, N.Y.: Edwin Mellen, 1991.

Molina, Tirso de (Fray Gabriel Téllez). *La Santa Juana, segunda parte.* In *Tirso de Molina: Obras dramáticas completas*, vol. 1, edited by Blanca de los Ríos, 825–65. Madrid: Aguilar,1946.

Moreto, Agustín, and Pedro Lanini y Sagredo. *Santa Rosa del Perú.* In *Parte treinta y seis [de] comedias escritas por los mejores ingenios de España*, edited by Joseph Fernández de Buendía. Madrid: Manuel Meléndez, 1671. http://www.trinity.edu/org/comedia/moreto/strosa.html.

Morrison, Robert R. *Lope de Vega and the Comedia de Santos.* New York: Peter Lang, 2000.

Myers, Kathleen Ann. "'Redeemer of America': Rosa de Lima (1586–1617), the Dynamics of Identity, and Canonization." In *Colonial Saints: Discovering the Holy in the Americas*, edited by Allan Greer and Jodi Bilinkoff, 251–75. New York: Routledge, 2003.

Otte, Enrique, and Guadalupe Albi Romero. *Cartas privadas de emigrantes a Indias, 1540–1616.* Mexico: Fondo de Cultura Económica, 1993.

Ribadeneyra, Pedro de. *Flos Sanctorum de las vidas de los santos.* Vol. 1. Madrid, 1761.

Root, Deborah. *Cannibal Culture: Art, Appropriation and the Commodification of Difference.* Boulder, Colo.: Westview Press, 1996.

Sánchez Lora, José L. *Mujeres, conventos y formas de la religiosidad barroca.* Madrid: Fundación Universitaria Española, 1988.

Segalen, Victor. *Essay on Exoticism: An Aesthetics of Diversity.* Translated by Yaël Rachel Schlick. Durham, N.C.: Duke University Press, 2002.

Strother, Darci L. *Family Matters: A Study of On- and Off-Stage Marriage and Family Relations in Seventeenth-Century Spain.* New York: Peter Lang, 1999.

University of Illinois Extension College of Agricultural,Consumer and Environmental Sciences, University of Illinois at Urbana-Champaign. "Turkey History and Lore." Urban Programs Resource Network. http://www.urbanext.uiuc.edu/turkey/history.html.

Villegas, Alonso de. *Flos Sanctorum.* Barcelona, 1748.

Weishan, Michael. "Pick a Pear: Background and History." In Village, Country Living, 1995–2003. http://magazines.ivillage.com/countryliving/garden/your/articles/0,,284660_294173-2,00.html.

Transatlantic Performances of Hybridity in Sor Juana's Baroque Festival, *Los empeños de una casa*

Michael J. Horswell

"nunca son pesadas las cosas que por agua están pasadas"
—From the "Sainete segundo," *Los empeños de una casa*

THE WORD "CROSSCURRENTS" IN THE TITLE OF THIS COLLECTION CONCERNING transatlantic crossings in early modern Spanish and Spanish American theater is a provocative term; crosscurrents, understood in its nautical meaning as "a current flowing at an angle to the main current" or in its rhetorical meaning as a "clashing or opposing opinion, influence or tendency," invites a discussion of the multiple crossings at play in Sor Juana Inés de la Cruz's baroque festival, *Los empeños de una casa* (1683).[1] Sor Juana's theater is often characterized as having flowed from the Calderonian school of classic Spanish theater.[2] Rather than only flow from it or even parallel with it, recent critics have begun to appreciate how Sor Juana's theater added to a crosscurrent that pulled the comedia in original directions as it crisscrossed the Atlantic to and from the periphery of empire.[3] Her critique of patriarchy in the play is well-known and contributed to the emerging protofeminist discourse disseminated by other seventeenth-century writers. Another compelling crosscurrent in Sor Juana's work is voiced through crossings of another sort: hybridization, the crossing or mixing of different breeds, races, cultures, ethnicities, or species and, in the case of Baroque theater, the combination of diverse poetic and performance genres. It is the performance of transatlantic hybridity that makes Sor Juana's play and Baroque fête, one of a few complete, extant Golden Age court festivals, unique and compelling, especially as the work relates to issues of mestizaje, transculturation, and an emerging Creole consciousness in the late seventeenth century.

Los empeños de una casa was ostensibly written and dedicated to celebrate the birth of a viceroy's son in the colonial city of Mexico and the arrival of a new archbishop.[4] There is, however, another birth staged and feted in the fiesta: that of a new subjectivity in the transatlantic literature and society of the Hispanic world. While the celebrated heir of the Spanish viceroyalty, José, is the American-born offspring of an European crossing between Italian and Spanish nobles, Sor Juana's fictional "newborn" is the precursor of a people eventually to be celebrated as the "cosmic race," the mestizo, the Mexican, the "crossbreed" of imperial, transatlantic miscegenation.[5] The Baroque spectacle of the comedia proved to be an auspicious vehicle for the introduction of this new subjectivity, affording the playwright a multivoiced, carnivalesque platform from which to perform several variations on the theme of hybridity. From the *loas* to the *sainetes* and from the *comedia* to the *final sarao,* the theatrical spectacle entertained its audience with allegories, metaphors, tropes, metadrama, and intertextualities that crisscrossed the Atlantic, transgressed the norms of viceregal and metropolitan culture, and above all, called into question the stability of renaissance humanists' epistemological paradigms of gender, race, and class. In short, the mixed-genre festival performed a unique commentary on transatlantic difference.

Octavio Paz, in his study of Sor Juana and the Baroque of New Spain, *Las trampas de la Fe,* asserts that artistic styles are always transnational currents that accept local particularities.[6] A variation on the transnational "estética de la extrañeza" [aesthetic of strangeness], the Mexican Baroque became, for Paz, the "colmo de la extrañeza" [height of strangeness] and the Creole, a self-conscious "ser extraño"[strange being].[7] I argue, however, that Sor Juana goes beyond merely adding local particularities to a transnational literary aesthetic. Sor Juana embodied the sense of difference expressed by the new "strange beings," crossing from the traditionally private space of women to the public space of colonial polemics, crossing to and from the court and the convent, and finally, crossing from New Spain to Old Spain through her writings. In her literary and theatrical works, she produces more than just aesthetic decoration in benign mimicry of the imperial Baroque by expressing an ideology of difference that challenges colonial hegemonies and imperial patriarchal culture. As Walter Mignolo has recently stated, "The colonial difference is the space where local histories inventing and implementing global designs meet local histories, the space in which global designs have to be adapted, adopted, rejected, integrated, or ignored. The colonial difference is, finally, the physical as well as the imaginary location where the coloniality of power is at work in the confrontation of two kinds of local histories displayed in different spaces

and times across the planet."[8] Sor Juana (Juana Ramírez de Asbaje) was born
in New Spain's San Miguel Nepantla.[9] The hybrid name of her birthplace (a
combination of a Christian saint and an indigenous Nahuatl word) sugges-
tively signals the kind of duality that would mark her writing; "nepantla" in
Nahuatl expresses the idea of "to be or feel in-between" or "torn between two
ways."[10] As a writing subject, Sor Juana moved in and beyond the liminal
space of the convent, a "multicultural," multiclassed place in which transatlantic intellectual currents clashed with local histories and experience of
Spaniards, Creoles, Indians, mestizas, mulattoes, and Africans. From this
local space she articulated her version of the transnational Baroque in what I
argue is a consistent evocation of the hybrid as an aesthetic and political
form of negotiating transatlantic culture, producing a carnivalesque confrontation between the local and the global. From this confrontation emerges
a consciousness of Creole identity and a challenge to imperial hegemony.

The transgressive potentiality of the Baroque was not just a colonial phenomenon. As John Beverley has pointed out, "the paradox of Spanish Baroque writing, both in the metropolis and the colonies, is that it was, like
postmodernism today, at once a technique of power of a dominant class in a
period of reaction and a figuration of the consciousness of the limits of that
power."[11] The American Baroque had the added intrigue and the cultural
specificity of working within and against the limits of coloniality and became
a semiautonomous literary movement that must be read, as Mabel Moraña
suggests, as an expression of the formation of a new "Hispano-American subject" who emerges, perhaps as "strange being," to confront the hegemony of
imperial ideologies and marginalizing colonial practices: "If it is true, then,
that in America reigned a 'Baroque of the State,' a theatricality and allegory of
imperial power through whose codes organic intellectuals of the Colony expressed themselves, it is no less true that an emergent ideology, that with time
would consolidate itself into an alternative political and economic project,
began to express itself and represent its social condition by means of the same
expressive models used by the dominator, but aesthetically re-articulated in
texts that today require a new reading."[12] Understood in the Gramscian sense
of being of the class she represents, Sor Juana might be considered a Creole,
"organic intellectual," though she excelled and surpassed in erudition most
traditional intellectuals of her time. Sor Juana is one of those "new subjects"
whose literary inventions reflect the unique consciousness of an emerging
class of Creoles. Her Baroque festival performs aspects of the hybrid condition of the Creole in the heart of imperial power, the viceregal court. As I will
show below, the hybrid is not a mere decorative Baroque conceit, but a

metaphor invoked in a subtle but striking call to usurp metropolitan hegemony. The new subjects of colonial Mexico, and by extension, some of the literary characters who populated the viceregal stages, are constituted by the
crossings common to the colonial condition. Reading them through the critical lenses of hybridity underscores the performative, antiessentialist discourse
that emerges from Sor Juana's writing and highlights the critique of the center
that hybrid subjects offer in colonial and transatlantic contexts. The crossings
I examine in this essay, and that inform the theoretical positions I adopt here,
work against notions of cultural fixity or essential identities. Hybridity is
about processes of identification that are in continual states of transculturation; Sor Juana as a writing subject, and some of her fictional characters,
make frequent reference to these transformations and the ideological implications of the new agencies that emerge from them.[13]

Sor Juana employed literary crossings, such as intertextuality and metafictional commentary, as well as dual cultural allusions that polysemically
evoked double meanings, to create difference in her mimicry of the fashionable comedia. Homi Bhabha has defined colonial mimicry as "the desire for a
reformed, recognizable Other, *as a subject of a difference that is almost the same,
but not quite.* Which is to say that the discourse of mimicry is constructed
around an ambivalence; in order to be effective, mimicry must continually
produce its slippage, its excess, its difference."[14] Sor Juana as a colonial subject
appropriating imperial literary and performative forms, asserted political
agency in a reproduction of these forms that became "at once resemblance
and menace."[15] The fiesta, I argue, is mimed back to colonial authorities, but
slips into an excessive hybridity that opens the imperial original to expressions
of difference from the periphery of empire. The various components of the
hybrid fiesta contributed to a heteroglossia that culminated in the original
voice of a Creole-mestizo colonial subjectivity. By reading the fiesta as a
whole, and not just the comedia itself, we appreciate how the theme of hybridity was staged in multiple ways. In this essay, I will analyze the *loa* [initial
prelude], scenes from the comedia, especially those related to the play's *gracioso* [buffoon], the *second sainete* [the interlude between act two and three],
and the *final sarao* [finale].

Sor Juana takes advantage of the subversive potentialities of the Baroque
festival that had long been part of the peninsular and European tradition.
Several critics have explored the relationship between the comedia and carnival, revealing how the popular energy of the streets crossed into early modern
theater. Peter Burke's study of popular culture in early modern Europe highlights how "Carnival may be seen as a huge play in which the main streets and

squares became stages, the city became a theatre without walls and the inhabitants, the actors and spectators."[16] Teresa Soufas has shown how "the Spanish comedia makes use of the collective traditions that are part of the popular revelry and festive inversions of Carnival which criticize and evaluate the political and moral dimensions of the then contemporary society."[17] Javier Huerta Calvo summarizes the commonality between carnival and drama: the "action" of jokes and parodies, the "setting" of relative freedom of the public street festival, the "characters" who represent the inversions of everyday life often portrayed on stage, the "language" of insults, jokes, and puns and finally the "performance," or the comedic gestures and performances of inversion and excess.[18] These aspects of the carnivalesque in the comedia are amplified in the larger context of the Baroque festival, which includes the preludes, interludes, and finales that function to recreate the atmosphere of carnival-like rituality in which the spectators gradually crossed from the space and time of everyday life into the theatrical space of mimesis and mimicry, of excess and joy, of grotesque inversions and eventual reestablishment of order. The dialogic nature of the fiesta, then, lends itself in its very form to expressions of hybridity in its message.

The loa was the first prelude, the first step in a crossing, in which the spectators were invited to pass from street to stage, from the uncontrolled canivalesque spirit of the processions and dances that accompanied the archbishop's arrival to the city, to the controlled action of the comedia. In the fiesta de *Los empeños de una casa* the loa consists of a dialogue among four allegorical figures who dispute what is life's greatest happiness and who end the prelude by concluding that the presence of the viceroy and family and the arrival of the archbishop are the greatest of all joys for New Spain. Sor Juana puts the traditional praise of the patrons in the mouth of Fortune, Chance, and Merit. Fortune announces the arrival of the vicereine as the "diosa de la Europa, deidad de las Indias" [goddess of Europe, deity of the Indies] while Chance welcomes the viceroy as he that "pisa/la cervix ufana/de América altiva"[steps on the proud cervix of haughty America].[19] Thus, imperialism and coloniality are enacted in the first lines, as a performance of the power that this couple embodies in the political structure of New Spain.

The Spanish subjugation of America, both physical and spiritual, had led to the hybridity Sor Juana represents as a leitmotiv throughout the fiesta. The epithets used to honor the vicereine bring into play the two continents that had clashed and come together under the tutelage of the Spanish monarchy and the Catholic Church.[20] The violence of the "encounter" is alluded to in the metonymic figure of the viceroy stepping on the neck of haughty America.

These laudatory remarks are the only lines of the loa that connect the allegorical dialogue to New Spain, but their directness, despite the conventionality of their utterance in requisite praise of the patrons, echoes the loas from Sor Juana's other profane and sacramental plays in which she more fully addresses issues of coloniality, protonational identity, and Creole subjectivity.[21] In this loa, and especially in her other theatrical preludes, which are beyond the scope of this essay, one appreciates the ambivalent slippage of colonial mimicry from courtly praise to colonial critique. In this sense, the "resemblance" of colonial mimicry crosses to become a potential "menace" to empire.

The mixing of literary and performance genres continues as the loa gives way to songs in honor of the countess and then to the comedia itself. *Los empeños de una casa* is a unique reworking of several Golden Age models, as Ángel Julián Valbuena Briones has commented, including such classics as Calderón's *Los empeños de un acaso, Mañanas de abril y mayo*, and *El Escondido y la tapada*. Read as colonial mimicry, Sor Juana stages difference through transgressive recharacterizations of stock character types from traditional cloak-and-dagger comedias and honor plays. Sor Juana's imitation of the originals produces ambivalent mirrors in which the mix-ups of the *enredos* [intrigues] become crossings of gender norms of patriarchy and colonial norms of race and class. Two characters stand out: the leading lady, Leonor, and the buffoon, Castaño. Leonor's resistance to the arranged marriage she eludes in favor of her chosen love, Don Carlos, is grounded in mimicry of traditional comedia types, ladies and *mujeres esquivas* [aloof, disdainful women], but spirals into an excess of even the most transgressive of models from the peninsula.[22]

Sor Juana's treatment of gender and sexuality in the play exposes the constructedness of those categories by staging characters who occupy liminal positions, perform gender crossings, and express desire for hybrid objects of affection. Georgina Dopico Black recognizes gender crossings in many of Sor Juana's texts, "moments that question strict gender binarisms and that are perhaps best seen as a striking appropriation of and contestation to the concept of mujer varonil [manly woman] that was so often applied to her authorial figuration."[23] Dopico Black's insightful readings of *Primero sueño*, "Autodefensa," and Romance 48: "Respondiendo a un caballero del Perú, que le envió unos barros diciéndole que se volviese hombre" lead her to conclude that Sor Juana created a "self-imposed somatic illegibility" as a "mode of resistance against readings that would make Sor Juana's body into that of a man, or even a perfect wife."[24] This resistance to the binarism of her day is echoed in Leonor's in-between position in the play. While her beauty and social position would suggest that she be the "perfect wife," her inclination to study created a renowned erudite woman who resisted the marriage proposals of all but her beloved Carlos. Leonor's choice, as Emilie Bergmann has argued, "departs from the norms of comedia plots in which intellectual women are subdued through marriage. . . . Leonor's marriage to a man she has chosen is both a concession to comic convention—the only ending possible for a work belonging to such a public genre as theatre—and a symbolic resolution to the problem of female autonomy."[25]

Leonor's desire for Carlos, however, is complicated by her characterization of his attractive, but ambiguous qualities. Carlos is depicted in a literary portrait during her famous monologue that introduces the spectators and Doña Ana to her predicament and to her beloved:

> Era su rostro un enigma
> compuesto de dos contrarios
> que eran valor y hermosura,
> tan felizmente hermanados,
> que faltándole a lo hermoso
> la parte de afeminado,
> hallaba lo más perfecto
> en lo que estaba más falto.
> (*Los empeños*, 225)

> [His face was an enigma,
> composed of two contradictions—
> manly strength and feminine beauty—
> so fortuitously harmonized
> that his beauty,
> lacking softness,
> found the greatest perfection
> in what it most lacked.]
> (*The House*, 47)

Carlos's beauty derives from sexual ambiguity and androgynous features. His face is an "enigma composed of two contradictions": the opposites of valor and beauty that function as metonymic signifiers of masculinity and femininity are crossed and "harmonized" to make "the greatest perfection." While Dopico Black astutely registers the potential homoerotic appeal of Leonor's attraction to the femininity of her chosen love, I wish to underline Leonor's, and by extension, Sor Juana's desiring of the hybrid.[26] The "greatest perfection" is not the essentialized masculine, or even the feminine, but something in between. This desire for the hybrid takes on even more resonant significance in the final scenes of the play when Don Pedro declares his desire for the cross-dressed gracioso, Castaño, functioning as Leonor's double. But before spectators were treated to the climax, they were entertained by the second sainete.

In this last interlude of the fiesta, Sor Juana continues to voice an imaginative and humorous reception of the comedia in her metatheatrical second sainete. In this satirical crossing from the fiction of the comedia to the metafiction of an interlude within an interlude, two bored audience members propose whistling at the actors of the representation of a comedia, *La Celestina*, now believed to have been a play written by Agustín Salazar y Torres that Sor Juana herself finished and perhaps polished.[27] Guillermo Schmidhuber has analyzed the historical references in this sainete to reveal how the metafictional discourse would have been a humorous series of inside jokes for the audience in the court and literary circles of New Spain.[28] The inside jokes expressed a carnivalesque satire of popular reception of theater in the periphery of empire and underscore the beginnings of a Creole consciousness, a consciousness of difference. The success of the sainete depends on a transatlantic metafiction that gives voice to the hybrid culture of New Spain, for the players work both sides of the Atlantic with their humorous allusions. The humor works because the Creoles, and the Spanish immigrants in New Spain, lived in a world of transculturation in which imperial and colonial cultures mixed and new forms emerged, including the transatlantic joke.

The fun begins with a burlesque complaint of the play's length and plot, voiced by Muñiz, who also expresses a preference for peninsular playwrights: "No era mejor, amigo, en mi conciencia, / si quería hacer festejo a su Excelencia, / escoger, sin congojas, / una de Calderón, Moreto, o Rojas . . . ?" [As I see it, wouldn't it have been better, friend, in order to celebrate his Excellency, to have chosen, without grief, a play by Calderón, Moreto or Rojas . . . ?] (*Los empeños*, 287). His friend, Arias, responds that he preferred the *Celestina* in which Muñiz had played a cross-dressed Celestina. Muñiz responds to Arias's foreshadowing of Castaño's transgendered performance in the third act by saying: "Amigo, mejor era *Celestina*, / en cuanto a ser comedia ultramarina: / que siempre las de España son mejores, / y para digerirles los humores / son ligeras; que nunca son pesadas / las cosas que por agua están pasadas" [Friend, *Celestina* was better, as an overseas play; those from Spain are always better, and to digest the humors, they are light; for things passed over water are never heavy] (*Los empeños*, 289).[29] Different from the peninsula productions, however, they are commenting on a play that came from New Spain: "Pero la Celestina que esta risa / os causó, era mestiza / y acabada a retrazos, / y si le faltó traza, tuvo trazos, / y con diverso genio / se formó de un trapiche y de un in-genio"[But the *Celestina* that caused you so much laughter was mestiza, and completed in fragments, and even if it was lacking a plan, it had plot lines, and with a diverse spirit it was formed from a sugar press and a genius] (*Los empeños*, 289).[30] This self-referential comment on the play Sor Juana and her contemporary Salazar y Torres wrote speaks to the hybridity of its creation, while foreshadowing, perhaps, the ingenuity of the mestizo who was about to retake the stage in the third act. As a counter to the earlier judgment that the good plays come from across the ocean, here the mixed play of Creole inge-nuity appeals to the new subjectivities of the growing local class of spectators. Just as Leonor desires the ambiguously (mixed) gendered Don Carlos and Don Pedro pines for the cross-dressed mestizo, here Arias yearns for the mes-tiza play, hybrid product of literary transculturation. Compared to the "light" Spanish plays, these mestiza plays are judged more ingenious.

The local further interrupts hegemonic comedia tropes in the climax of the sainete. As Schmidhuber has shown, these last verses refer to another Sor Juana contemporary, Luis Sandoval y Zapata and the fortune he made and lost in sugar mills and literature, respectively, perhaps an allusion to the pre-carious nature of local economies and literary ambitions.[31] The sainete ends with one last jab by a local, the well-known university professor and play-wright Francisco de Acevedo, whose play the audience, led by Arias and Muñiz, are said to be hissing. Muñiz's Creole identity is confirmed by his in-ability to pronounce the peninsula sibilant "s": "que no acierto a pronunciar la ese" [I cannot pronounce the "s"] (*Los empeños*, 291). The agitated Ace-vedo, in dismay over the deafening whistles and hisses, provides the counter-point, denouncing his detractors as recently arrived "peninsulares" [Spaniards from the peninsula]: "Gachupines parecen / recién venidos, / porque todo el teatro se hunde a silbos" [They appear to be recently arrived Gachupines (nickname for peninsular-born Spaniards) because the entire theater collapses in whistles] (*Los empeños*, 291). We are left with an ambivalent performance of mimicry, in which the players represent, through metatheatrical discourse, a local scene of comedia reception in which the hybrid mestiza play is com-pared to the peninsula original. The hybrid, "made from fragments" and "of diverse spirit," must defend itself in the hostile world of critical gachupines, of Calderons and Moretos, of the transnational Baroque.

The third act reaches its climax with the mestizo gracioso defending him-self in the hostile world of comedic intrigues, stealing the show, and perhaps showing the gachupines a thing or two about Creole ingenuity. Castaño dressed as Leonor, is not only an ambiguously gendered object of desire in this famous scene, but a mestiza one, as well. In the first two acts of the play, Castaño's transatlantic liminality was limited to audience perceptions of how his body and name signified racial difference in relationship with the rest of the characters and by his use of language.[32] Whereas the reader does not learn of his physical traits until the third act, the viewing audience would have made the connection between his appearance, what he himself later characterizes as "morena" [dark-skinned] (*Los empeños*, 302), (assuming a darker-skinned actor played the role) and the suggestiveness of his name, "Chestnut."

From the chaotic, carnivalesque atmosphere of the fiesta emerges this character who embodies the hybridity that will shape the "New" and "Old" worlds. While Sor Juana playfully suggests, in the prelude and second interlude, and, as we shall see, in the finale, that the audience begin to embrace this new reality, it is with the coming out of Castaño that her transgressive and liberating views are fully staged. In the action of the play, Castaño has migrated from New Spain to Toledo and is employed by the play's leading man, Don Carlos. Typical of most buffoons of the comedia, Castaño finds himself at cross-purposes with his boss, who sends him on a hopeless errand despite Castaño's incessant hunger and fear of being apprehended. Though the "hungry buffoon" is a common trope in the peninsular comedia, Castaño's identification as mestizo and Mexican suggests a possible double cultural allusion performed by Sor Juana; the trope conforms to the conventions while at the same time it calls forth an image of the inferior material conditions of the racialized Other from New Spain.

This reading of the subversive potential of hybrid colonial, subaltern subjects is supported by Castaño's comic, yet poignant, transatlantic identification with his "patron saint," the famous Mexican picaro [rogue] from the mid-seventeenth century, Garatuza: "¡Quien fuera aquí Garatuza, / de quien en las Indias cuentan / que hacía muchos prodigios! / Que yo, como nací en ellas, le he sido siempre devoto / como a santo de mi tierra" (*Los empeños*, 301) [I wish Garatuza was here! / In Mexico he is said to have / performed many miracles / while disguised as a priest. Since I was born there, / I always worshiped him / as the patron saint of my homeland.] (*The House*, 115). His invocation of this New World, cross-dressing rogue (who disguised himself as a priest to carry out his crafty tricks) combined with his next intertextual reference, this time to Calderón de la Barca, leads him to the idea of donning Leonor's clothes in order to escape from the house to the street unnoticed: "inspírame alguna traza / que de Calderón parezca, / con que salir de este empeño!" (*Los empeños*, 302) [help me to escape these trials / by inspiring a scheme for me / worthy of the great playwright, Calderón] (*The House*, 115).[33] Castaño performs his subjectivity through these intertextual references that speak to both the peninsular, metropolitan origins of the comedia and to the American, peripheral references that mark the transatlantic crossings of theatrical works. Moreover, Castaño humorously elevates Garatuza to the stature of "patron saint of my homeland," subtly displacing the ideal of Catholic beatification of charitable and miraculous actions and substituting instead a rogue as exemplar of what it takes to survive in colonial Mexico.

By mixing allusions to "New" and "Old World" cultures, Sor Juana's Castaño brings to the stage a hybrid character who metonymically reproduces the conditions of the marginal mestizo-criollo in relation to the Spanish dominant class and discourse on purity of bloodlines. Castaño's references to marginal outlaws like Garatuza continues as he completes his transformation into a *tapada* [veiled woman]. In yet another direct address to the audience, Castaño imagines himself being identified with the infamous *tapado,* Antonio de Benavides, another "cross-dresser" who impersonated a marquis and royal official in New Spain and who was executed some months after the play was performed.[34] Benavides's crossing is marked by the same gender ambiguity Castaño will perform, as the buffoon intimates with his earlier invocation of Garatuza, "oh tú, cualquiera que seas, / bien esgrimas abanico / o bien arrastres contera" (*Los empeños,* 302) [Oh, Garatuza, whoever you were, whoever you are, / whether waving a fan or wearing a sword] (*The House,* 115). The word *tapada* in the *germanía* [slang] of early modern Spain had the additional meaning of *buscona* or prostitute in the language of the marginal communities, a possible double meaning that would have caused more laughter and would have further signaled Castaño's mimicry of and alignment with the marginalized in Spanish society.[35] Sor Juana is known to have interceded on Benavides's behalf, which encourages us to interpret Castaño's imitation of this real-life *tapado* as a not-so-subtle commentary on viceregal justice. Here again, the playwright voices a consciousness of the local that challenges imperial ideologies. The implicit critique is uttered by the buffoon, as often is the case in Baroque theater; but in this case the allusion to a local hero who had challenged the colonial order takes on added significance given that the fool in question is racially marked. As if he, or Sor Juana, realizes the dangers of these roguish crossings, however, Castaño comically reminds the audience, the viceroy, and archbishop that his dressing up is all part of the play: "Pues atención, mis señoras, / que es paso de la comedia; no piensen que son embustes / fraguados acá en mi idea, / que yo no quiero engañarlas, ni menos a Vuexelencia" (*Los empeños,* 304) [Please remember, ladies, that this is a play. /

Don't think that I / hatched this scheme myself. / I don't want to fool any of you, / especially not Your Excellency.] (*The House*, 117). The deceit is reserved for Don Pedro, who falls for his disguise and declares his love for Castaño-Leonor in the next scene.

These allusions to crossings, both from the peninsula and from New Spain, were the lead-in to Castaño's famous gender-crossing performance. Castaño as Leonor heightened the buffoon's satirical function, as Christopher Weimer has observed. The satire is staged through Castaño's drag performance, a kind of mimicry of absolute gender categories that destabilizes any notion of fixity. Here the subaltern experience of the rogue alluded to above is crossed with a performance of female subalternity through a comic monologue that surely will live on as a masterpiece of the genre. As Julie Greer Johnson has compellingly argued, Sor Juana elevated the comic fool to the heights of comic hero, breaking the stereotype by investing him with the subversive role that called into question patriarchal norms. Dopico Black's insightful Butlerian reading emphasizes how his performance denaturalizes gender norms while providing Sor Juana a way to rehearse the illegible body in parodic excess of traditional honor scripts.[36] Dopico Black concludes that Pedro's "perpetual bachelorhood" resulting from his misreading of Castaño's cross-dressed body "suggests the irreconcilability of his desire (metonymically displaced from Leonor to Castaño) with institutional sanction."[37] If we extend her interpretation to think about this final scene in terms of Creole/mestizo-Spanish relations, then Castaño's cross-dressing becomes an attempt at passing not just as a woman, but also as a Spanish, presumably white, leading lady. Pedro's disavowal, then, stages a rejection of the Creole, subaltern Other, a problematic body in the racial economy of the empire. Pedro's desire for the hybrid ends in an anxiety-ridden abjection of that which is now part of the Spanish imperial identity, both in its gendered and its racial dimensions.

The fiesta closed with an elaborate sarao, a spectacle of crossings that brought to the stage a diverse group of "four nations": Spaniards, Africans, Italians, and Mexicans.[38] The sarao invited the spectator to cross back to the carnivalesque space of dance and music, as multiple choruses, a musical group, and the four dancing nation-groups began an intricate series of entrances and stage crossings timed with alternating choral interventions. The crisscrossing of bodies and voices invokes the hybridity leitmotif yet again. No spectator could have ignored the allusion to the diverse crossings from Europe and Africa that brought the nations together to celebrate the triumph of love over obligation in homage to the patrons of the fiesta. But the hybrid empire, as represented in the loa, is formed of an implicit subjugation of one nation to another: Sor Juana has the "Mexicans" summoned to render to the three "deities" of Spanish colonialism: the count, countess, and their son. Only after this call to submission do the four nations unite, as directed by the stage directions, in a finale of dance and song (*Los empeños*, 339). Again, as in the loa, Sor Juana embedded in the requisite laudatory language toward her patrons a crosscurrent that subtly invoked an image of difference and the ambivalent coloniality of power.

The submission of the Mexicans, however, is to the viceroy, the Monarch's stand-in, a colonial mimic of imperial power wielded by the sovereign. Could we be viewing, therefore, yet another crossing, in this case a subtle change of allegiance from Spain to a new imperial center, New Spain? In his analysis of Sor Juana's ballad, also dedicated to the viceroy's son, José, Félix Duque argues that the poet saw in the Cerdas, a family with pretensions to the throne dating back for centuries, an alternative to the Hapsburg decadence of Carlos II.[39] Her ballad's expression of miscegenation as the future of the empire, and a recentering of the capital of that empire in the Americas, is startling:

> Crezca gloria de su patria
> y envidia de las ajenas;
> Y América, con sus partes,
> las partes del Orbe venza.
> En buena hora Occidente
> traiga su prosapia excelsa,
> Que es Europa estrecha Patria
> a tanta familia regia.
> Levante América ufana
> la coronada cabeza,
> el Águila Mejicana
> el imperial vuelo tienda.
> Pues ya en su Alcázar Real
> donde yace la grandeza
> de gentiles Moctezumas,
> nacen católicas Cerdas.
>
> [Grow, glory of your homeland
> and the envy of others;
> and America, with your parts,
> defeat those other parts of the globe.

Fortunately the West
brings here its illustrious lineages,
for Europe is a narrow fatherland
for such a grand royal family.
Proud America, raise
your crowned head;
Mexican eagle,
take imperial flight.
For now in your royal palace,
where lies dead the greatness
of pagan Montezumas,
Catholic Cerdas are born.][40]

Here again, the hybrid plays a subversive role; the Creole, this time cross-dressed in the feathers of the Mexican eagle, destabilizes imperial power and chooses the Mexican-born José as her future, a Catholic Cerda born in the Mexican/Aztec capital. The polysemic words *católicas* and *gentiles,* juxtaposed in an antithesis that reflects the coloniality of the imperial relationships (Christian versus pagan), also signify more transgressive ideas: *católico* as universal and *gentil* as noble, and thus recoverable in the Creole effort to constitute a useable history and heritage in the formation of a mestizo *patria,* one that befits the majesty of the mixed heritage José, now of too great of stature for "narrow" Europe.

Like this ballad, the sarao from *Los empeños de una casa* presents the same choice of allegiance, made not out of obligation, but out of love inspired by a Creole consciousness. As the four nations crisscross the stage, José is introduced to the Mexicans in a pair of analogies suggestive of botanical hybridity. First, Sor Juana invites the Mexicans to the party: "¡Venid, mejicanos; / alegres, venid, / a ver en el sol / mil soles lucir!" (*Los empeños*, 338) [Come, Mexicans; / joyfully come! / to see in the sun / a thousand suns shine bright]. The sun, as bicultural symbol, resonant in both Aztec and Christian symbology, becomes a leitmotif in this passage. Sor Juana's sun is one made of many suns, suggestive of the inclusive tone she sets in this finale to her fiesta, and illuminates José's parents, the viceroys. This American, mestizo sun grows the white carnation and the purple jasmine: "Y al clavel nevado, / purpúreo jazmín, / fruto de una y otra vid: / José, que su patria / llegó a producir / en él más tesoros / que en su Potosí." (*Los empeños*, 339). [And to the snowy carnation, / purple jasmine, / fruit of different vines: / José, his homeland / managed to produce in him / more treasures / than in Potosí.] These majestic flowers, originally imported from the Near and Far East and used in ceremonial contexts in classical antiquity, are the fruit or offspring of different vines or lineages, just as José was the "fruit" of his mixed-heritage parents and of New Spain. In a reference to the famous wealth derived from the mines of Potosí, Sor Juana reminds the spectators that the future ruler derives his power not from the Old World, but from America's riches.

This budding Creole consciousness is appealed to yet again in one of the last images of the sarao in which another metaphor of botanical hybridity is invoked to represent, ideally, the future viceroy, José: "Y al José generoso, que de troncos / reales, siempre ramo floreciente, / es engarce glorioso que vincula / los triunfos de Laguna y de Paredes,"(*Los empeños*, 341). [And to generous José, who from royal trunks / always a flowering bouquet, / is a glorious link that connects / the triumphs of the Lagunas and the Paredes.] José, the primogeniture engendered from two royal family trees, is the "flowering bouquet" that links the "Old World" families together, but is born in the "New World." The subsequent lines suggest that this royal Creole will be nurtured not only by his European parents, but will also be formed by the native culture of New Spain. Sor Juana calls for the rendering of tribute to José in the form of sacrifices, a double allusion, I would argue, to both the cults of classical antiquity, in line with her earlier allusions to pagan gods, and to the cults of the indigenous Americans: "¡venid a dedicar, en sacrificios / de encendidos afectos obedientes, / la víctima debida a sus altares, / la ofrenda que a su culto se le debe!" (*Los empeños*, 341). [Come dedicate, in sacrifices / obedient burning affections, / the suitable victim on your altars / the offering that your cult is due.] One can imagine the Mexicans being directed to move toward the honoree, thus highlighting again the hybrid nature of New Spain. The conceit of the sarao is brought to closure, however, in lines that seem to discredit the actual practice of sacrifice by reminding the audience that it is the intention of the person making the offering that matters most, not the actual blood of the victim:

> Y en la aceptación suplan sus aras,
> donde la ejecución llegar no puede,
> las mentales ofrendas del deseo
> que ofrece todo aquello que no ofrece:
> pues a lo inmaterial de las deidades,
> se tiene por ofrenda más solemne
> que la caliente sangre de la fiera,
> la encendida intención del oferente.
>
> (*Los empeños*, 341)

[And in accepting, replace your altars
where execution cannot,
with mental offerings of desire
that offers all it does not offer:
For the immaterial deities,
regard as a more solemn offering
than the hot blood of the beast,
the burning intention of the offerer.]

Here, the historical body of the Aztec sacrifice ceremony is subjugated to the Christian notion of symbolic sacrifice. Sor Juana does not challenge the coloniality of that subjugation, but she does summon once again the performance of hybrid forms of Mexican culture in homage to the newborn Creole, a tribute inspired, according to the choruses, by love and good intentions. Here again, she recuperates a usable heritage with which to forge an acceptable Creole consciousness, nurturing the future of New Spain, and, indeed the world, through syncretic images of religiosity. As the sarao invites spectators to prepare to cross back into everyday life from the rituality of carnival, evoked in the dances, songs, and allusions to ceremonial rites from both pagan and Catholic traditions, Sor Juana draws her Baroque festival to a close with the requisite rhetorical humility of traditional early modern dramatists and a final exaltation of the viceregal family.

The rhetorical humility of the last lines pales in comparison with the grandeur of the fiesta as a whole Baroque spectacle and with the Creole pride that emerges from Sor Juana's writing. The polysemic nature of this essay's epigraph reveals this consciousness: "nunca son pesadas las cosas que por agua están pasadas" [for things passed over water are never heavy]. What was first uttered as a contemptuous comment on New World theater can now be appreciated as a reference to the transatlantic crossing of the mestiza comedia from the periphery to the metropolis. Not merely a "transplanted" Baroque play, but a transculturated celebration of a new subjectivity, expressed from a mixture of "fragments" and "genius" that crossed the local with the global in a critical commentary on imperial hegemony. Castaño the buffoon played the hero through his own form of ingenuity: conquering through deceit a Spanish leading man in the capital of the empire, while Creole José was feted as the possible American displacement of the European center. All crossings that leave the audience laughing yet thinking, perhaps, of how new currents of possibility flowed to the Hispanic comedia . . . and how crosscurrents flow both ways across the Atlantic.

NOTES

1. Neufeldt and Guralnik, *Webster's New World Dictionary,* 331. For biographical information on Sor Juana Inés de la Cruz, see Paz, Leonard, and Sabàt de Rivers, *Sor Juana,* especially chapter one. Paz and Leonard also portray the intellectual and cultural context in which the nun lived and worked.

2. For this connection, see Valbuena Briones, *"Los empeños de una casa."*

3. Susana Hernández Araico has recently discussed how the play "exponentially intensifies the cloak-and-sword intrigue for which Calderón remained the acknowledged master" (*"Los empeños,"* 324) and how original twists to the plot make the work stand out in the tradition (325).

4. Hernández Araico gives a succinct review of the history of the possible performances of the play and the ancillary texts (ibid., 316–20). Her article also discusses the importance of considering the fiesta as a whole.

5. The term "cosmic race" comes from José Vasconcelos's essay on Mexican and Latin American identity, *La raza cósmica.*

6. Paz complicates his overall notion of New Spain's "transplanted literature" by rejecting the idea that the baroque in New Spain is an expression of "literary or Creole nationalism." (*Las trampas,* 85).

7. Ibid., 86.

8. Mignolo, *Local World,* ix.

9. Paz, *Las trampas,* 96.

10. Mignolo, *Local World,* x. Anzaldúa, *Borderlands / La Frontera,* 100.

11. Beverley, *Against Literature,* 63–64.

12. Moraña, *Viajes al silencio,* 60-61. My translation.

13. For more on hybridity and colonial and postcolonial discourse, see Bhabha, *Location of Culture,* García Canclini, Mignolo, *Local World,* and Cornejo Polar, *Escribir.* I have found Mabel Moraña's "Antonio Cornejo Polar" very helpful. For discussions of transculturation, see Ortiz, *Cuban Counterpoint,* Rama, Spitta, *Between Two Waters,* and Horswell, "Introduction."

14. Bhabha, *Location of Culture,* 86. Emphasis in the original.

15. Ibid.

16. Burke, *Popular Culture,* 182.

17. Soufas, "Carnival," 315.

18. Huerta Calvo, "Carnaval," 40.

19. Inez de la Cruz, *Los empeños,* 208. All citations are taken from the version of the fiesta found in *Obras selectas de Sor Juana Inés de la Cruz,* edited by Georgina Sabàt de Rivers and Elías L. Rivers. Hereafter cited in the text. All translations from the loa, sainetes, and the sarao are my own and strive to privilege clarity of meaning over poetic integrity. Translations of the comedia are taken from David Pasto's translation, *House of Trials.*

20. The greatest praise is reserved for the archbishop, who is greeted with a periphrasis that years later will invoke great irony, given the misogyny and intolerance with which Aguiar y Seijas will attack Sor Juana.

21. Martínez-San Miguel, in her reading of the loa from *El Divino Narciso,* as well as the auto itself, argues that Sor Juana gave voice to subaltern colonized subjects in order to propose a change in the colonial order (*Divino Narciso*). Díaz Balsera recognizes an emergent "feminine

Creole consciousness" in *El Divino Narciso* in the way that Sor Juana rewrites Calderonian autos (*Divino Narciso*).

22. For a classic study of the "*mujer esquiva,*" see McKendrick, *Women and Society.*

23. Dopico Black, *Perfect Wives,* 174.

24. Ibid., 178.

25. Ibid., 200.

26. Ibid., 182.

27. Guillermo Schmidhuber recovered the lost play. He has given his opinion of its history and analyzed the play in chapter four of *Three Secular Plays.* Paz comments on the metafictional aspects of the sainete and on references to the *Celestina,* highlighting the transgressive nature of Sor Juana's adoption of the *Celestina* as a subject matter, given her position as a nun (*Las trampas,* 435).

28. Schmidhuber, *Three Secular Plays,* 115–20.

29. This line, which also serves as the epigraph to this essay, can be interpreted in several ways. Is Sor Juana making fun of the frivolity of Spanish comedias? "Pasar por agua" [pass through water] could mean "aguar," that is to attenuate, in this case, the seriousness of the plays. Or, the character could be referring more literally to the geographic crossing of the plays "over" the waters of the ocean. I will return to this phrase below.

30. Sor Juana's wordplay in these lines invokes multiple meanings. The word "trapiche" means a sugar or olive press, and refers to the business dealings of Luis Sandoval y Zapata, as explained below. But, the verb "trapichear" connotes shady dealings, perhaps comical given Sandoval's business standing in New Spain. Though the noun form would be "trapicheo," here the play on words may have resonated with the audience, as did the double meaning of "ingenio" (sugar mill and creative genius).

31. Schmidhuber, *Three Secular* Plays, 116.

32. Paz has observed that Castaño "habla como los mexicanos y así introduce una nota localista en la acción" [talks like the Mexicans and therefore introduces a local touch to the action of the play] (*Las trampas,* 436).

33. Manuel Antonio Arango describes this famous Mexican rogue, who was "born in Puebla in 160, baptized with the name Martín Villavicencio Salazar, disguised himself as a priest, said Mass in the Cathedral of Mexico for seven years, and traveled much of the country fooling the civil authorities and the Inquisition. They say that when raising the Eucharist he would ask himself: 'Where will these Masses end, Garatuza?' He was captured and sentenced to suffer 200 lashes in the *auto-de-fé* of 1648, some three years before Sor Juana was born" ("Contribución," 299).

34. Irving Leonard offers a description of the political context of this historical character, highlighting how his case became the talk of the viceroyalty and how Sor Juana openly defended him, asking for the viceroy's clemency through a poem she wrote and dedicated on his son's birthday (*Baroque Times,* 161–62). Dopico Black reproduces a fragment of the poem and remarks that the "allusion to el Tapado betrays the tenuousness of the line between transvestism (in the broadest sense of the word) on and offstage" (*Perfect Wives,* 191–92).

35. I appreciate Yolanda Gamboa bringing this secondary meaning of the word to my attention. José Luis Alonso Hernández's *El lenguaje,* records the word as "la buscota, generalmente nocturna, pero no siempre, que, cubierta con un manto la cara y dejando sólo una parte al descubierto, con frecuencia un ojo la parte de la cara correspondiente, recorría las calles de la ciudad en busca de clientes"(40).

36. Dopico Black, *Perfect Wives*, 192, 200.

37. Ibid, 200.

38. As Hernández Araico has pointed out, the choice of the four nations represented in the sarao reflects Sor Juana's homage to the two European nations represented by the viceregal couple (Italy and Spain) and "reduces the theatrical representation of the world to two parts—a bicultural Europe (Spain-Italy) and a multicultural America which extratextually encompasses all four nations mentioned"("Los Empeños," 324).

39. Duque, "La conciencia del mestizaje," 25–26.

40. Ibid., 25. My translation.

WORKS CITED

Alonso Hernández, José Luis. *El lenguaje de los maleantes españoles de los siglos XVI y XVII: La germanía: Introducción al léxico del marginalismo.* Salamanca: Ediciones de la Universidad de Salamanca, 1979.

Anzaldúa, Gloria. *Borderlands / La Frontera.* San Francisco: Aunt Lute Books, 1987.

Arango L., Manuel Antonio. *Contribución al estudio de la obra dramática de Sor Juana Inés de la Cruz.* New York: Peter Lang, 2000.

Bakhtin, Mikhail. *The Dialogic Imagination: Four Essays.* Edited by Michael Holquist, translated by C. Emerson and M. Holquist. Austin: University of Texas Press, 1981.

———. *Rabelais and His World.* Translated by Helene Iswolsky. Bloomington: Indiana University Press, 1984.

Beverley, John. *Against Literature.* Minneapolis: University of Minnesota Press, 1993.

Bhabha, Homi K. *The Location of Culture.* London: Routledge, 1994.

Burke, Peter. *Popular Culture in Early Modern Europe.* London: Temple Smith, 1978.

Casa, Frank, Luciano García Lorenzo, and Germán Vega García-Luengos, comp. *Diccionario de la comedia del Siglo de Oro.* Madrid: Editorial Castalia, 2002.

Cornejo Polar, Antonio. *Escribir en el aire.* Lima: Editorial Horizonte, 1994.

Díaz Balsera, Viviana. "Mal de Amor y alteridad en un texto de Sor Juana: *El Divino Narciso* reescribe la Calderón." *Bulletin of the Comediantes* 49 (1997): 15–33.

Dopico Black, Georgina. *Perfect Wives, Other Women: Adultery and Inquisition in Early Modern Spain.* Durham, N.C.: Duke University Press, 2001.

Duque, Félix. "La conciencia del mestizaje: el Inca Garcilaso y sor Juana Inés de la Cruz." *Cuadernos hispanoamericanos* 504 (1992): 7-31.

García Canclini, Nestor. *Culturas Híbridas: Estrategias para entar y salir de la modernidad.* Mexico City: Grijalbo, 1990.

Greer Johnson, Julie. "Sor Juana's Castaño: From Gracioso to Comic Hero." *South Atlantic Review* 66, No. 4 (Fall 2001): 94–108.

Hernández Araico, Susana. "Sor Juana's *Los empeños de una casa*—a Baroque Fête and a Theatrical Feat." In *Hispanic Essays in Honor of Frank P. Casa*, edited by A Robert Lauer and Henry W. Sullivan, 316–42. New York: Peter Lang, 1997.

Horswell, Michael J. "Introduction: Transculturating Tropes of Sexuality, *Tinkuy,* and Third Gender in the Andes." In *Decolonizing the Sodomite: Queer Tropes of Sexuality in Andean Colonial Literature.* Austin: University of Texas Press, 2005.

Huerta Calvo, Javier. "Carnaval." In *Diccionario de la comedia del Siglo de Oro,* Frank Casa, et al., comp. Madrid: Editorial Castalia, 2002.

Inés de la Cruz, Sor Juana. 1683. *Los empeños de una casa. Obras selectas de Sor Juana Inés de la Cruz.* Edited by Georgina Sabàt de Rivers and Elías L. Rivers. Barcelona: Editorial Noguer, 1976.

———. *House of Trials.* Translated by David Pasto. New York: Peter Lang, 1997.

Leonard, Irving A. *Baroque Times in Old Mexico.* Ann Arbor: University of Michigan Press, 1959.

Martínez-San Miguel, Yolanda. "Articulando las múltiples subalternidades en el *Divino Narciso.*" *Colonial Latin American Review* 4 (1995): 85–104.

McKendrick, Melveena. *Women and Society in the Spanish Drama of the Golden Age: A Study of the Mujer Varonil.* London: Cambridge University Press, 1974.

Merrim, Stephanie. "*Mores Geometicae:* The 'Womanscript' in the Theater of Sor Juana Inés de la Cruz." In *Feminist Perspectives on Sor Juana Inés de la Cruz,* edited by Stephanie Merrim, 94-123. Detroit: Wayne State University Press, 1991.

Mignolo, Walter. *Local World Histories / Global Designs; Coloniality, Subaltern Knowledges and Border Thinking.* Princeton: Princeton University Press, 2000.

Moraña, Mabel. "Antonio Cornejo Polar y los debates actuales del latinoamericanismo: Noción de sujeto, hibridez, representación." *Revista de crítica literaria latinoamericana* 50 (1999): 19–27.

———. *Viajes al silencio: Exploraciones del discurso barroco.* México: Facultad de Filosofía y Letras, UNAM, 1998.

Ortiz, Fernando. *Cuban Counterpoint: Tobacco and Sugar.* Translated by Harriet de Onís. Durham, N.C.: Duke University Press, 1995.

Paz, Octavio. *Sor Juana Inés de la Cruz o Las trampas de la fe.* México City: Fondo de Cultura Económica, 1982.

Rama, Angel. *Transculturación narrativa en América Latina.* México City: Siglo 21, 1982.

Sabàt de Rivers, Georgina. *En busca de Sor Juana.* Mexico: Facultad de Filosofía y Letras, UNAM, 1998.

Sabàt de Rivers, Georgina, and Elías L. Rivers, eds. *Obras selectas de Sor Juana Inés de la Cruz.* Barcelona: Editorial Noguer, 1976.

Schmidhuber, Guillermo. *The Three Secular Plays by Sor Juana Inés de la Cruz.* Lexington: University of Kentucky Press, 2000.

Soufas, Teresa. "Carnival, Spectacle, and the *gracioso*'s Theatrics of Dissent." *Revista Canadiense de Estudios Hispánicos* 14, No. 2 (1990): 315–30.

Spitta, Sylvia. *Between Two Waters: Narratives of Transculturation in Latin America.* Houston: Rice University Press, 1995.

Valbuena Briones, Ángel Julián. "La particularidad de *Los empeños de una casa,* de Sor Juana Inés de la Cruz, ante la tradición calderoniana." *Hispanic Journal* 18, No. 1 (1997): 159–68.

Vasconcelos, José. *La raza cósmica-The Cosmic Race, A Bilingual Edition.* Trans. Didier T. Jaén. Baltimore: Johns Hopkins University Press, 1997.

Weimer, Christopher Brian. "Sor Juana as Feminist Playwright: The *Gracioso*'s Satiric Function in *Los empeños de una casa.*" *Latin American Theatre Review* 26, No. 1 (Fall 1992): 91–98.

Picaros, Saints, and the New World in Cervantes's *El rufián dichoso*

Eric J. Kartchner

THE "DISCOVERY" OF THE "NEW" WORLD DIRECTLY OR INDIRECTLY AFFECTED every aspect of European life and thought, particularly of Spanish life. What would soon become "America" quickly converted into a land of dreams and of nightmares. In Spanish society of the sixteenth and seventeenth centuries, upward mobility, especially in the social and economic realms, was practically nonexistent. This fact, coupled with the empire's need for soldiers and colonizers, inspired many of the society's traditionally underprivileged to seek their fortune across the Atlantic where the long arm of tradition and authority would lose some of its strength should it attempt to control or to discipline would-be convention breakers. Cervantes, burdened by debt, inspired by adventure, sought to undertake the risks and opportunities of the New World on more than one occasion, to no avail. This failure to test the possibilities of American shores in the flesh did not, however, curb the limits of his imaginational boundaries. In his play *El rufián dichoso* [*The Fortunate Ruffian*] we witness the transformation of a conventional Spanish picaro into a successful and respected member of Mexican society.[1] Although Cervantes makes no attempt whatsoever to concretize Mexican culture or geography, in this essay I explain that the concept of America plays a fundamental role in the development of the plot, providing a means whereby Cervantes can critique Spanish traditions and society while simultaneously pointing to a path for Spanish redemption. First, I will show how Cervantes seemingly bends the ordinary boundaries of picaresque literature by transforming an ordinary Spanish pícaro into an extraordinary Spanish holy man; this metamorphosis, however, seems to be motivated by pride, the antithesis of saintliness. Next, I demonstrate that, despite the main character's manifest pride, a flaw common to all picaros, this ruffian, unlike his literary contemporaries, actually seems to be successful in discarding the moral and social baggage that prevents other picaros from truly ascending the social and moral ladder. I will suggest that the concept of America offers the possibility of this transformation.

FROM PICARO TO SAINT:
SUBVERSIVE TRANSFORMATIONS

In critics' attempts to elucidate Cervantes's writings, multiple theories and hypotheses have emerged. Some researchers hold Cervantes's work as a pillar supporting the patriarchal institutions of the day; other investigators emphasize the opposite: a subversive element lightly cloaked in uncensurable rhetoric.[2] Although most Cervantes criticism has focused on his narrative, which is generally perceived to be of greater aesthetic worth, the *Ocho comedias y ocho entremeses nunca representados* [*Eight Plays and Eight Farces, Never Performed*] have received significant attention, especially in recent years, due, in part, to the author who wrote them but also to their increasingly appreciated value as literary artifacts. Of the plays, *El rufián dichoso* is unique in that it is the only example of a religious comedy, being based, loosely, on historical reports of the transformation of a repentant sinner.[3] The play superficially tracks the life of an innkeeper's son from roguery to sainthood: the first act deals with his life as Cristóbal de Lugo [Christopher of Lugo], student turned delinquent in Seville; the second act outlines the nature of his repentance and his transformation into Cristóbal de la Cruz [Christopher of the Cross], a friar in Mexico; and the third act, which also takes place in Mexico, displays his saintly sacrifice for an allegedly wicked woman, along with his suffering, death, and miraculous sanctification.

Both religion and the underworld are common themes in Cervantes's writing and are blended expertly in works such as *Rinconete y Cortadillo*, in which one sees the carnivalesque figure of Monipodio satirize both church and state, or in *Don Quijote*, in which both non-pious priests and falsely penitent picaros abound. If we recall the genesis of other famous ruffians of the day, we may notice similarities with the rogue in Cervantes's play, albeit with significant differences. Lazarillo, Pablos, and Guzmán, three of the most famous literary picaros, share similar conditions and motives, particularly the desire to change their circumstances. However, these contemporaries to Cervantes's Lugo fail to manifest the type of interior changes that might help them achieve the inner peace that eludes them. They give lip service to repentance but concentrate their actions on improving their social and economic status, a motivation reflected in and emphasized by their choice of the word *medrar* [to improve] to characterize their efforts. Medrar, of course, does not allude to moral or spiritual betterment but specifically to the desire for upward social mobility and for improved financial standing. Lugo, like other rogues, was born into unfortunate circumstances and spends a good part of his life attempting to supplement the meagerness of his birthright. In contrast, however, to the typical picaro, Lugo manifests dissatisfaction less with monetary instability than with the inability to control how others perceive him. In the case of Guzmán, Pablos, and Lázaro, most critics would probably agree that little real transformation takes place, that the authors either condemn the character's motives or, to satisfy contemporary societal views, prevent any real change from occurring. A careful reading of *El rufián dichoso* may reveal that Cervantes, unlike Alemán, Quevedo, and the author of *Lazarillo de Tormes*, allows his picaro to undergo true transformation.[4]

Some critics believe that Cervantes's own patriotism and religiosity denies the possibility for subversive readings of this religious drama, describing the play as an endorsement and reinforcement of traditional socioreligious discourse. But why should a religious comedy in the hand of Cervantes escape the conventional and thematic twists experienced by every other genre he explores? Consider, for example, *La española inglesa* [*The English Spanish Girl*], a text long described by critics as an idealistic romance well removed from reality. Carroll B. Johnson has carefully demonstrated that, far from unrealistic, the text is replete with historicity, and that behind the apparently straightforward approval of marriage and aristocracy lies a subversive critique of the selfishly monopolistic practices of the nobility as well as a disguised endorsement of the burgeoning bourgeoisie. Few critics have ventured to challenge the apparent adherence to patriarchal authority demonstrated in *El rufián dichoso*. By adjusting our focus, however, to see beneath the veil of orthodoxy, it becomes quite possible to read many of the seemingly pious passages as subtle attempts to denude certain socioreligious practices. *El rufián dichoso*, like many other Cervantine texts, is capable at least of multivalent extractions from its readers if not intentional subversive discourse of the author. The title itself, as in so many of Cervantes's works, suggests that interpretation is multifaceted. *Rufián* [ruffian] customarily conjures up qualifiers more sinister or less admirable in Spanish than *dichoso* [fortunate]. Equally, dichoso carries a wide range of connotations, from "virtuous," "fortunate," and "happy," to "unlucky" or "bothersome." Certainly each of these adjectives can be applied to the innkeeper's son at some point in the play. In addition, many are relevant simultaneously, each reflecting a different character's perspective regarding a particular event or attitude. The text, therefore, would seem to suggest that interpretation is varied if not open, or, in the words of Nicholas Spadaccini and Jenaro Talens, the "reader is thus invited to bring to the reception of *El rufián* his or her own codes for the production of meaning."[5]

As the play begins we find Cristóbal de Lugo, a self-proclaimed and novice ruffian, seeking to force a tenured colleague to recognize his superiority. As words turn to blows, the local authorities enter the scene, at which point Lugo's challenger flees. Pride clearly motivates the conflict. This same pride moves Lugo to hold his ground when outnumbered by the local lawmen. He refuses to turn himself in, taunting and challenging them. The evening patrol recognizes him and immediately desists from its attempts to detain him. Lugo, they reveal, much to his dismay, is protected by the local inquisitor, his relative and master. No one from the constable's office seems willing to risk a confrontation with the inquisitor by detaining Lugo. Although Lugo would like to believe that it is his *macho valor*, his supposedly intimidating presence, that frightens the constable, we later learn that the inquisitor has freed Lugo from jail no less than seven times, a fact that would suggest that it is indeed possible to overpower and arrest the young man; the problem is in the ability to keep him incarcerated. The inquisitor's interference on behalf of Lugo reveals the corruption or at least inconsistency in the Spanish system of moral maintenance. The inquisitor's lax attitude toward his youthful charge is not dissimilar to that of Rodolfo's father in *La fuerza de la sangre* [*The Force of Blood*], who, as we remember, gave his son a key to the outer door of the house and allowed his son unfettered and unmonitored access to the street, thus permitting, if not encouraging, incidents such as the rape of Leocadia. In *La fuerza de la sangre*, the narrator chastises the negligence of Rodolfo's father in particular and broadens the scope of his attack to include fathers throughout Spain who are failing in their parental duties. *El rufián dichoso*, of course, does not have a narrator. We, the reading public, must determine the extent to which the author attempts to critique social customs.

Our first direct introduction to the inquisitor is through a prostitute who, irreverently and erotically, complains that Lugo does not give her the attention that she needs. One might expect an inquisitor to send her marching. Not so. The inquisitor Don Tello invites her in and admonishes her to hide where she can listen while he clarifies the matter with Lugo. What on earth is he going to clarify? Does he plan to tell Lugo to take better care of his prostitutes? Why, in the first place, would a prostitute dare to seek the inquisitor's protection? The incident inspires these and other questions, but the answers are not forthcoming. Lugo remains haughty in his exchange with Don Tello, and, despite the inquisitor's threats and chastisements, the young panderer rudely interrupts his master's discourse and dismisses himself without permission upon hearing that a fellow pimp has been arrested by the constable. The inquisitor shows no anger, no negative reaction, no real desire to discipline. He merely inquires as to the nature of the escapade. Despite the absence of narratorial denunciations, the weak nature of the inquisitor and his favoring of delinquents over lawmen may represent a criticism of the contemporary dictators of morality.

It infuriates and humiliates Lugo that people render him deference on account of the inquisitor, that his own presence does not cause them to tremble. Stanislav Zimic explains this in terms of Adlerian psychology, proposing that Lugo, despite his bravado, suffers from a self-conscious sense of inferiority, "su espíritu revoltoso está por esto ansioso e impaciente en extremo en poder ostentarse a todos en su verdadero ser" [for this reason his rebellious spirit is extremely anxious, and he is impatient to flaunt himself before everyone in his true light].[6] This prideful desire to dominate others manifests itself throughout the text. As William A. Stapp eloquently demonstrates in opposition to most critics, pride is a frailty that Lugo will not fully overcome until after his death. Stapp argues that pride is the constant throughout the play, particularly, that it is Lugo's only moral defect, and that he never fully repents of his pride. Textual evidence, however, may suggest the presence of other weaknesses. A rufián, of course, was a cross between a hit man and a pimp. Physical violence and sexuality were an inseparable part of the definition. Stapp contends, however, backed by notable critics such as Joaquín Casalduero and Jean Canavaggio, that Lugo has conquered carnal desires.[7] Jenaro Talens and Nicolas Spadaccini noncommittally suggest otherwise in the introduction to their edition of the play, and Zimic openly argues that sexuality is an important subtext, that readers or spectators would have understood implicitly that Lugo had a long history of sexual escapades.[8] In a different context, Spadaccini and Talens also suggest that readers' expectations would have included, "at least potentially, a critical understanding of other texts, a relationship with other systems of meaning or social and discursive norms," thereby allowing us to conclude that Cervantes's contemporary readers would have understood the underlying nature of a rufián.[9] The principal textual evidence used to justify arguments both for and against Lugo's dominance of lechery is a brief exchange between Antonia the prostitute and the inquisitor Don Tello:

Tello:	¿Bien le queréis?
Antonia:	No lo niego;
	mas quiérole en parte buena.
Tello:	El madrugar os condena.
Antonia:	Siempre es solícito el fuego.
Tello:	En otra parte buscad
	materia que le apliquéis,
	que en mi casa no hallaréis
	sino toda honestidad;
	si el mozo da ocasión
	que le busquéis, yo haré
	que desde hoy más no os la dé.
Antonia:	Enójase sin razón
	vuesa merced; que, en mi alma,
	que el mancebo es de manera,
	que pueda llevar do quiera
	entre mil honestos palma.
	Verdad es que él es travieso,
	matante, acuchillador;
	pero, en cosas del amor,
	por un leño le confieso.
	No me lleva a mí tras él
	Venus blanda y amorosa,
	sino su aguda ganchosa
	y su acerado broquel.
Tello:	¿Es valiente?
Antonia:	Muy bien puedes
	sin escrúpulo igualalle
	y aun quizá será agravialle,
	a García de Paredes.
	Y por esto este mocito
	trae a todas las del trato
	muertas: por ser tan bravato;
	que en lo demás es bendito.[10]

Tello:	You love/want him well?
Antonio:	I deny it not;
	but I love/want him in a good place.
Tello:	Look in another place
	for something to apply to your fire,
	since in my house you will find
	nothing but chastity;
	if the young man gives you the opportunity

	to look for satisfaction here, I will ensure
	that from now on he will not give it to you.
Antonia:	You anger without cause,
	sir; on my word,
	the youth is such
	that wherever he may be
	he outperforms the most chaste
	It is true that he is mischievous,
	murderous, and pugilistic;
	but in matters of love he is a blockhead.
	What draws meto him
	is not soft and amorous Venus,
	rather his sharp hook knife
	and his steely shield.
Tello:	Is he valiant?
Antonia:	You may very well
	without scruples compare him,
	though perhaps it would insult him,
	to García de Paredes.
	This explains how this young man
	keeps all his prostitutes
	worn out: due to his inflated valiancy.
	On all other accounts, he is a saint.

If we choose to read this as a straightforward text, then we are compelled to believe the words of Antonia when she states that Lugo is hands down the most chaste man that she knows. If, however, we see reason to doubt a prostitute; if we see a woman so sexually aroused that she overcomes her fear of the inquisitor in order to ask for the whereabouts of her means of satisfaction; if in the course of her conversation with the inquisitor she senses that the inquisitor intends to restrict her access to Lugo should he suspect that Lugo is veering from sexual purity; might not her hyperbolic description of his chastity be a red herring? It is not, she claims, soft and loving Venus that makes her chase him; rather, his sharp and hard weapons.[11] One could read that she is not emotionally attached, that she merely desires to put to her advantage the "hard and sharp weapons" that Lugo seems to have at his disposal. It is, in fact, these weapons that have left all of the prostitutes in the vicinity breathless, bless his chaste soul. I proffer that Lugo's approach to sexuality parallels his pride. He seems not to be gentle and doting in his conquests; rather, he is violent and domineering. His desire, evident from the beginning of the play, is to dominate all—men, women, even God—and to force them to adjust to his will, his demands, his whims. He is not interested in sex or money, the obvious fruits of pimping. He seeks to control.

Lugo's desire to control manifests itself in every scene of the opening act. First he attempts to dominate a senior ruffian. Interrupted, he asserts his authority over the constable. Next a noble woman begs him to make love to her. Zimic astutely notes that the refusal to satisfy her desires does not automatically imply a lack of interest in sexual gratification; rather, for Zimic, "Cervantes nos muestra cómo el rufián, de costumbre mujeriego, rechaza a una mujer muy seductora, por el mero hecho de que poseerla en ese momento no puede servirle en absoluto para gratificar su ilusión de importancia personal o para apuntalar su íntima inseguridad" [Cervantes shows us how the ruffian, normally a womanizer, rejects a very seductive woman simply because the act of possessing her in that moment in no way serves to gratify his illusion of personal importance or to prop up his intimate insecurity].[12] But it is not the refusal, alone, that seems to give pleasure to Lugo. In addition, he alerts her husband as to her intentions. Although he does not reveal to the near-cuckolded gentleman the object of his wife's lust, merely to mention the betrayal of her love is to flaunt his dishonor before him. Doña Mencía lost blood for lesser offenses in Calderón's *El médico de su honra* [*The Surgeon of His Honor*]. The point of this scene is not to highlight Lugo's resistance to sexual temptations but rather to underscore his insatiable desire to control others. From the unfortunate gentleman, Lugo turns to Don Tello, refusing him the respect that he deserves as master, as inquisitor, and as a father figure, a member of his own family. Then he once again asserts his authority over the constable, forcing him to release a fellow pimp, and he exacts promises of fidelity from all involved in the incident. The night continues with more bullying and impositions, the point of each incident being less to obtain sex, money, food— anything physical—than to exercise control over the participants.

The destructive direction of Lugo's life comes to an abrupt halt when, after challenging God, the one entity that eludes his control, his fortunes are reversed. Lugo has never been able to win money from a certain Gilberto. Unable to tolerate this lack of supremacy, he has scheduled a card game. His friend Lobillo offers him a marked deck. Lugo, however, prefers a different path: "Juro a dios omnipotente / que, si las pierdo al presente, / me he de hacer salteador" (Cervantes *El rufián,* 340) [I swear to God Almighty that, if I lose here now, I will become a plunderer]. He is set to control his own destiny and refuses to win by any means other than his own natural abilities. Even his psuedo oath to God is more a challenge, a threat, than a plea or a promise. He seems to want to deal with God in the same way that he deals with man: through intimidation and force. When Lugo wins the card game—not only winning, but acquiring more money in that one game that he had squandered in all his previous losses—he is not quite sure how to react. To accept the money and continue his present lifestyle would be to acknowledge that God controls him. If, however, he chooses to give himself to God, he will remain in control, the choice would be his. Leaving his old life behind, Lugo metamorphoses into Fray Cruz, dedicating himself to God, to meditation, to fasting, and to self-flagellation in an effort, through his own works, to pay for his past sins and to earn his entry to heaven.

Religious practices and beliefs in Spain during Cervantes's lifetime, and within the chronology of the text, allowed little room for personal interpretation. Faith was good; works, essential. But what kind of works? Were prayers, fasting, and flogging sufficient to redeem oneself, or were acts of charity also required? And what about Christ's role in the process of redemption? Spanish Catholics of Erasmian bent may have felt some uneasiness with regard to certain practices of the Iglesia Católica Apostólica Española [Spanish Apostolic Catholic Church], as Unamuno's character San Manuel Bueno [Saint Emmanuel the Good] would later call it.

Zimic makes a connection between Cervantes's Cruz and Unamuno's San Manuel, stating that he considers Cruz's sacrifice to be greater than San Manuel's, "porque el consuelo religioso que Manuel ofrece a sus feligreses no implica, *ipso facto*, una correspondiente tortura o perdición para él. La falta de fe de Manuel—que es su martirio—no depende en absoluto de sus relaciones con los demás"[13] [because the religious comfort that Emmanuel offers to his parishioners does not imply, *ipso facto*, a correspondent torture or perdition for him. Manuel's lack of faith—which is his martyrdom—does not depend at all on his relationship with others]. I find that neither part of Zimic's argument withstands deconstruction. One could debate whether San Manuel's inner torment was exacerbated or tempered by his tireless service to his flock. Likewise, there is more than a small possibility that Cruz's suffering does nothing to alleviate the afflictions of others. As a rufián, Lugo exercised authority over others in an effort to control them in order to feel better about himself. As a priest, Cruz exercises control in the form of resistance over the temptations that devils and demons lay before him as he attempts to secure his own redemption. In both circumstances his efforts can be viewed as self-centered. I agree with Stapp that Cruz's religious redirection does not include retraining in humility.[14] When Don Tello visits him, Cruz seems lacking in gratitude and respect (contrary to Zimic's reading). He appears to revel in his position of religious authority, in having the man who practically raised him and who formerly scolded his indiscretions now ask for his blessing and kiss his hand. Cruz's final opportunity to relinquish control to God comes when Doña Ana, a sinner of the worst kind, refuses to confess her sins and to ask for God's mercy, believing herself to be unworthy of salvation. Rather than convince her of the boundless mercy of Christ and of His power to redeem, Cruz offers to exchange his own good works for her sins, guaranteeing her entry to heaven on his word alone.

On one level of interpretation, Cruz can be viewed as a metaphor for Christ: he willingly makes the "disinterested decision" (Spadaccini and Talens, *Shattering Glass,* 94) to take upon himself the sins of another in order to provide for that person's salvation. This comparison, however, presents a complication and contradiction of motives: Christ sought the will and the glory of his Father, and, according to the accounts of his believers, he was expressly authorized to expiate the sins of others; Cruz, from a certain perspective, seems to seek his own glory, usurping the role of Christ as savior; Cruz promises that he personally can guarantee Doña Ana forgiveness and eternal life rather than promising her that as a servant of Christ he will plead that Christ will forgive her her sins. He seems to have an egotistical audacity and personal knowledge that Christ has accepted his good works and has given him permission to transpose their effects from himself onto another. On another level of interpretation, the whole confession incident may be a type of self-serving perversion of Catholic dogma. Although critics such as Patricia Varas suggest that "Cruz es un ejemplo de piedad, humildad, y caridad" [Cruz is an example of piety, humility, and charity], it is also true that Lugo always wanted to be recognized for his own merits; he constantly strove to accomplish some feat that would clearly set him apart from his past and his present, that would solidify his reputation and exalt his honor.[15] Just before he chose to dedicate himself to God, he also vowed to become eternally famous. Does he perhaps see in Ana an opportunity to realize his ambition? When Ana agrees to give Cruz her sins, Cruz tells Fray Antonio, the former Lobillo, to go to the convent and announce the good news to the Reverend Father and to have everyone say a prayer of thanks for this miracle. Is he broadcasting the event for himself, for Ana, or for God? The answer may lie in God's response. Doña Ana confesses her sins and rises to heaven in glory. As she enters into God's glory, Cruz is covered with leprosy, a disease that will plague him for another thirteen years before he passes away. Stapp suggests that Cruz's indomitable pride lies at the root of the supposed apparition of demons as well as many other of the supposed miracles that Cruz performs: "Recordemos que no nos habríamos enterado de estas visiones si el buen fraile no las hubiera publicado, y se juzgan verdaderas precisamente porque las cuenta un fraile santo" [Let us remember that we would not have become aware of these visions if the good friar had not publicized them, and they are believed to be true precisely because a holy friar recounts them].[16] Stapp postulates that Cruz becomes leprous because his works were not sufficient to pay for Ana's sins, hence God burdened Cruz with the remainder of her sins, and he continued to suffer until he had paid for them ("Dichoso," 442). Although this explanation is plausible, I find another more appealing. Ana was received into heaven because at the last minute she confessed her sins and turned to God. Cruz was punished for his pride in order to teach him who really was in control. For the remainder of Cruz's life, he slowly ascended the ranks of the priesthood. By the end of his life, he controlled spiritually the greater part of the land he lived in, yet God did not release him from his leprosy until after his death, nor did he allow him to die quickly. God exercised ultimate control over both Ana and Cruz.

It is difficult to know what Cervantes himself intended to portray with this play; regardless of his intentions, however, it may be possible to interpret many of the apparently pious passages as subtle ironies that reveal something different from the obviously apparent. In religion, in territorial expansion, in the underworld, and in politics, the desire for control often overpowers all other sentiments and reasoning. Lugo and Cruz are not necessarily tremendously different. Both, perhaps, pridefully seek to control the people around them. How fitting that this plot of fame, of desire, of control, that this spiritual conquest of a sinner reluctant to recognize the Spanish God, would unravel in the New World.

A NEW WORLD:
POSITIVE TRANSFORMATIONS

Curiously enough, despite Cervantes's documented desires to travel to the New World, the Americas rarely appear in his work. Many critics have demonstrated that Cervantes regularly makes direct and indirect reference either to the New World or to the effect that its existence has created on the Old. *El rufián dichoso*, however, is the only Cervantine work whose events purportedly unfold on the transatlantic continent. The dramatist takes pains to state explicitly that the second and third acts of the play take place in Mexico (were he not to emphasize this point by unequivocally stating it, the reader would have no other way to ascertain this fact, due to the complete absence of local dress, fauna, vegetation, dialect, or other autochthonous indicators). If Cervantes's plays in general have attracted little attention from scholars or dramatists over the preceding centuries, this particular, seemingly insignificant detail "a Mexican setting" has attracted even less. Glen F. Dille indicates that, notwithstanding the New World setting for part of the play, "Cervantes's own interest in America was limited" ("Plays," 91) and that, essentially, his view of the New World "could be characterized as effectively no view at all, or at least no positive view" (90). As we know, however, recognizing the opinions of an author in a text can be difficult, and appreciably more so with skillful and playful writers. Since Cervantes was very familiar with the foreign and the "exotic," having spent significant time in Italy, Algeria, and Portugal; since on more than one occasion he sought to receive permission to travel to the Americas; and since he (or his readers) often find ways to critique or comment on society and tradition through his texts; it is interesting, at least, and provocative that he would choose the New World as the location for the metamorphosis of his picaro-saint. A closer reading may reveal that rather than producing a nonview or a negative view of America, the text casts the New World in an optimistic role, a place full of possibilities for miraculous change and positive regeneration.

By the time Cervantes set his foot on the stage, Spanish supremacy in Europe was headed toward its decline, and the colonization, subjugation, and evangelization of the New World had yielded as many troubles as treasures. Of the many men that set sights on New Spain for adventure and riches, relatively few achieved the financial success of individuals such as the fictional Carrizales in Cervantes's *El celoso extremeño* [*The Jealous Extremaduran*]. And although Carrizales was able to return to Spain, procure a beautiful young bride, and conceal her in a prison-like mansion, he was not able to purchase respectability, wisdom, or honor. Critics have pointed to the semantic similarity of *Carrizales* and *descarriar* [to lead astray, to wander from the path]; Cervantes's text, in fact, seems to suggest that Carrizales's fate was a direct result of wandering. Dille, perhaps, would suggest that the text's criticism of wandering is a reflection of what Dille deems to be Cervantes's negative attitude toward the New World. We know, however, that Cervantes had fond memories of Italy, yet this affection did not interfere with his criticisms of young men who traveled from Spain to Italy in search of sexual adventures, if not riches. Remember, for example, the case of Rodolfo, in *La fuerza de la sangre* [*The Force of Blood*]. For some critics, Rodolfo represents—on a certain level—Cervantes's depiction of the moral depravity of the Spanish elite males. That an author would cause a fictional persona of questionable character to visit a particular country does not necessarily indicate that the country itself exemplifies the author's conception of corruption. It is equally possible that the reasons for choosing America, Italy, the Netherlands, or elsewhere for his protagonists' travels tell us more about literary conventions and historical reality than about Cervantes's own interest or non-interest in the country as a country. The act of wandering from home, of deviating from the correct path, perhaps speaks more to moral issues than to geographical antipathy. I suggest that, in the case of Cervantes, America as a destination does not necessarily represent, as Dille claims, "a dumping ground and place of refuge for society's dregs."[17]

A survey of the literature and history of Spain's colonization of the New World suggests that Carrizales's inability to be fully reintegrated into Spain and Spanish society despite his newly found American riches was a fate experienced by more than one *indiano*.[18] Perhaps their inability to readapt is due more to the questionable, often illegal or inhumane methods by which they acquired their wealth than to the fact that it was gained in a particular location. One can imagine that many of those who left Spain with the intention to get rich and then to return to their homeland had a change of heart after arriving in the New World. Perhaps many decided that to return would be economically implausible or no longer desirable. The New World was a land of discoveries, of possibilities, of miracles, of change.

If we admit that there is an undertone of negativity toward the endeavors of the indiano in *El celoso extremeño*, we must also recognize the differences between a friar and an indiano. Early on in *El rufián dichoso*, there is reference to the general association of the indiano, or, in this case, a synonym, *perulero*, to the unsavory elements of society.[19] In the first act, Lagartija, a young delinquent with aspirations of becoming a ruffian of the stature of Lugo, attempts to impress Lugo by boasting of the indecorous deeds he plans to perform that will make him wildly wealthy: "Pues de él espero / salir presto a otro ejercicio / que muestre ser perulero" (Cervantes, *El rufián*, 328) [Since from it I hope to quickly pass to another enterprise that promises to be lucrative]. It is very unlikely, especially considering the author in question, that the choice of perulero is gratuitous in a drama that will have its final setting in Mexico and whose plot is based more or less on the "truthful" accounts of historical figures. Both Canavaggio and Zimic underscore Cervantes's creative license with the historical accounts of Fray Cruz's life, but there is indisputable evidence and critical agreement that the real events did, indeed, unfold in Mexico, a fact that Cervantes chooses to maintain and to highlight in the didascalia through reminders to the reader of this "never performed play" that the action really did occur as portrayed. This emphasis on the "truthfulness" of otherworldly events—and I am referring, here, not only on the events portrayed in the New World as compared to the Old, but also to the appearance of devils, of heavenly voices, and of miraculous events—leads the reader, in retrospect, to examine more closely the events that unfold in Seville. These events, too, according to most critics, find their inspiration in historical leads, but Cervantes makes no attempt to certify their truthfulness in the stage directions.

If we return to *El celoso extremeño*, we will remember that Carrizales, as a young man, set out from Spain, made a fortune in the New World—perhaps by questionable means—and returned to his homeland. Extremadura had little to offer him before he left, financially or socially, and for this very reason he chose to leave Spain behind for a land of greater economic promise. He was unable, however, to root the motherland out of his heart, nor, for that matter, out of his head: he took with him all that Spain had taught him and had failed to teach him. Hence, his purpose for being in the New Spain was selfish and limited. His return to his native land, as we have already reviewed, perpetuated attitudes that he acquired long before his sojourn in America. Cervantes underscores the selfish nature of exploiters through Loaysa's conquest of Carrizales's fortress and, additionally, by sending Loaysa off to Las Indias after Carrizales's death, leading the reader to suspect that Loaysa will repeat the cycle of Carrizales's egotistical wanderings.

The circumstances surrounding Lugo's departure for America are similar, but significantly different. Although Lagartija makes linguistic reference to the bounty of the New World, Lugo gives no indication of a desire to seek economic fortune across the ocean. As the dominant rufián in Sevilla, the acquisition of goods is not, at his particular youthful age, a preoccupation. He takes what he pleases when he pleases. Interestingly enough, contrary to the miserly Carrizales, Lugo, nicknamed "Roque" (Cervantes, *El rufián,* 334) by those that know him, is a type of Spanish Robin Hood. Rather than "stealing," he forces the proud to recognize his superiority and accepts their peace offerings, as in the scene with the *pastelero* [pastry baker].[20] When Lugo does have money that he is fortunate enough not to lose in gambling, he has a reputation for distributing it down to the last *real* to the poor, as in the scene with the blind man.[21] At the moment of act 1, Lugo has lost practically all his earthly possessions while gambling, a fact that does not seem to concern him in the least, since, he reports, if he loses what he owns playing cards, he knows how to take "double revenge" (Cervantes, *El rufián,* 340), suggesting that he can take by force what he loses by chance. Thus, as Dille implies, both Carrizales and Lugo are societal problems, but readers may sense a difference, that the young Carrizales was a man like Loaysa, a clever but unsuccessful lad without a clear future, while Lugo, on the other hand, though a rufián, seems to act with purpose and direction, succeeding in all he does, earning the fear and/or respect of all. Carrizales appears to leave Spain poor, traveling to the New World to seek riches. Lugo, on the contrary, while gambling wins back in one night a hundred times more than he had lost previously; thus, in addition to the fact that it does not seem to be in his nature to be preoccupied by money, at the end of act 1 Lugo has more money than he needs—he even turns down the generous offer of the rich husband who seeks to repay him for averting his public dishonor (Cervantes, *El rufiana,* 342).

At the conclusion of act 1, Lugo consciously determines to change the direction of his life. His mentor, Tello, had already announced his decision to extract Lugo from his knavish lifestyle: "Bien iré a la Nueva España / cargado de ti, malino" [I will indeed go to New Spain, burdened with you, evildoer] (Cervantes, *El rufián,* 337). But Lugo takes no notice of his benefactor's objectives until he, himself, arrives at the independent decision to abandon his villainous life and to dedicate himself to holy works. Hence, when Lugo sets off for the New World, his goal is not to exploit the land and the people, not even, in fact, to preach and to convert. Principally, Lugo desires to compel God to recognize that he is sorry for the misguided actions of his life up to that point.

One could argue, perhaps, that to a certain extent the New World serves as an escape for both Lugo and Carrizales in which they can selfishly dedicate themselves to acquiring that which they believe will bring them happiness, forgiveness for the former, riches for the latter. Carrizales, however, after extracting his fortune, leaves the New World with no indication of having left it better than he found it. Even in Spain he dies a lonely, dishonored, miserable man; and, although he donates the majority of his fortune to charitable causes, he is remembered for his weakness—his jealousy—not for his money, which, in reality, he distributed not out of a spirit of philanthropy, but rather, to prevent it from falling into the hands of his young rival. On the other hand, our friar, Lugo, or Cruz as he is known in Mexico, diligently labors to procure his own eternal salvation, but not, of course, at the expense of others. In offering to take upon himself the sins of Doña Ana, a vile and godless woman, as reported by the text, Cruz seems to demonstrate his love for the people of his new home and his desire to serve them and to help them abandon evil. Cruz, unlike his former self, Lugo, persuades through example and generosity rather than force and intimidation. His tools are a Rosary and a kind word, not a dagger and a threat.

During a time when there were still heated debates regarding the value of the indigenous people of the New World, it is pleasing at least and, indeed, credible to imagine that Cervantes, a man who suffered much and witnessed much suffering, envisioned the New World as a place where a well-intentioned Spaniard could begin to rectify the social and moral problems of the Old. Perhaps, contrary to Dille's proposition, Cervantes views the New World as a place of hope, of change, of salvation; a place where miracles can happen, a place where socioeconomically unfortunate Spaniards of sound moral principles can escape from the social, moral, and even political decline of the Peninsula. Lugo's journey, much different from that of Carrizales, was unidirectional: from Spain, to Mexico, to Heaven. In Spain, he advanced to the top of his rufián class; in Mexico, he was elevated by his peers to the highest echelons of his religious order; and, in the end, Mary, the Lord Jesus, and a host of angels welcomed him into a heavenly glory. Perhaps, indeed, Cervantes has a positive view of America; in *El rufián dichoso,* at least, one can view the New World as gateway to heaven, as an escape from corruption and status quo.

CONCLUSION

The final words of Diana de Armas Wilson's fascinating study on the interpretation of Cervantine dreams are, "Reader, *you* decide" (emphasis in original) (Wilson, "Cervantes," 80). When discussing Cervantes's theater, it is particularly important to remember that the principal mode of reception, contrary to much drama, is through the written word. This fact slightly alters the task of the dramatist and of the audience, who become, respectively, author and reader, and while we might construct in our minds a theatrical setting, we recognize that the author was conscious of his audience of readers and, therefore, of the individual performances that each reader would stage in his or her mind. Were a director to stage the play, he or she would present certain aspects of the text according to his or her reading. Each director, of course, would interpret and stage the play differently, and, for that matter, each performance would be different. In my review of *El rufián dichoso,* I have presented a variety of readings, including two of my own. I suggest first that the text presents Lugo/Cruz as a figure whose pride dominates his actions throughout his life, even and especially when he takes upon himself the sins of another. Later, I propose that we may read that same culminating event as a suggested solution to the problems of decadence in the religion, politics, and culture of seventeenth-century Spanish society. Although the readings compete for the same signifiers, they are not incompatible: Cruz, "the cross," ends his days proudly ascending to heaven from Mexico. In Cervantes's play, the New World becomes a place where true transformations are possible, where picaros can become saints, where sinners can be exalted, where men can rise from the socially restrictive circumstances of their birth to become famous, powerful, and internally changed. Mexico, like the Christian cross, becomes a symbolic spiritual as well as temporal destination. Of course, the play may be interpreted in other ways. Reader, you decide.

NOTES

1. All translations are mine. In the case of key words and titles, translations are normally provided only for the initial occurrence.

2. See, for example, Casalduero, *Sentido* and, more recently, Sears, *Marriage.* See Friedman, "Cervantes's *La fuerza de la sangre*" and Johnson, *Cervantes,* for example.

3. An account of the historical Fray Cristobal de la Cruz is reproduced from the *Historia General de la Orden de Santo Domingo, y de su Orden de Predicadores* [*General History of the Order of Saint Domingo, and of his Order of Preachers*] in Hazañas y la Rua's introduction to his edition of the play.

4. Edward H. Friedman reminds us that change from within a religious order was more likely from in the contemporary society than change from without (*Unifying Concept,* 107). Perhaps for this reason Cervantes chose to frame this drama within the genre of the saint's play.

5. See Spadaccini and Talens, *Through the Shattering Glass,* 100.

6. See Zimic, "La caridad," 107.

7. See Casalduero, *Sentido,* 108, and Canavaggio, *Cervantès,* 363. See Stapp, "Dichoso," 415–20.

8. See Zimic, "La caridad," 96.

9. See Spadaccini and Talens, *Through the Shattering Glass,* 93.

10. See Cervantes, *El rufián dichoso,* 336. I use Valbuena Prat's edition of the *Obras completas* and cite the page number.

11. Antonia's sexuality is not central to my argument, although I recognize that it is problematic to suggest that she and the other prostitutes seek sexual satisfaction from Lugo, a domineering and violent male. Examined biologically and socially, however, it does not seem at all strange that an unprotected female would seek out the most dominant male; one can also make the argument that, although Lugo is domineering and willing to commit violence, he is not violent when violence is unnecessary, and he is even compassionate—kind—to those who are weak and dispossessed; it is probable that his dominance and violence would be sublimated into virulence in sexual matters. This would explain why the women continue to seek him out, why Antonia values his "hard" and "sharp" weapons and refers to him otherwise as a saint. This matter could be explored in another essay.

12. See Zimic, "La caridad," 106.

13. Ibid., 145.

14. See Stapp, "Dichoso," 432.

15. See Varas, "*El rufián dichoso,*" 16.

16. See Stapp, "Dichoso," 438–39.

17. See Dille, "The Plays," 91. By countering Dille's argument, I do not mean to deny the general socioeconomic status of many if not most emigrants from Spain to the New World, nor do I close my eyes to the negative consequences of the conquest, of colonization, of evangelization, of slavery, of continued transatlantic domination of the newly formed viceroyalties, etc.

18. An *indiano*, at the time, was a Spanish immigrant who returned to Spain after having made a fortune in the Spanish "Indies."

19. A *perulero*, was a synonym for *indiano*, the reference, of course, being Perú.

20. See Cervantes *El rufián dichoso*, 335.

21. Ibid., A *real* is a former silver coin of Spain and Spanish America, equal to one eighth of a peso.

WORKS CITED

Canavaggio, Jean. *Cervantès dramaturge: Un théâtre à naître*. Paris: Presses Universitaires de France, 1977.

Casalduero, Joaquín. *Sentido y forma del teatro de Cervantes*. Madrid: Gredos, 1966.

Cervantes Saavedra, Miguel de. *El rufián dichoso*. In *Obras Completas*, edited by Angel Valbuena Prat, 325–64. Madrid: Aguilar, 1960.

Dille, Glen F. "The Plays of Cervantes, Lope, Calderón and the New World." *La Chispa* 1987: 89–97.

Friedman, Edward H. "Cervantes's *La fuerza de la sangre* and the Rhetoric of Power." In *Cervantes's* Exemplary Novels *and the Adventure of Writing*, edited by Michael Nerlich and Nicholas Spadaccini, 125–26. Minneapolis, Minn.: Prisma Institute, 1989.

———. *The Unifying Concept: Approaches to the Structure of Cervantez's Comedias*. York, S.C.: Spanish Literature Publications Company, 1981.

Hazañas y la Rua, Joaquín. Introducción to *Los rufianes de Cervantes: "El rufián dichoso" y "El rufián viudo,"* by Miguel de Cervantes. Sevilla: Librería e impresora de Izquierdo y Compañía, 1906.

Johnson, Carroll B. *Cervantes and the Material World*. Urbana: University of Illinois Press, 2000.

———. "*La española inglesa* and the Practice of Literary Production." *Viator* 19 1988: 377–416.

Sears, Theresa Ann. *A Marriage of Convenience: Ideal and Ideology in the* Novelas ejemplares. New York: Peter Lang, 1993.

Spadaccini, Nicholas, and Jenaro Talens. *Through the Shattering Glass: Cervantes and the Self-Made World*. Minneapolis: University of Minnesota Press, 1993.

Stapp, William A. "Dichoso por confiado." *Anales Cervantinos* 25–26 1987–88: 413–52.

Talens, Jenaro, and Nicholas Spadaccini, eds. *El rufián dichoso/ Pedro de Urdemalas*. By Miguel de Cervantes. Madrid: Cátedra, 1986.

Varas, Patricia. "*El rufián dichoso*: una comedia de santos diferente." *Anales Cervantinos* 29 1991: 9–19.

Wilson, Diana de Armas. "Cervantes and the Night Visitors: Dream Work and the Cave of Montesinos." In *Quixotic Desire: Psychoanalytic Perspectives on Cervantes,* edited by Ruth Anthony El Saffar and Diana de Armas Wilson, 59–80. Ithaca, N.Y.: Cornell University Press, 1993. 59-80.

Zimic, Stanislav. "La caridad 'jamás imaginada' de Cristobal de Lugo: Estudio de *El rufián dichoso* de Cervantes." *Boletín de la Biblioteca de Menéndez Pelayo* 56 1980: 85–171.

Sigüenza and Sor Juana's *fiestas alegóricas*: An Inquiry into *Redemptive Hegemony* and Its Dissolution

Bradley J. Nelson

ONE OF THE MORE SELF-REFLEXIVE MOMENTS IN THE *LIBRO DE BUEN AMOR* occurs when Juan Ruiz's ironic avatar tells the one about the Roman and the Greek who face off in a literal mano a mano (21–31).[1] As the *arcipreste* tells it, the Romans, who have just defeated their more cultured neighbors, paradoxically suffer from what can only be called an inferiority complex. Admittedly having no laws of their own, they demand that the Greeks hand over their *ciencias* as part of the spoils of war. The Greeks refuse the request, however, stating that the Romans—barbarians that they are—not only do not deserve their laws, but they wouldn't understand them even if they had them. The Romans dispute this point and compel the Greeks to agree to a public test of their merit, with the sole stipulation being that the weapon of choice give neither party an unfair advantage. The Greeks arrogantly give their consent, not realizing that in agreeing to such a condition they have effectively surrendered their symbolic superiority, for the medium of exchange will be hand gestures and not alphabetic language. This sets up a very instructive—and hilarious—encounter between two mute *letrados*, one who uses and interprets hand signals as symbols of religious doctrine, while the other sees and produces gestures that threaten physical violence to his competitor. In the end, everyone is happy, except perhaps the "serious" reader, who finds no release of tension in Ruiz's "resolution": the Greek tells his compatriots that the Roman correctly answered two questions concerning theological doctrine; the Roman, for his part, assures his comrades that the Greeks will not be bothering them anymore thanks to the graphic and emphatic description of the bodily harm that will come to them if they persist in their insults. In quite Bakhtinian fashion, the shifts in context produce wildly varying readings according to contrary, yet simultaneously power hungry, ideologies.

There are many ways in which Ruiz's ambiguous exemplum illuminates some of the more pressing issues of transatlantic studies. Among them we could cite the following: the too-often-missed encounters that occur in what Mary Louise Pratt terms the "contact zone"; the polyvalence or resistance of linguistic signs of all types; the importance of the body as both site and medium of carnivalesque symbolic exchanges; the construction of cultural legitimacy and its relation to imperialistic violence; the performance of culture versus its so-called objective status; and, not least, the role of contingency and misunderstanding in the production of meaning and history. Following the lead of the arcipreste, the object of this study is to explore the interconnected issues of agency, transgression, and subversion and their relation to recent theorizations concerning the Baroque and the problematic of *Criollo* national consciousness in New Spain. At the center of this transatlantic encounter will be the identification and elucidation of what Walter Benjamin terms a historical monad: "a configuration pregnant with tensions [between] the homogeneous course of history . . . and a revolutionary chance in the fight for the oppressed past."[2] In short, I will compare and contrast the rhetorical and symbolic strategies employed by Carlos de Sigüenza y Góngora and Sor Juana Inés de la Cruz in their respective allegorical monuments celebrating the arrival of Tomás de la Cerda, Marqués de la Laguna, to New Spain in the year 1680: Sigüenza's *Teatro de virtudes políticas* and Sor Juana's *Neptuno alegórico*. By considering a series of similar yet contradictory aspects of these works, I hope to demonstrate how Sor Juana challenges Sigüenza's attempt to incorporate Aztec history into a homogeneous and unilateral narrative of universal history by unveiling the contingent nature of her own allegorical performance and, in so doing, rescues both a largely "oppressed" past and the historical viability of the subject of representation.

The symbolic strategies I will analyze coincide in large part with the (mis)encounter at the heart of Juan Ruiz's ingenious and unresolved narration, which frames at least three contrasting modes of representation. The first is the a priori claim (by the Greeks) to symbolic authority, which exemplifies what Lacan calls "the subject supposed to know"; the second is the theatrical performance of linguistic and cultural appropriation, or conquest, in the figure of the Roman savant; finally, we have the placement of the reader in a position from which it is impossible to determine which interpetation of the event is more correct. I will frame the discussion of these strategies within a theoretical dialogue of sorts between Catherine Bell's notions of "ritual

agency" and "redemptive hegemony," and the analytical space opened up by
Slavoj Žižek's reading of Lacanian psychoanalysis, in particular his position-
ing of the subject in relation to a "constitutive lack."[3]

I claim that whereas Sigüenza y Góngora constructs a self-legitimating,
i.e., redemptive, version of American history that acts to reinforce the allegorical readings of history on which peninsular political legitimacy and superiority rest—even as it rearranges that same history—Sor Juana, for her part,
deconstructs the rhetorical tropes that support and represent the voice of historical authority itself (*the subject supposed to know*), opening up and maintaining a nebulous indeterminacy in the space where Sigüenza situates a
positive notion of criollo identity.[4]

By moving away from *meaning* toward the analysis of authorial *activity*,
this discussion foregrounds a more practice-oriented understanding of the
Baroque as a particular strategy, or series of strategies, involved in the appropriation, deployment, and/or subversion of institutionalized modes of representation consistent with the appearance of modernity.[5] The central thesis of
José Antonio Maravall's *Culture of the Baroque*, that "the culture of the
baroque is an instrument to achieve effects . . . [in which] a simple *static guidance by presence* had to give way before a *dynamic guidance controlling by activity*," will be a key point of reference.[6] The cultural artifacts in question,
moreover, could not be more representative of the mercurial Baroque encounter between visual art, verbal acrobatics, theatricality, political power, and
religious festival. Within what has been universally considered a culture of
spectacle, the occasion of densely ornamented, *temporary* arches and/or ceno-
taphs—in this case, the triumphal arch and cathedral façade celebrating the
arrival and installation of the Marqués de la Laguna as viceroy of New
Spain—focusses critical and theoretical discussions even more closely on the
moment of cultural performance.[7] Often the only records we have of these an-
tithetically named "ephemeral monuments" are the verbal descriptions and
interpretations of the emblematic, hieroglyphic, and pictorial decorations that
adorned them. In the words of Sor Juana herself, "que como es tan formal
vuestra grandeza, / inmateriales templos os dedica" [since your grandeur is so
formal, it dedicates immaterial temples to you].[8]

The overwhelming sensorial and verbal excesses of these spectacles seem at
first (or even second) glance to reflect a cohesive and unified image of imperial
sovereignty and religious orthodoxy. In colonial studies, this perception of
achieved hegemony with respect to Spain has often been used to place into
sharper relief the cultural and historical specificities of the Latin American experience. Following the lead of Lezama Lima, Severo Sarduy, and Alejo Car-

pentier, Mabel Moraña locates in the historical moment and marvelous and confusing symbolic strategies of the Baroque, "the seed, as yet unformed, of national identities."[9] She is seconded by Alfredo Roggiano, who writes, "a nascent art is nothing more than the result of a being, a people, a nation, that is being born and will create itself with everything that is necessary and appropriate to its freedom and independence."[10] This *organicist* image of a nascent cultural identity also has been used to describe Spain itself, as Henry Kamen observes in his recent book *Empire*. Kamen also notes, however, that organic national metaphors are more closely related to the narrative practices of the historian than to the cultural tensions whose concrete effects the historian seeks to place in "correct order": "It is sometimes claimed that the secret of [imperial] success was the emergence of 'Spain' as a nation. The potential for overseas expansion, however, was never dictated by its potential as a 'nation state'. The peninsular territories known collectively as 'Spain' did not begin to develop as a nation before the eighteenth century."[11] Although national identity is certainly a central motif of Baroque literature, as in the case of Baroque spectacles themselves the relation of these "nationalistic" discursive practices to a transhistorical entity that could be called Spanish or criollo national identity is more problematic than first appears. Critics such as Rolena Adorno and John Beverley challenge these historicist points of view and take a rather suspect view of the enthusiastic valorization of a phenomenon as loaded with contingencies and contradictions as is the case with national identity. Beverley in particular advocates for a "psychoanalysis of the imaginary," reading the revalorization of the Baroque by the Latin American avant-garde as a "neurosis of the failed identities of Latin America."[12] For Beverley, Latin American national identities are no less prone to historical manipulation than other ideological constructions. As in the case of Maravall's understanding of baroque *guided* culture, national identity is perhaps better understood as a type of symbolic beachhead, assembled and erected in the face of a sea of historical transformations.[13] In this view, Sigüenza and Sor Juana's texts not only reflect contrasting historical reactions to what David R. Castillo terms *the Baroque condition*, they also can be used to place current critical postures into sharper relief. To demonstrate this point, I will analyze three deceptively similar moments in the two allegorical texts: the construction of the narrative voice; the use of the biblical figure of Absalom; and the use or misuse of allegory in the construction of an image of monarchical sovereignty.

Sigüenza begins his *Teatro* by linking his personal aspirations to those of the new viceroy, to whom he offers his work in order to extoll his fortune, which "elevaráse . . . a superior eminencia si obtengo el que con cariño se acepte este Triunfal Teatro de las Virtudes Políticas, en que las que en V. E. pueden servir de modelo augusto para que se reforme aquéllas, se aplauden inmortales" [my fortune will rise to greater eminence if I secure your fond acceptance of this Triumphal Theater of the Political Virtues, in which these held by Your Highness may may serve as a stately model so that those may be reformed, be applauded as immortal].[14] By framing the success of his own practice within the reformation, or transformation, of the ruling practices of the monarch, Sigüenza exemplifies Catherine Bell's understanding of ritual discourse. "Ritualization is perceived to be the most effective type of action to take in two over-lapping circumstances: 1) when the relationships of power being negotiated are based not on direct claims but on indirect claims of power conferred; and 2) when the hegemonic order being experienced must be rendered socially redemptive in order to be personally redemptive."[15] The ritual agent first establishes his own authority *indirectly* by taking for granted the legitimacy of the institution whose interests he merely seeks to shore up. The historically situated act of *redemption* of this institution then "naturally" leads to his own legitimacy. Once again, Bell: "One appropriates and thereby constructs a version (usually neither very explicit nor coherent) of the hegemonic order that promises a path of personal redemption, that gives one some sense of relative dominance in the order of things, and thereby some ability to engage and affect that order."[16] The *Teatro* will fulfill the first circumstance when Sigüenza ingeniously links Aztec genealogy to the tribes of Abraham, subsuming a very selective version of "American" history into the universal genealogy of the Hebrews. Thus, although Sigüenza offers an alternative genealogy to rival that of the Habsburgs, one that he translates out of the still emerging history/mythology of the Aztec empire, his posture with respect to the workings of allegorical discourse mimics rather than deconstructs symbolic modes used by Spanish elites to construct their own cultural and political dominance.

As for the second movement, this occurs when the author embeds his activity within the act of narration; if the narrative is successful he, along with his Aztec-criollo revision of colonial history, will be carried along with it to his own redemption. His self-transposition into the body of his imaginative text begins when he likens himself to that most conventional figure of cultural authority, the bee, traveling from literary flower to literary flower collecting the nectar and wisdom of the ages. In his reading of the first *empresa* of the triumphal arch, he further anchors his authorial activity within the genealogy of the Aztec emperors through his reconstruction of the etymology of Huitzilopochtli, the name of the first king of the Aztecs. Citing Torquemada, he notes that the name is composed of two parts: "*huitzilin*, que es el pajarito que llamamos chupa-flores, y de *tlahuipochtli* que significa nigromántico o hechicero, que arroja fuego, o como quieren otros de *opochtli*, que es mano siniestra" [*huitzilin*, which is the little bird we call a hummingbird, and from *tlahuipochtli* which means necromancer or sorcerer, who throws fire, or as others say from *opochtli*, which is the left hand].[17] What earlier seemed to be a rather obvious *excursus* on the bee now can be fully appreciated as an attempt to naturalize and mystify Sigüenza's authority over colonial history, as the cultured bee and imperial hummingbird become superimposed one over/under the other. Indeed, Sigüenza's version of Aztec history will be superior to that of the Aztecs themselves, whose first king's grasp on things was tainted due to his sinister (*siniestra*) inclinations. Later, an empresa on sacrifice will see the hummingbird morph into a pelican—the most Christological of all emblematic motifs—as Sigüenza symbolizes the Aztec king Chimalpopocatzin with the marine bird who opens its own breast so that its young can feed on its blood. The pelican will change shape yet again and become an anamorphic dove/phoenix, which rises from the smoldering body of Cuahtemoc, who was tortured with fire by the Spaniards for refusing to return the treasures *he* stole from *them*. As in the case of the hummingbird, Sigüenza plays with both pagan and Christian symbolism, simultaneously investing the Aztec's smoldering body with a Catholic meaning while foregrounding its ontologically inferior, i.e., pagan (phoenix), status.

Although we glide through nominally different historical events and colonial encounters with the help of Sigüenza's bird imagery, in the end all of the empresas are framed within the ideals of wisdom, heroism, and sacrifice, and embedded in an allegory of universal destiny. As a result of this play with allegorical historical tropes, there is an undeniable feeling that we have witnessed this progression of events somewhere before. Following Bell's paradigm, the rhetorical naturalization of Sigüenza's reassemblage of classical, biblical, European, and American cultural history and mythology is characteristic of the unconscious assumptions of *ritual agents*, who "do not see themselves as projecting schemes; they see themselves only acting in a socially instinctive response to how things are. Thus, the production and objectification of structured and structuring schemes in the environment involve a misrecognition of the source and arbitrariness of these schemes. These schemes tend to be experienced as deriving from powers or realities beyond the community and its activities, such as god or tradition, thereby depicting and testifying to the ultimate organization of the cosmos."[18] I am not saying that Sigüenza is completely unconscious of the ideological risks he takes here but rather that his rhetorical posture repeats rather than challenges conventional historical discourse of the Baroque and thus underlines the unconscious symbolic assumptions of Counter-Reformation Spain. The imperial reader may disagree with Sigüenza's thesis, but (s)he cannot reject the structural order of things without calling into question the Crown's own manipulation of languages, texts, and bodies.

To appreciate how the erasure of contingency and "arbitrariness" from the scene of translation occurs, it will be useful to look at Sigüenza's deployment of the figure of Absalom, King David's fratricidal and rebellious son. What is interesting about Sigüenza's use of Absalom is its simultaneous brevity and audacity. Without explaining why he has chosen this example from hundreds of possible citations, Sigüenza refers to a monument of Absalom in the Old Testament Book of Kings: "Y denominó el monumento con su nombre, que hasta el día presente se denomina monumento de Absalón" [And he called the monument by his name, which until this day is called the monument of Absalom].[19] This monument is then cited as a model that should serve "de espejo" [as a mirror] for rulers, "para que de allí sus *manos* tomen ejemplo, o su autoridad y poder aspire a la emulación de lo que en ellos se simboliza en los disfraces de *triunfos* y alegorías de *maenos*" [so that from there their own hands take an example, or so that their authority and power aspire toward the emulation of that which is symbolized in them in the disguises of *triumphs* and allegories of *maenos*].[20] But why Absalom, the reader is left to ask. A probable answer can be found in Sor Juana's *Carta atenagórica*, in which she uses the disobedience and intransigence of Absalom to illuminate the generous and even excessive forgiveness of the king. For Absalom not only murdered his brother, he also usurped the kingdom of Hebron from his father. According to the Book of Kings, it is the second act that motivates Joab to kill him, in spite of David's protests, and so it is most likely the second transgression that is monumentalized by Sigüenza. For the less informed reader, however, the more memorable effect arises from the superimposition of the biblical monument onto the geographical stage of the Aztec pyramids, which repeats other anamorphic combinations we have already seen.

For Bell, such ambiguity is indicative of ritual practice and actually works to Sigüenza's advantage in the reconfiguration of the cosmos to account for the origins of a specifically American ruling class. Rodríguez Garrido notes a similar reconstruction of the universe in a sermon by Espinosa Medrano on the Virgin of Guadalupe: "The first step he takes toward addressing the issue of a saint born and raised on American soil consists of situating the New World within the universal meaning of the divine plan."[21] In Sigüenza's case, following the bee-hummingbird, dove-phoenix, and monument-pyramid *conceptos*, Neptune is posited as the progenitor of both African and American civilizations. Linking Neptune to biblical genealogies, however, requires some exceedingly deft, etymological sleight-of-hand. To begin, Sigüenza takes advantage of a rather fortuitous, which is to say accidental, similarity between the names Nepthuim and Neptuno: "Que Nepthuim sea hijo de Misraim consta del Génesis, pero que de Misraim sea hijo el mitológico Neptuno es lo que necesita de prueba" [that Nepthuim is the son of Misraim is clear from Genesis, but that Misraim is the son of the mythological Neptune is what requires proof].[22] One might point out here that the chaotic history of biblical translation and retranslation is acutely constitutive of the alphabetic happenstances that will be seized upon by the author. Nevertheless, in order to reinforce the link between biblical and mythological, or pagan, figures Sigüenza now connects Isis to the Hebrew Isc, "como si dijese 'is-is' es decir 'varón-varón'" [as if saying "is-is" is to say "male-male"].[23] Sigüenza's point has to do with the "costumbre" of naming "doctrinas" after their inventors, in this case the *Wisdom of Isis*. This *varón-varón* effectively attaches Isis to Misraim through this doctrinal understanding of genealogy, and now the change is complete: "Si Isis es la misma Sabuduría de Misraim no hay razón para que Misraim no se confunda con Isis, con que siendo Nepthuim hijo de Misraim habrá de ser Neptuno hijo de Isis, según la doctrina y enseñanza y de Misraim según la naturaleza" [If Isis is the selfsame Wisdom of Misraim there is no reason that Misraim cannot be confused with Isis, thus Nepthium being the son of Misraim, Neptune will have to be the son of Isis according to doctrine and instruction, and (son) of Misraim according to nature].[24] In the movement from doctrine to nature, Sigüenza effectively transfers the "pagan" wisdom of Isis to the sacramental body of biblical genealogy; or as Pierre Bourdieu would put it, "culture becomes nature."[25] In the end, the inheritors of the Aztec kingdom become equals to the Spaniards in matters of genealogy and sovereignty, as the American pagans are ethnically cleansed, so to speak, of any bad blood.

The cumulative effect of the *Teatro* can be described as a multiplicity of sameness, wherein Sigüenza's revisionist project legitimizes itself without questioning the institutional roots of Habsburg Spain; quite the contrary, he constantly borrows symbolic capital from Spain in order to increase the homeland's value by recognizing the illustrious past and legitimate present of the Criollo "nation." As Sam Cogdell notes, "for the criollo it is also necessary to affirm his identity with that which is Spanish in order to assure himself of the protection of imperial power, at the same time as an attempt is made to present just reasons for a policy that incorporates the foundations of the tradition of the criollos and defends their interests over those of peninsular Spaniards."[26] Bell's definition of ritual discourse helps us understand how the unsettled ambiguities of Sigüenza's *obra* actually lead the reader toward the perception of closure: "Ritualization does not *resolve* a social contradiction. Rather it catches up into itself all the experienced and conventional conflicts and oppositions . . ., juxtaposing and homologizing them into a loose provisional systematicity. . . . Moreover, this orchestrated deferral of signification never yields a definitive answer, a final meaning, or a single-act—there is no point of arrival but a constant invocation of new terms to continue the validation and coherence of the older terms. . . . This totality, the full potential of which is never fully grasped, [is] thus never fully subject to challenge or denial."[27] The antagonism between empire and colony is not so much resolved as displaced and reorganized in a way that preserves peninsular hegemony while opening a space for legitimate, criollo political empowerment. This historical synthesis corresponds to Žižek's understanding of the Hegelian dialectic: "The only shift that effectively occurs is subjective, the shift of our perspective (i.e., all of a sudden, we become aware that what previously appeared as conflict *already* is reconciliation)."[28] The Aztecs always-already were Spanish, and as such, the author merely uncovers a truth that had been hidden up until now. Understanding how Sigüenza both transgresses and redeems peninsular hegemony, however, introduces a new problem, since there does not appear to be a space for those Baroque cultural practices which, rather than project social antagonisms toward the horizon, actively work to reveal the arbitrary nature of the symbolic practices themselves. In other words, where is Juan Ruiz?

Refusing to be embedded in the allegorical superstructure that dominates Sigüenza's emblematization of history, Sor Juana foregrounds a different understanding of subjectivity in her *Neptuno alegórico*, one in which her historically framed role as "vanishing mediator" between language and meaning is taken to an institutional level.[29] By situating her voice and its product within the arbitrary and contingent act of performance Sor Juana destabilizes the point of articulation of universal allegories of divine right. Once this edifice crashes to earth, she attempts to ground the legitimacy of monarchical power in concrete acts of mercy—the redemption of the *other*—as opposed to the language of genealogical and historical necessity. At the same time, she takes advantage of the vacuum at the center of the Baroque signifier of *desengaño* to place the unspoken agenda of her allegorical tour de force both in front of and beyond the gaze of the spectator/reader.

She begins the prologue of her allegorical reading of the paintings and decorations of the cathedral façade with one of the most recognizable emblem-hieroglyphics of the Baroque: "un círculo . . . por ser símbolo de lo infinito" [a circle . . . because it is a simple of infinity].[30] Rather than detach the hieroglyphic from its antique context in order to recycle its generic form within a political allegory, however, Sor Juana emphasizes *this* circle's theological function and meaning according to the Egyptians themselves, where the image does not so much represent as negatively suggest the infinite nature of the gods. Unlike Sigüenza's preemptive insistence on the universal presence of *Novohispano* identity, Sor Juana points a suggestive finger at the negative element at the heart of signification and subjectivity: "Como eran cosas que carecían de toda forma visible; y por consiguiente, imposibles de mostrarse a los ojos de los hombres (los cuales, por la mayor parte, sólo tienen por empleo de la voluntad el que es objeto de sus ojos), fue necesario buscarles jeroglíficos, que por similitud, ya que no por perfecta imagen, las representasen" [Since they were things that lacked any visible form; and therefore, impossible to display to the eyes of men (who, for the most part, have for the use of their will only that which is the object of their eyes), it was necessary to search for hieroglyphics for them, which through resemblance, and not through a perfect image, represent them].[31] The gap that Sor Juana opens through this constitutive difference between transcendent idea and terrestrial, or historical, sign is analogous to the psychoanalytical understanding of language, wherein "the symbolic order, the universe of the Word, *logos*, can only emerge from the experience of this abyss."[32] By beginning with a "sacred" sign, the poet effectively foregrounds all representation as a fictional approximation; there will be no infallible criterion for judging the truth of mundane, terrestrial representations on this stage. Who is right, the Greek doctor or the Roman ruffian? Neither will have any ultimate claim to truth in Sor Juana's scheme.

This enunciatory vacuum is *performed* by the *Neptuno*'s authorial voice when Sor Juana tells how she was compelled to take on this allegorical labor due to the desire of her *Venerable Cabildo*, who aspired to imitate God in his choice of "instrumentos flacos."[33] In the section entitled "Razón de la fábrica alegórica, y aplicación de la fábula," she writes:

> Le pareció que era, para pedir y conseguir perdones, más apta la blandura inculta de una mujer que la elocuencia de tantas y tan doctas plumas: industria que usó el Capitán Joab en el perdón de Absalón con la ofendida Majestad de David, conseguido por medio de la Tecuites, no porque juzgase más eficaces

los mentidos sollozos de una mujer no conocida, ignorante y pobre, que su autoridad, elocuencia y valimiento, sino porque el rayo de la ira real incitada a los recuerdos del delito, no hiciera operación en el sujeto flaco, pues éste siempre busca resistencias para ejecutar sus estragos.[34]

[It seemed to him that to ask for and secure pardons, the uncouth softness of a woman was more suitable than the eloquence of so many and such learned pens: a skill that Captain Joab used for the pardon of Absalom with the offended Majesty of David, obtained through Tecuites, not because he judged the feigned sobs of an unknown, ignorant and poor woman to be more effective than his authority, eloquence and favor, but so that the ray of royal rage incited to the memories of the crime, would not take effect upon the feeble subject, since it (royal rage) always seeks opposition on which to execute its destruction.]

There are two aspects of this passage that are inextricably related to both the epistemological instability of Sor Juana's allegorical performance and the model of monarchical practice she privileges throughout the work. First, she compares both her authorial role and rhetorical tone with the uncultured meekness of Tecuites, a woman paid to emit *mentidos sollozos* [feigned sobs] in order to soften the rigor of a (morally bankrupt) king driven by vengeance. This moment in the text can be seen as the culmination of her earlier effort to break the transcendental, or organic, relationship between word and meaning, material letter and immaterial idea, etc. What had been to this point a type of philosophical and historical severing of universal meaning from the immanent practice of signification becomes embedded in the strategically circumscribed activity of the writer herself. These *mendacious sobs* mark the point of enunciation as a formal function disjointed from any ontological or epistemological substance, an empty spatial coordinate at the center of the arrangement of oppositions and hierarchies that she is constructing. This is also the case in Žižek's understanding of the subject of language, whose "unity is guaranteed only by the self-referential symbolic act, that is, 'I' is a purely performative entity, it is the one who *says* 'I'."[35] One can start to see already that Sor Juana's erasure of certitude has only partly to do with the melancholy induced by Counter-Reformation *desengaño*, as she interprets the transcendental *meaninglessness* of mundane history as an opportunity for an earthly sense of historical agency arising from the liberation from symbolic necessity.

The goal of Tecuites, my second point, is to lead the king toward a reconsideration of his punitive rigor. Just as the success or failure of Tecuites hinges on her ability to redeem the king from his own desire for vengeance, his actions, in turn, should not automatically exercise his divine right by carrying out the (just) punishment of his son's crimes but rather allow the redemption of the *other*. Thus, Sor Juana's formal role and activity as authorial voice are immanently tied to the more forgiving, or open-ended, form and function of knowledge and power she configures. She is much more interested in what we might call a negative representation of power, present only in concrete and contingent gestures of lenience and mercy, than in lending legitimacy to positive and violent assertions of universal justice. Her posture subverts the model of *redemptive hegemony* outlined by Bell, in that 1) the legitimacy of political action does not come from outside the actions of the ritual agent, say, in the trascendental body of absolutist sovereignty but rather is inseparable from a "self-referential symbolic act"; and 2) in order for the ritual act to be considered socially, or institutionally, redemptive it must first be individually redemptive with respect to the *other*: "que la confianza fuese en la *piedad* a que movería el sujeto y no en la fuerza de los argumentos" [that the trust be in piety-pity that the subject stirs up and not in the force of reasoning].[36] Not content to theorize, Sor Juana will now project a working model of her reformed "authority" onto the mythological figures decorating the arch.

As she moves from the characterization of her authorial voice to the object of her discourse, Sor Juana prepares the reader spectator—rhetorically, the viceroy himself—for the flight back into antiquity by returning to the topic of fabulous representation. After outlining the unimaginable greatness of the marquis, the poet proceeds to infantilize the representative of Spanish hegemony as quickly as she deified him. The Marqués de la Laguna, as is well known, is metamorphosed into Neptune, "emperor of the oceans, islands and straits." Yet, as soon as Neptune makes his entrance, his mother(s), "Opis o Cibeles," are brought onto the scene, "la cual llamaron *Magna Mater*, y creyeron ser madre de todos los dioses, y aun de las fieras" [whom they called *Magna Mater*, and believed to be the mother of all the gods, and even of the wild beasts].[37] The rest of the "Razón" is dedicated to subjecting the legitimacy and actions of Neptune to the preeminence and wisdom of his mother(s). For Paz, "Sor Juana's process of transformation tended to intellectualize and internalize Neptune in order to convert him, the stormy god who was the progenitor of terrifying monsters like Polyphemus and the giant Antaeus, into a civilizing deity whose attributes were sapience, culture, and art."[38] Paz identifies these new attributes as masculine in nature, which is not surprising considering his similar *masculation* of the nun's poetic activity itself. Whereas in the *Neptuno*, even the most masculine symbol of virility and power, the bull, is transformed into the cows that are sacrificed to the wisdom of Isis, quite literally "cowed," as it were.[39]

I would like to return for a moment to the apparent confusion that Sor Juana creates when she openly vacillates between Opis, Cibeles and, later, Isis as mother(s) of Neptune because it exemplifies another strategy that works against the conventions of allegorical and authorial legitimacy as practiced by Sigüenza. In emblematic discourse, authorial citation is generally deployed according to the medieval model of *auctoritas* (Minnis), in that the meaning of the emblematic image is fixed by locating a single source in antiquity, or by reaching a consensus among equal authorities. In Sigüenza, we have already seen how any differences or contradictions between Nepthuim, Misraim, Neptune, and Isis are elided by framing them all within a doctrine of "Sabiduría." Sor Juana, on the other hand, constantly subverts and reconstructs the authority of her discourse by underlining the circumstantial nature of her etymologies, many times self-consciously subverting an authoritative consensus she herself has constructed. Unlike Sigüenza's movement toward apparent closure, Sor Juana leaves the authorial question in a consciously rendered fog. Her readings of the *lienzos*, on the other hand, repeatedly return to the theme of the cloud, which becomes an evanescent symbol of her epistemological open-endedness even as it activates her immanentist ontological model. By following these clouds, we can plot a course out of her labyrinthine deconstruction of allegorical certitude and move toward an alternative regime.

Sor Juana's commentaries on the paintings present a coherent program of mythological gestures in which Neptune, although seldom by his own design, intervenes on behalf of mortals who are in *dire straits*, so to speak. In the *segundo lienzo*, he is persuaded by Juno to pacify his oceanic ire, which is destroying an unnamed Greek city. Like a cloud, Juno appears in the heavens "con regio ornato, en un carro que por la vaga región del aire conducían dos coronados leones" [with regal adornment, in a chariot which was driven through the indistinct region of the air by two crowned lions].[40] As will be the case throughout the piece, Neptune behaves like a good son and obeys his mother's superior wisdom. In the fourth painting, he saves Aeneas from the rage of Achilles by hiding him in a cloud so that the cross-dressing, Greek demigod cannot annihilate the future progenitor of Rome. In the case of both epic heroes Sor Juana privileges moments in their lives in which Christian piety, not to be confused with Roman piety or poetic justice, checks the exercise of violence.[41] Furthermore, although Sor Juana had previously used the term *numen* to refer to the viceroy's ability to calm and channel the waters of Mexico, this deity will from now on take the form of a cloud, a particularly uterine image that is more fully developed later on. In the fifth painting, the "tutelar numen de las ciencias" [guardian deity of knowledge] virtually becomes a uterus by enveloping the centaurs, "maestros de las ciencias en la antigüedad" [masters of knowledge in antiquity], in a cloud and delivering them from the jealous rage of Hercules.[42] This image of wisdom, in the figure of the centaurs enclosed in the ephemeral embrace of Neptune—whose presence is indicated exclusively through his act of redemption—is then used by Sor Juana as a model for the relationship that the marquis should have with the *conquistadores*, the centaurs of New Spain. Admittedly, Sor Juana, like Sigüenza, uses classical allusions to legitimate the standing of the "New Rome," beseeching the viceroy to protect it from the ire of Hercules (an allusion to the Catholic kings' and, later, Carlos I's twin *empresas, non plus ultra* and *plus ultra*). Nevertheless, the evanescent nature of the cloud penetrates and destabilizes the perceived permanence of symbolic edifices, inverting Bourdieu's emblematic theorum on culture and nature. The vacuous nature of the cloud effects a insubstantiation of cultural and institutional monuments, including her own.

Neptune's self-restraint has nothing to do with the legitimacy of his actions—or the letter of the law—rather he *performs*, acts out, the wisdom and mercy that come about through the *suspension* of symbolic necessity. The predominance of nebulous imagery, moreover, can be read as an allusion to the Virgin of Guadalupe, future master signifier for American independence. In Jaime Cuadriello's monumental contribution to *El divino pintor*, the Mexican art historian studies how the marvelous creation, or appearance, of the *tilma* of Juan Diego is eventually framed within a nationalist discourse of legitimacy, but not before being used by painters in New Spain to legitimize the noble status of their art.[43] What I am suggesting here has only partly to do with this type of institutional legitimization, even though Sor Juana herself admittedly seeks and requires such official protection. Sor Juana Inés de la Cruz, in her theoretical (anti)frame as well as her rhetorical performance, employs a mythological allegory to subvert patriarchal models of authority and configure an open and immanentist model of political as well as personal legitimacy.[44] And although she herself is criolla, mestiza, and an oppressed subject of a regime driven by universalizing tendencies, I do not think that the strategies she outlines here should be automatically equated with the construction of an alternative nationalist discourse.[45] None of the examples mentioned to this point dwells on the legitimacy or illegitimacy of mercy with respect to the concrete, historical recipients of benevolence, many of which, in fact, have done something to bring righteous judgments down upon themselves. It is the very discourse of political power and its dependence on narratives of transcendental identity that is on trial here.

This reading of *Neptuno alegórico* cannot pretend to be convincing in an exhaustive sense. A search for univocal meaning would contradict both my own method as well as the point I am trying to make concerning Sor Juana's use of allegory. Still, the rhetorical deployment of the Virgin of Guadalupe is not an isolated phenomenon in Baroque Spain and New Spain. In *Los trabajos de Persiles y Sigismunda*, Cervantes advocates for a similarly redemptive understanding of knowledge and power by placing the forgiving figure of the Virgin at the center of his Baroque masterpiece.[46] In both cases, the contestation of metaphysical certitude and universal truths can be interpreted through Ellie Ragland-Sullivan's reading of the Lacanian formula, "Woman = symptom." By way of contrast with the signifier that guarantees male subjectivity as "completely determined" by the symbolic order, "Woman was Lacan's signifier for the anti-thesis of masculine certitude."[47] In other words, for Lacan, Woman—not as female "subject" but as patriarchal (non)signifier—acts as the symptom of the impossibility of ideological closure, the excess (un)meaning that allows us to identify the contingent and arbitrary nature of its judgments and claims. Can we not use this thesis to approach the ideological significance of Sor Juana's multiplication of Neptune's mothers, or her recurrence to cloud imagery? This inconclusiveness, or lack, in the symbolic order is also mentioned by Bell, who observes that ritual discourse only *appears* to reach closure when, in fact, its dependence on polyvalent symbols in combination with the historically grounded body of the ritual agent precludes such closure. Bell's method of studying ritual emphasizes the practical, which is to say, strategic, situational, partially blind, and power-seeking nature of ritual practice in order to reveal its relationship to power. Sor Juana employs a similar method that deconstructs its own legitimacy while offering a different model based on the relaxation of the signifier, which can lead to more creative possibilities.

The conclusions of this essay largely agree with those critics of Sor Juana who recognize an emergent feminist discourse of freedom that productively opposes Baroque regimes of containment. I would add, however, that Sor Juana's symbolic strategies preclude the historicist conception of an evolving and, therefore, "natural" identity, insisting rather on the performative nature of identity as a response to the lack of an absolute guarantor of certainty. Or, as she states in the *Carta atenagórica*, "Dios . . . quiere más parecer escaso, porque los hombres no sean peores, que ostentar su largueza con daño de los mismos beneficiados . . . antepone el aprovechamiento de los hombres a su propio opinión y a su propio natural" [God . . . wants to seem scarce, so that men are not worse, rather than to show off his generosity to the detriment of the selfsame beneficiaries . . . he places the improvement of men before his own opinion and his own nature].[48] I take this to mean that "man" is left to work things out as best she can with the tools at her disposal, while resisting the temptation to fill in the divine space or surpass the material limits of her existence with a fabricated, or feigned, symbolic necessity. The imperative for Sor Juana is, rather, the recognition and even the activation of the "symptom" as opposed to the allegorical fixing of contingency within a false sense of meaning-destiny. By valorizing mundane endeavors as the result of a voluntarily absent creator, Sor Juana injects a positive and liberating, historical activity into the Baroque vacuum and consequently redeems human agency, including of course her own. Returning to Benjamin, where Sigüenza seeks to wrap his ritual vision of American history ever more tightly in a unilateral and homogeneous discourse of necessity, Sor Juana goes about her business in a much more playful and open-ended way, staging moments in which symbolic necessity is checked in order to redeem exemplarily imperfect subjects.

NOTES

1. Ruiz, *Libro de buen amor*. The Greek, for his part, says that when he held up one finger to signify that there is only one God, the Roman responded with three fingers, thus correctly recognizing the three-in-one nature of the Trinity. When the philosopher proceeds to hold up the palm of his hand to show how God holds dominion over all, he reads the Roman's showing of a fist as demonstrating that God holds the whole world in his fist. The Roman, in the meanwhile, interprets the single finger of the Greek as a threat to poke out his eye, to which he responds by showing two fingers and his thumb, thus showing the Greek that he will not only poke out both his eyes but also break his teeth. Later, when the Greek threatens to cuff him upside the head (with the palm of his hand), the Roman shakes his fist "que·l daría a él una tal puñada, / que en tenpo de su vida nunca la vies vengada" [I'd give him such a clout, / that in his lifetime you would never see it avenged] (25).

2. Benjamin, *Illuminations*, 262.

3. Žižek, "Cartesian Subject."

4. The "subject supposed to know" is a projected gaze of absolute authority that guarantees that the world and one's actions in the world make sense; or, more precisely, it preserves the ideological illusion that the world as one sees it exists independent of one's actions while affirming the "logic" of one's aims and desires: "we assign to individuals the position of God's inconceivable will" (Žižek, *For They Know Not*, 167).

5. Beverley, "Gracián."

6. Maravall, *Culture of the Baroque*.

7. Commenting on the particular heterogeneity of these festivals in colonial Iberoamerica, Petra Schumm notes, "Images as well as baroque festivals, prove themselves as points of departure for the flourishing of hybrid imaginaries wherein elements of the indigenous cultures sub-

sist and reformulate themselves in the undersoil of christian representations" (*Barrocos y modernos,* 17).

8. Cruz, *Obras Completas,* 810.

9. Moraña, *Relecturas del Barroco,* 231.

10. Roggiano, "Para una teoría."

11. Kamen, *Empire,* 36–37.

12. Beverley, "Nuevas vacilaciones sobre el barroco," 225.

13. Beverley writes, "If gongorism wore and wears the sign of a certain kind of radicalism it should remain clear that the poetic revolution that it signifies in the seventeenth century develops precisely *instead of,* and in certain measure *against,* a true social revolution of the estatist and colonial Spanish system" (Lazarillo, 96).

14. Sigüenza y Góngora, *Obras históricas,* 229.

15. Bell, *Ritual Theory,* 116.

16. Ibid., 208.

17. Sigüenza y Góngora, *Obras históricas,* 285.

18. Bell, *Ritual Theory,* 206.

19. Sigüenza y Góngora, *Obras históricas,* 234.

20. Ibid.

21. Rodríguez Garrido, "Espinosa Medrano," 157.

22. Sigüenza y Góngora, *Obras históricas,* 249.

23. Ibid.

24. Ibid., 249-50.

25. Bourdieu, *Outline of a Theory of Practice,* 2.

26. Sam Cogdell, "Criollos," 248.

27. Bell, *Ritual Theory,* 106.

28. Žižek, *Organs without Bodies,* 14.

29. In this context, *vanishing mediator* is understood according to Žižek's reading of the function of Protestantism in Max Weber's analysis of the passage from medieval to bourgeois society: "the point not to be missed is that one cannot pass from medieval 'closed' society to bourgeois society immediately, without the intercession of Protestantism as 'vanishing mediator': it is Protestantism which, by means of its universalization of Christianity, prepares the ground for its withdrawal into the sphere of privacy" (Žižek, *For They Know Not,* 183). In our case, Sigüenza in particular and Catholicism in general become the vanishing mediators between Aztec "paganism" and criollo protonationalism. As in Weber's scheme, the universalization of Western classical and biblical culture allows Sigüenza to articulate the passage from paganism to nationalism.

30. Cruz, *Obras Completas,* 777.

31. Ibid.

32. Žižek, "Cartesian Theater," 258.

33. Cruz, *Obras Completas,* 779.

34. Ibid.

35. Žižek, "Cartesian Theater," 264.

36. Cruz, *Obras Completas,* 779; my emphasis.

37. Ibid., 780.

38. Paz, *Sor Juana,* 161.

39. Cruz, *Obras Completas,* 782.

40. Ibid., 790. Georgina de Sabàt de Rivers informs us that the city is the Greek city of Inaco. ("El *Neptuno* de Sor Juana," 67).

41. James D. Garrison's illuminating study of the transformation of the concept and function of *piety* throughout almost two millennia of Western literature begins by considering the meaning of piety with respect to what many would consider to be the more dubious actions of Virgil's Aeneas: his abandonment of Dido; and his execution of the prostrate Turnus. Garrison makes it clear, however, that Aeneas's actions are consistent with a Roman understanding of filial piety, which in psychoanalytical terms would coincide with the absolute obedience to the Father of the Law. A popular Renaissance emblem of filial piety shows Aeneas carrying his father Anchises on his back, although the emblematic motif is interpreted in many different ways. What we see in Sor Juana, by contrast, judges the piety of one's actions within relation to the love that is shown, not directly to the Father of the Law, but rather to God's creation on earth (see *La Carta atenagórica*).

42. Cruz, *Obras Completas*, 793.

43. Cuadriello comments on a particularly ingenious fusion of religious and nationalist ideology in an eighteenth-century painting of the Virgin of Guadalupe by Joaquín Villegas, in which the figure of the dove is mirrored by an emblematic image of the eagle in the foreground of the painting: "On this occasion, everything happens in front of the emblematic presence of the Mexican and apocalyptic eagle already prefigured as the means so that the miracle takes place, as was read in the book by Sánchez. This bird of solar nature is the atlas who lends the Woman of the Apocalypse her wings so that she escapes the beast and is, at the same time, the blazon of the Mexican Empire already converted to the faith, because it can fixedly look at the sun of God; and, therefore, is the exclusive beneficiary, together with her chicks, of such a peerless deed as the inscription prays: Two wings of a great eagle are given to the woman" ("El obrador trinitario," 176). We have already seen such symbolic hybrids in Sigüenza's *Teatro*.

44. Although this distinction between transcendentalist and immanentist aesthetics is one that I have been studying for several years, informed largely by the work of Benjamin and Bakhtin concerning the relation of the body to allegory both in the Renaissance and the Baroque, the reader will recognize the influence of Hardt and Negri's *Empire*.

45. I should clarify that I am using these adjectives in cultural and symbolic terms and not in terms of blood genealogy, although the latter distinctions are no less problematicaɪ

46. Nelson, "*Los trabajos.*"

47. Ragland-Sullivan, "Sexual Masquerade," 53.

48. Cruz, *Obras Completas*, 825.

WORKS CITED

Adorno, Rolena. "El sujeto colonial y la contrucción cultural de la alteridad." *Revista de crítica literaria latinoamericana* 14 (1998): 55–68.

Bell, Catherine. *Ritual Theory, Ritual Practice*. New York, Oxford: Oxford University Press, 1992.

Benjamin, Walter. *Illuminations*. Edited with an introduction by Hannah Arendt. Translated by Harry Zohn. New York: Schoken Books, 1968.

Beverley, John. *Del* Lazarillo *al sandinismo: Estudios sobre la función ideológica de la literatura española e hispanoamericana*. Minneapolis, Minn.: Prisma, 1987.

———. "Gracián o la sobrevaloración de la literatura (Barroco y postmodernidad)." In Moraña, *Relecturas del Barroco*, 17–30.

———. "Nuevas vacilaciones sobre el barroco." *Revista de crítica literaria latinoamericana* 14 (1998): 217–27.

Bourdieu, Pierre. *Outline of a Theory of Practice*. Cambridge: Cambridge University Press, 1977.

Castillo, David R. "Horror (Vacui): The Baroque Condition." To appear in a forthcoming volume of *Hispanic Issues*.

Cogdell, Sam. "Criollos, gachupines, y 'plebe tan en extremo plebe': Retórica e ideología criollas en *Alboroto y motín de México* de Sigüenza y Góngora." In Moraña, *Relecturas del Barroco*, 223–43.

Cruz, Sor Juana Inés de la. *Obras Completas*. México City: Porrúa, 1987.

Cuadriello, Jaime. "El obrador trinitario o María de Guadalupe creada en idea, imagen y materia." In *El divino pintor: La creación de María de Guadalupe en el taller celestial*, with Prologue by Jaime Cuadriello. México City: Museo de la Basílica de Guadalupe, 2001.

Garrison, James D. *Pietas from Virgil to Dryden*. University Park: Pennsylvania State University Press, 1992.

Hardt, Michael, and Antonio Negri. *Empire*. Cambridge, Mass: Harvard University Press, 2000.

Kamen, Henry. *Empire: How Spain Became a World Power, 1492–1763*. New York: Penguin, 2002.

Lacan, Jacques. *The Four Fundamental Concepts of Psychoanalysis*. Edited by Jacques-Alain Miller, translated by Alan Sheridan. New York: W.W. Norton and Co., 1981.

Maravall, José Antonio. *Antiguos y modernos*. Madrid: Alianza, 1986.

———. *Culture of the Baroque: Analysis of a Historical Structure*. Translated by Terry Cochran,Forword by Wlad Godzich and Nicholas Spadaccini. Minneapolis: University of Minnesota Press, 1984.

Moraña, Mabel, ed. "Barroco y conciencia criolla en hispanoamérica." *Revista de crítica Literaria latinoamericana* 14 (1988): 229–51.

———. *Relecturas del Barroco de Indias*. Hanover, N.H.: Ediciones del Norte, 1994.

Nelson, Bradley J. "*Los trabajos de Persiles y Sigismunda*: una crítica cervantina de la alegoresis emblemática." *Cervantes* 23, No. 2 (2004).

———. "The Marriage of Art and Honor: Anamorphosis and Control in Calderón's *La dama duende*." *Bulletin of the Comediantes* 54, No. 2 (2002): 407–42.

Paz, Octavio. *Sor Juana or, The Traps of Faith*. Translated by Margaret Sayers Peden. Cambridge, Mass.: The Belknap Press of Harvard University Press, 1988.

Pratt, Mary Louise. "Arts of the Contact Zone." *Profession* (1991): 33–40.

Ragland-Sullivan, Ellie. "The Sexual Masquerade: A Lacanian Theory of Sexual Difference." In *Lacan and the Subject of Language*, edited by Ellie Ragland-Sullivan and Mark Bracher, 49–80. New York: Routledge, 1991,

Rodríguez Garrido, José A. "Espinosa Medrano, la recepción del sermón barroco y la defensa de los americanos." In Moraña, *Relecturas del Barroco,* 149–72.

Roggiano, Alfredo. "Para una teoría de un Barroco hispanoamericano." In Moraña, *Relecturas del Barroco,* 1–15.

Ruiz, Juan, Arcipreste de Hita. *Libro de buen amor.* Edited by Alberto Blecua. Madrid: Cátedra, 2001.

Sabàt de Rivers, Georgina. "El *Neptuno* de Sor Juana: Fiesta barroca y programa político." *University of Dayton Review* 16 (1983): 63–73.

Schumm, Petra, ed. *Barrocos y modernos: Nuevos caminos en la investigación del Barroco iberoamericano.* Frankfurt: Vervuert, Ibero-Americana, 1998.

————. "El concepto 'barroco' en la época de la desaparición de las fronteras." In Schumm 13–30.

Sigüenza y Góngora, Carlos de. *Obras históricas.* Edited by José Rojas Garcidueñas. México: Editorial Porrúa, 1983.

Žižek, Slavoj. "The Cartesian Subject versus the Cartesian Theater." In *Cogito and the Unconscious,* edited by Slavoj Žižek, 247–74. Durham, N.C.: Duke University Press, 1998.

————. *For They Know Not What They Do: Enjoyment as a Political Factor.* London: Verso, 1991.

————. *Organs without Bodies: On Deleuze and Consequences.* New York: Routledge, 2004.

————. *Tarrying with the Negative: Kant, Hegel, and the Critique of Ideology.* Durham, N.C.: Duke University Press, 1993.

Colonial Imbalances
of Old Cañizares

Vicente Pérez de León

CERVANTES'S INTERLUDE *THE JEALOUS OLD MAN* IS ABOUT HOW THE MAIN character, Cañizares, tries his best not to let anyone seduce his wife. The uncertainty that keeps the plot alive is related to the possibility of the wife, Lorenza, realizing her dreams of a fully sexual relationship that is absent in her marriage with Cañizares, thereby risking her 'honra' in the context of the tradition of the Spanish drama of honor. The evident relationship between this play and *The Jealous Man of Extremadura* will be reevaluated in this essay to interpret aspects of the old man's personality that define him, especially analyzing his *celos,* a word that in Spanish means both "zeal" and "jealousy," and its relationship to the conquest and colonization of the Americas. As we try to make sense of the allegory that pervades the play and study the different possibilities of administering a human being to which one has property rights in Early Modern Spain, we find explanations of Cañizares's behavior in his previous literary incarnation as Carrizales, an emigrant to the New World. Indeed, with historical and literary sources, we can construct an allegorical reading of *The Jealous Old Man* in which the interlude makes a subtle, implicit comment on the transnational flow of riches from the Indias to Spain. This interpretation is represented chiefly by Cañizares and his zeal to contain his weath within the confines of his house. This study of the play will be complemented with an analysis of the crucial vital moment, or ages, of Lorenza, Cañizares, Cristina, Ortigosa, and the young seducer, *el galán,* using some of the ideas and theories presented in the treatise *Examen de Ingenio para las ciencias* de Juan Huarte de San Juan. Through the interweaving of the two readings, we show how Cervantes creates a dichotomy New World/Old World and posits that the only way to relieve the tensions between the two is by means of an economic and sexual go-between, Ortigosa.

The drama and universality of the themes of *The Jealous Old Man* are stressed through different means. Among them, we find the creation of characters that do not conceal the imbalances typical of the different ages represented in the play: adolescence, youth, maturity, and old age.[1] In this sense, we are studying an interlude that invites us to reflect upon the natural transformations inherent to the different stages of the life of women and men and their consequent behaviors. However, in this particular Cervantine universe, the tendencies typical of the different ages become factors that bring characters to an unavoidable destiny, either through an absence of attitudes appropriate to their vital moments, or because of behaviors that correspond too closely to what is expected physiologically and psychologically of their respective ages. A clear example is how Cañizares seems to be unable to escape his own curse of being extremely jealous.

Cañizares is old and rich; if we compare his origins with those of the almost homonymous main character of the exemplary novel *The Jealous Man of Extremadura,* the former's wealth could have come from spending most of his previous existence in Spanish America. Cañizares also thinks that his marriage is, somehow, the culmination of the life of a man who has demonstrated his social success by the accumulation of recognized wealth: a home, a servant, and material abundance, all of which are recognized by the society in which he lives as symbols of success. We can affirm that although there is not a specific reference in *The Jealous Old Man* to Cañizares being an *indiano,* an interpretation of this play could be made using elements from the construction of the character of Carrizales, bearing in mind the behaviors and circumstances of the two characters common to other Spanish emigrants to the Indies of their times.

There are several points that support a reading of Cañizares as an indiano based on his relationship with the main character of Cervantes's exemplary novel, which has a very similar plot. Due to the necessary brevity of the interlude, we assume that the omitted details of the play can be filled in with others from the almost homonymous narrative, since the interlude is essentially a comic version of the novel. There are many similarities that lead to a common interpretation of aspects of both texts. For example, we note the presence of the same main characters: the unhappy young married wife, the jealous old man and the young *galán,* and the similarity of the names of both characters—Cañizares/Carrizales—among others. A connection between the old husbands and the New World is confirmed when we find out that almost half of the immigrants to the Indeas were either Andalusian or from Extremadura (Sánchez-Albornoz, "Transatlantic Transfer," 28), as is the main character of the novel, trapped in a plot similar to the one of the old man of

our interlude. In fact, in the years of the emigration of Cañizares and Carrizales, they were probably as zealous (*celosos*) as other Spaniards to get riches
from the New World: "Most of them (emigrants from the middle strata),
however, came from the middle strata of the towns. They constituted an am-
bitious group eagerly looking for social promotion. The newly discovered
lands promised them ample reward for their *zeal*" (30).[2] Both protagonists are
conditioned by similar life events. Both had to delay their marriage and both
have a pragmatic wedding/pact. A younger wife is exchanged for money as if
both Carrizares and Cañizares wanted to achieve something impossible:
buying a younger age, returning to their lost time of youth.

These are exactly two of the factors who characterized persons that emi-
grated from the Castilian town of Brihuela: "Going to the Indies could delay
marriage somewhat, especially for men, who usually needed a few years to establish themselves after emigrating . . . The relations between spouses probably comprised a mixture of affective ties and pragmatic concerns" (Altman,
"Transatlantic Ties," 131). The ultraprotective master of the interlude puts off
marriage for so long, in fact, that he finds a wife that could easily be his
grandaughter, ideally suited to take care of his typical age-related health problems. The error of this classic and necessarily conflictive equation in *The Jealous Old Man* stems from the fact that there seems to be no awareness of the
basic truth that both ages are usually associated with desires naturally and di-
ametrically opposed and which are, therefore, very hard to satisfy in harmony.
Cañizares thinks that he is doing the right thing in trying to prevent his wife
having contact with the outside world of male and female friends, thus im-
peding a natural desire of the young. His wife, on the other hand, thinks she
is right to claim what she is denied in her marriage to an old man. Jealousy
will never let Cañizares live in peace; desire without consummation is consuming his young wife. So natural fatality dictates, in these cases, that neither
can avoid a destiny complicated by different interests. The disparity of ages
between husband and wife and the old man's impotence make Lorenza a mere
commodity that the old man is using at his will simply because he has the
right to do so according to commerce laws: he wanted a wife, he had money,
and as in the case of Carrizales, Cañizares seems to have *acquired* her to marry
him, as he somewhat confesses to his compadre (Cervantes, *Eight Interludes*,
136).[3] The marriage is also a spatial inversion of the characters. Cañizares, in
my reading, comes from a New World with old ideas, while Lorenza is living
in the Old World with subversive ones.

The materialism of the old man becomes an attitude toward life and
makes of his wife just another possession—the most valuable and, ironically,

the most dangerous one. The owner of the house has concentrated all his energies on only one aspect of his existence: obtaining wealth and social recognition for his value. Although he has succeeded in this, the world will make him see that this path is not the right one. There exists the added circumstance that the respective desires of both parties in the marriage are thwarted by the impossibility of the dissolution of a union in which both are unhappy. The social pressure of the code of honor is an unavoidable law that appears at the end of the old man's existence as a problematic shadow that will not let him live in peace. Cañizares has done what he thought was the right thing in order to be successful in his society—getting rich and marrying to live out his life in peace with his wife. Paradoxically, he is unhappier than ever.

Like David in the Bible, the old man seems to use his wife to regain lost vigor, relying on the ancient idea that sleeping with a warm young female would help keep an old man healthy.[4] Cristina alludes to this interest of old men in young females (135), and Cañizares himself confirms this same idea when he recognizes that he married Lorenza in order to be accompanied on his last journey (136). This last wish, the only one that he cannot fulfill with money, is the one that never will be realized. As he confesses to his best friend, the terrible logic of Cañizares clashes with the reality of daily life with his teenage bride: "*Cañizares*: See here my good friend, when a man in his seventies marries a girl of fifteen, either he's out of his mind or he's in a hurry to move on to the next world. I'd scarcely wed little Mistress Lorenza, expecting to find in her my joy and companion—someone to be at my bedside to close my eyes when I die—when I was beset by a whole host of trials and vexations" (136).

In *The Jealous Old Man*, the first glimpse of Cañizares is obtained through a dialogue between Lorenza and her best friend and neighbor, Ortigosa, outside of the presence of Cañizares. Ortigosa, responding to Lorenza's complaints, proposes to bring into the house a young fellow to suffocate the desire of the young lady. From the very beginning of the play the space of the house/colony is invaded by the struggle and tension between the jealousy of the old man and the unsatisfied desires of Lorenza and her niece, Cristina, with the meddling of the neighbor Ortigosa. In these first lines we can also appreciate that this play is about the conflicts brought on by generation and gender gaps, and the opposing points of view that result from inflexible reasoning: "*Cristina*: Jesus! What a disgusting old man! All night long it's 'Bring me the bed pan, empty the bed pan; get up Cristinica and fetch me hot cloths, my belly's killing me.' Or, 'Where are my pills? My kidney stone's playing me up.' There are more salves and potions in his room than you'd find in an apothecary's shop. As for me, I'm scarcely old enough to dress myself, yet I have to nurse him. Cluck, cluck, cluck, he coddles his aches and pains like an old broody hen! I don't know which makes him more impotent, his hernia or his jealousy!" (133).

Ortigosa's role serves to accelerate the action of the interlude in a way similar to that of the student in *La cueva de Salamanca*. It can also be appreciated as an attempt to exceed the limits and possibilities of her traditional role as a character, since the neighbor is, at the same time, not only a character, but also an actress, and in some way even an author of the play. She is also the only character, with the exception of Cañizares, with the capability to place herself inside and outside the house, connecting, this way, public and private spaces.[5] This female character has the power to re-write the plot in Lorenza's favor, taking a symbolic stand in opposition to the old, oppressive, and jealous male. Ortigosa also has the fundamental role of precipitating the action toward adultery and making the worst nightmares of the old man come true, a fact that is recognized by Cañizares at the conclusion: "Well, Mistress Ortigosa, if it hadn't been for you, none of this would have happened" (143). In this sense, the neighbor provides an infusion of capital to the stagnant "economy" of the old man's world.

The wisdom of Cañizares, based on the knowledge of the material world from which he has enriched himself and created a harmonious environment in agreement with society's demands, cannot withstand the sharpness of a neighbor who knows what the old man ignores or seems to have forgotten. It is the unsatisfied desire of the young that leads the protagonist to the mistake of thinking that his wife will ultimately respect the institution of Catholic marriage and will submit to the husband's will under any circumstances: "Lorenza is as innocent as a dove, and so far she understands nothing of such goings-on" (137).

Right after the first conversation of the three women, in which they discuss Lorenza's problem, the husband of the young lady and his best friend occupy the space abandoned by them. As they are of the same age, the conversation serves to make even more obvious Cañizares's problem due to the logical understanding and empathy of the compadre. Thus, the reality of this conflict has been considered from two different and opposite points of view. The audience becomes the judge of a specific case from the very first lines of the interlude; they have both opposing testimonies. The tone of Cañizares's dialogue is surprisingly just and humane for a character that traditionally had the role of not just a miser, but also of an abused cuckold in other short plays. This kind of character very rarely, or never, had such moments of personal reflection:

> *Friend:*   I'm of the same opinion. All the same, if Mistress Lorenza never leaves the house and no one enters it either, how is it you are still not satisfied, my friend?
>
> *Cañizares:*   I'm afraid that Lorenza may soon find out what she's missing. That would be terrible—so terrible that I'm frightened just to think about it. My fear drives me to desperation and so my life is miserable. (137)

In the same way as the shepherdess Marcela did in the first part of *Don Quijote*, the old man, surprises the reader with a perspective that is personal, intimate, and at the same time familiar to any human being who may well feel empathy for his problem. In the specific case of Cañizares, we can clearly appreciate the conflict of a man who does not have enough energy to satisfy his wife and is very worried about her desires. We can affirm that the old man of this interlude is a tragic character thrown into a drama that is trying to transform him in a carnivalesque way into a happy cuckold. Cañizares cannot go against a destiny marked by his imbalanced feelings as an old man, and his suspicion will even force him to bar his best friend from his house:

> *Friend:*   I should like to go in with you and see Mistress Lorenza.
>
> *Cañizares:*   I'll have you know, sir, there's an old Latin saying, "Amicus usque ad aras": in other words, a man must do everything for his friend except what offends God. So I say "usque ad portam," "Friendship as far as the door." No one crosses my threshold. Farewell my friend, and forgive me.
> *Cañizares* goes into the house
>
> *Friend:*   Never in my life have I seen a man who was so cautious, so jealous or so unreasonable! He'll be hoisted with his own petard and die of the very sickness he dreads so much. (137)

What we can interpret as a radical attitude would seem less so if we take into account the typical behaviors of people in their last stage of life, among which Huarte de San Juan points out six vices attributed by Aristotle to old men: cowardice, cheapness, suspicion, resentment, shamelessness, and disbelief.[6] The profile of our main character corresponds to most of them. For example, in an extreme case of the old man's distrust, he tries to avoid, by any means, letting in anything with a masculine name: "he seals the doors and windows, patrols the house at all hours, and chases away all the male cats and dogs" (135). Just observing these kinds of actions, we can conclude that he is

imbalanced because of his age.[7] However, no matter how many precautions
are taken, the climax of the play would be, eventually, the act of union between Lorenza and a young man. He will enter the house thanks to a plan orchestrated by Ortigosa; as this scheme unfolds, the old man will be *blinded* in
order to not be able to see the unavoidable:

> *As they lift the piece of tapestry and display it, a young man slips in behind it.*
> *Cañizares looks at the picture.*

> *Cañizares:* Ah, the charming Rodamonte! What's that little fellow in a cloak
> doing in my house? If he knew how little I care for disguises and
> that kind of thing, he'd make himself scarce. (139)

The arrival of the young male will take place in a space under the control of
the old man, the house. The act of coming into the room in order to enjoy
Cañizares's wife is an invasion of his home, a space protected by the honor
code as a place that belongs to the woman's sphere, something that is materi-
alized in the institution of marriage.[8]

The tension between what is demanded by the rules of honra and what is
imposed by the men and women's ages is solved with the final victory of unavoidable physical desire. The poetic justice of this play seems to dictate that,
just as the imbalances of the old man are hard to control, so too are those of
his wife. Like the old man's jealousy, the desire of the young wife is hard to
contain, even with a strict code of honor or other social pressures. Lorenza finally enjoys the aspect of the sacrament of marriage that she had been denied.
The young woman allows us to prove that the material wealth offered by the
old man is insufficient when the body lacks the necessary vitality to enjoy it.[9]
The space of the house invaded by the jealousy of the old man has finally
become balanced by the consummated imbalanced desire of his wife. The interlude has solved the original imbalance, as well as the particular one of
Lorenza. The unavoidable has happened thanks to an anonymous young man
who could be any man with whom the audience could identify. Thus the play
projects the public's desire for revenge against the attempt by the old man to
take control of a dramatic space that was making life difficult and suffocating
for the people who shared it with him.

In summary, in this interlude, there is, a deep reflection on the imbalances
inherent to the different ages of human beings as they are carefully described
in the treatise *Examen de Ingenios para las ciencias* of Juan Huarte de San Juan.
The decline of natural ingeniousness makes the old husband unable to prevent the union of the two young people who are beginning to discover an ad-

mirable ingenuity that eventually will disappear as they grow older (Huarte, *Examen*, 244–45).

Cristina, the niece, is likely a teenager; Lorenza is young as is the anonymous man; Ortigosa is middle-aged; Cañizares is an old man, just as his fellow compadre. In the particular case of the protagonist, Cañizares is not able to control his tendencies. Although theoretically Lorenza, being in her late teens, should find herself in a balanced age, her actions do not show her to be so. [10] It might be that her behavior, like her husband's, and in some ways like that of Tomás Rodaja in *El licenciado Vidriera*, results from not having been able to enjoy fully and in its specific moment the stage of existence that she was supposed to live, which is why Lorenza seems younger than she really is. This is a fundamental feature of her personality in the development of the actions of this play. In this regard, the *Examen de ingenios para las ciencias* states that the young have a temper that is hot and dry and that is why "no hay maldad de que no esté tentado el hombre en esta edad: ira, gula, lujuria, soberbia, homicidos, adulterios, robos, temeridades, rapiña, audacia, enemistad, engaños, mentiras, bandos, disensiones, venganzas, odios, injuria y protervia . . . en la juventud está el cuerpo más destemplado, por esto obra el ánima con más dificultad las obras virtuosas y con más facilidad las viciosas [There is no evil by which a man is not tempted in this stage of life: rage, gluttony, lust, arrogance, murder, adultery, stealing, temerity, theft, boldness, hostility, deceit, lies, gangs, quarrels, revenge, hate, affront, perversion. In youth, bodies are more unbalanced. That is why it is more difficult for the soul to achieve virtuous acts, and it is also easier to accomplish vicious actions]" (Huarte, *Examen*, 268, trans. mine).

The conflicts inherent in the placement of characters at such different life stages within the same dramatic space eventually come to a head as different worldviews, old and new, try to satisfy their respective, contradictory desires. Indeed, *The Jealous Old Man* also reflects the impossibility of governing a space in which an attempt is made to establish an almost dictatorial authority. The house becomes something like a colony ruled by a government that is distant and alienated from exterior events. Cañizares, as the Spanish Monarchy, is not able to manage all the energy that emanates from his teenaged wife, his profaned gold of Perú, and decides to keep it isolated from the world. [11] The final beneficiary of the most valuable possession of the old man is a young man who easily and effectively liberates the energy accumulated over years by young Lorenza. Thus, we can venture that there are hints of allegory in this interlude about the erroneous policy of accumulation and dispersal of riches acquired in Spanish America and the extreme efforts to

keep them out of circulation. The stealing of youthful energy and the conser-
vation of wealth within the walls of the house are two facts that are combined
with the intangible desire of the young wife, making the metaphor reach ab-
stract levels that lead us to reflect on the economic policy of the Spanish
Empire at beginning of the seventeenth century. The theft of riches and their
accumulation in a peninsula that is cut off from a world that does not share
its own views causes tensions. The ease with which the anonymous young
man seduces and steals the most precious jewel of the old man is indicative of
something that was noted by many commentators and politicians of the
times. The wealth of Spanish America came to the Peninsula with difficulty
due to constant attacks and weather conditions (Lynch, *Hispanic World*,
267–86) and vanished very fast, usually passing to European bankers to
defray the costs of absurd wars conceived in the minds of jealous (zealous),
old, powerful men.[12] The deception woven by Ortigosa—letting the young
man into the house under the cover of a wall hanging—shows the frailty of
the political and economic system on which the Spanish empire of the Aus-
trias was based (Elliott, *Spain*, 7–25). The inflexible position of the old indiano is futile, showing his double impotence—political and sexual—in the
face of the adultery that is committed in his own bedroom and narrated by
his own wife for her own and others' pleasure and to the frustration of the old
man. His erroneous strategy has to do with not having paid enough attention
to the needs of the army of women confined to his properties. This union of
the three women is actually characteristic of the interlude, not of the narrative, as we cannot find powerful and intermediating female characters in the
novel. It seems as if the three women together were able to achieve anything
they wanted in the carnivalesque interlude, an impossible scenario in the serious exemplary novel. Cañizares is not able to cope with the adversity of his
fallen world, based on taking advantage of seemingly less civilized human
beings; he is just realizing the expectations of the greedy Europeans of his
times to the New World:[13] "By the seventeenth century the New World con-
jured up visions in the European consciousness of gold and silver in abundance and of native Indian peoples lacking the rudiments of civility. These
visions consciously or unconsciously shaped the attitudes and reactions of
seventeenth-century colonists, differentiating them from the first generation
of European arrivals, whose expectation of the New World had been formed
exclusively in Europe" (5).

Lorenza opens the doors to the transformation of her body through sexual
enjoyment. She was not only in an unfair marriage, but also trapped in a reduced space of sensations in a situation that is hard to maintain in the face of

the constant temptations that other women were suggesting daily in the house.[14] The conclusion, intentionally dual and ambiguous, redistributes the guilt shared through the dynamics of the decisions that are made by the different characters in their natural situations.[15] The old man retains and contains his most valuable jewel bought with his indiano money, and apparently only loses part of it—her honor—a small and almost necessary concession in order to continue enjoying the abuse implicit in marrying a much younger wife. Lorenza commits an adultery that is existentially necessary. She knows that the institution of marriage is unchallengeable in a confessional state, so with the help of more experienced women she will try to take advantage of the few opportunities for enjoyment available under a totalitarian system of government. She is able to get what she wants, and she gets ready for a promising future when she will be able to dissimulate in front of her husband as she escapes with the anonymous young man. Lorenza establishes a dialogue with other unhappily married young women of other interludes, especially with Mariana in *The Divorce Court Judge*, a character who refuses to live in a monastery as an alternative to spending the rest of her life with her old husband: "To hell with that! A fine idea to shut me away!" (Cervantes, *Eight Interludes*, 15). Lorenza's evolution in the play goes from innocence to experience, from ignorant to learned; she does not enrich Cañizares's life as she learns through experience and through the help of two other women. Rather, she rebels, with her ingenuity, against the control exercised by the old indiano.

The same defect that Cañizares criticizes in Ortigosa—taking advantage of Lorenza's lack of experience in order to give her bad advice—he himself had shown in marrying a woman too innocent to choose a husband. Lorenza appears in the play as manipulated by other experienced characters who have influenced her decisions. The female neighbor's bad influence is part of the final moral of both the exemplary novel and the interlude. Thus, in *The Jealous Old Man*, Cañizares confesses to his best friend that where women "come to grief and fall from grace is in the house next door, with other women friends. A false friend keeps more things hidden than a dark night. More plots are conceived and delivered in that friend's house than in any public place" (137).

The deceived husband is right in some sense, because Ortigosa really is responsible for the plan that has made a cuckold of him. Mature and experienced characters need to exchange few words to really know what both are capable of doing. Ortigosa understands Lorenza's problem and tries to solve it in her own way. The weaving of the three women works out perfectly.

Cristina is like a chorus of Lorenza and also pretends to have a young friar with whom to pass time. Ortigosa is to blame for what has happened, or so Cañizares thinks. The keys controlled by the go-between open the doors of the world to Lorenza: "*Cañizares*: So you see, good sirs, what confusion and turmoil this neighbour has caused me and how right I am to be wary of my neighbours" (144).[16]

Ortigosa is just the tool, an intermediary to make true the pleasures that Lorenza wants to experience with a man who is not her husband. Ortigosa seems to project her desires onto those of the young lady, sharing interests and views and opposing the mercantilist view of the old man. Ortigosa appears happy with the rewarding contemplation of Lorenza's desires fulfilled, her motivation far from the lust for money and material compensation of the traditional Celestinesque archetype that she *seems* to represent in the interlude.

Cañizares's old friend is a character who makes the stupidity of his compadre even more evident when he is not even allowed to enter into the house of Cañizares. The sentence that the friend enunciates when he says good-bye to Cañizares is very significant, implying that Cañizares's perdition will come from his own impotence: "He'll be hoisted with his own petard and die of the very sickness he dreads so much" (137). The old man finally loses all his credit, if he ever had any, and the indiano is forced to adapt to the customs imposed by the three Spanish women. The abuser of Lorenza has been abused, and the natural order is restored through a promising future of more young men for her. The anonymous young man has no voice in the play, something that brings him close to an archetype of youth, a symbol of the libertarian air that has entered the oppressive house. He is also sex in its pure state, without social class or condition. He is full of virility and joy, far from the rakish young Sevillian of *The Jealous Man of Extremadura*. The final return of the seducer of the novel to the Indies is indicative of his association with the desperation of the hopeless. The *galán* in the interlude is, on the other hand, a purely comic character that disappears symbolically without any allusion to the New World, although he has definitely contributed to create a new one inside Cañizares's house.[17]

What happens in the closed and excessively protected space of the old man's house suggests different conclusions on an allegorical level. The jealous old man is a character that, to some extent, represents the rigidity, the immobility of the Hispanic empire, the interruption of the flow of energy—youth—and its reduction to a space where it can not expand. Lorenza symbolizes a juvenile openness to the world for the purpose of knowing it through experience, the freshness of the young colony that suggest a modus operandi based on activity and the movement of energies, not on their accumulation and stagnation. The anonymous young man collaborates with Lorenza in order to create more dynamism in the play. He represents, in theory, an economy based on the free flow of capital. His mere presence helps to speed up the action. Structurally, his role is also similar to that of the *furrier* (quartermaster) in the interlude of *El retablo de las maravillas,* because it serves the purpose of uncovering an injustice and completing the play with the climax of adultery.

Ortigosa is used as the final excuse of the old man to justify his own errors. In addition, she keeps the characters from becoming polarized and contributes to the ultimate balance of the play. With her wise advise and with almost no effort Ortigosa is like the Genovese lender who channels the gold to the young man. Her cunning is remarkable, because she is able to see Lorenza's problem from a holistic perspective, taking advantage of her own experience in order to attain her final objective of benefiting Lorenza. The now happier wife, who represents a material object for the old man, might also be a possession that is easily stolen by the young man right in front of the husband and is symbolically taken far from the house/bank where she has been stagnating.[18] The play constitutes, in this sense, some kind of a chess game between two old Spaniards—a male, Cañizares, and a female, Ortigosa. They have different and contrary opinions about freedom and the life of the young.

In this reading, *The Jealous Old Man* postulates a contradiction between personal freedom and the institution of marriage as a rule of social order. But at the same time, just as in *The Divorce Court Judge,* in the end the conjugal union overcomes the complaints against its oppressiveness. Still, the lack of free will in one of the married parties challenges the concept of an ideal life-long marriage. The conclusion of the play presents the unpremeditated revenge by a young seducer that culminates with the social ridicule of the oppressor. The old man is punished with the liberation of feminine energy that he had kept isolated and idle, something that turns out to be impossible in the Spanish society depicted in the play. Lorenza, as the American gold, is an energy that needs to change hands. The demystification of the happy and idealized marriage that takes place through its supreme negation—adultery—makes the walls of the house, and the inhabitants' own lives, shake. Curiously enough, the way in which the adultery is presented in the interlude has been the object of many controversial opinions. Cervantes's readers cannot completely believe that the author of *Don Quijote* has been able to present the sexual act so explicitly:

Lorenza: You should see the gentleman my good fortune has brought me! He's young and good-looking, with black hair. His breath smells like orange blossom.

. . . .

Lorenza: This is far from being a joke. So far, in fact, that it couldn't go any further!

Cristina: Dear Lord, what madness and folly! Tell me, Aunt, is my little friar there too?

Lorenza: No, Niece, he isn't. But he'll come next time, if neighbour Ortigosa is willing.

Cañizares: Lorenza, say what you will, but stop using that word neighbour. Just to hear it I'm all of a tremble.

Lorenza: Thanks to the neighbour, I'm all of a tremble too.

Cristina: Dear Lord, what madness and folly!

Lorenza: Now I see you for what you are, wretched old man. Until now the life I've lived with you has been a sham. (141)

We could conclude that these words of Lorenza serve as a kind of revenge against the long-term punishment or abuse imposed by Cañizares. Although the adultery is openly taking place in his own house, he cannot recognize it. This way, he can still be married and is somewhat more balanced—his power and zeal have been reduced, but Lorenza's have too, as her youthful imbalance has been equilibrated. In fact, in the final scene, in which Cañizares apologizes to his neighbor and opens his soul to his wife, shows a humanized character, far from the ridiculed cuckold favored by the audience of the baroque interlude:

Cañizares: I'd be obliged, sirs, if you'd leave us now. I thank you for your good offices; my wife and I have made peace with each other.

Lorenza: I'll keep the peace on condition you ask the neighbour to forgive you for harbouring any unkind thoughts against her.

Cañizares: If I had to ask forgiveness of all the neighbours I've thought about unkindly, there'd be no end to it. All the same, I do ask Mistress Ortigosa to forgive me.

Ortigosa: I forgive you here and now. Let's say no more about it. (143)

If we compare the interlude with the exemplary novel, we see that the ending of both works is very different. The Indies have an indubitable presence in the novel, adding circular closure to the narrative: "Loaysa empieza donde Carrizales acaba, en la impotencia, y que al igual que Carrizales huye a las Indias, calificadas por Cervantes de 'refugio y amparo de los desesperados de España' [Loyasa begins where Carrizales ends, in impotence, and just as Carrizales, he flees to the Indies, a place Cervantes calls the 'refuge and shelter of the desperate people of Spain']" (Percas de Ponseti, "Escondido," 144, trans. mine). On the other hand, the interlude ending perpetuates a situation that has developed from the plot of the play: "A marriage based on deceit will continue to thrive on deceit" (Wardropper, "Ambiguity," 25). Thus, Cañizares turns out in the end to be an impossible character, a man who has built a life around a combination of static and dynamic valuable material elements with a very materialistic philosophy. In the end both static (the house) and dynamic (Lorenza) values get out of control thanks to the skills of an experienced woman and the presence of a young man. The old man has not been able to impose his will; he is not able to create and govern his imagined ínsula because the inhabitants—including his own wife—do not identify themselves with Cañizares's values. This way of exercising power does not work in the peninsular society where imposition seems to be answered with a revolutionary reaction, at least in the carnivalesque microworld of the interludes.

Finally, the song that concludes the play offers an exemplary reconciliation. Instead of pointing to a cleansing of the honor of the wife, as was demanded in the *comedias,* or a beating of the cuckold, as was expected in the baroque interlude, dancing and singing serve to elevate the happy tone of the play and to distance it even from the final bitterness of the death of the old man in the exemplary novel: "Quarrels in June at the Feast of St. John / The rest of the year are forgotten and gone" (144). On the other hand, the play leaves many unanswered questions. Is Lorenza completely responsible of her adulterous behavior, or was she negatively influenced by her neighbor? Is the old man guilty of the fate of his wife because of his excessive jealousy, or are the neighbor's bad advice, the generation gap, and his own lack of sexual energy the ones to blame? Does the husband know that he has been deceived? Does Cañizares apologize to Ortigosa and reconcile with his wife, knowing that he has been deceived? The most reformist element of the play is probably in these unanswered questions that are enunciated so that the idle readers / spectators can resolve them by contrasting what has just been read or seen on the stage with their own experience.

Notes

I want to thank both Olga Markoff-Belaef and Mindy Badía for their kindness in reading previous versions of this essay.

1. Javier Huerta has pointed out the relevance of the different ages of women in *The Jealous Old Man:* "a la mujer se la ve en sus diferentes fases: aparece en la edad vieja, Ortigosa, que es la mujer que ayuda a cometer la transgresión; aparece la mujer en su fase casi adolescente, que es la Cristinica que está pinchando a la casada para que realice el adulterio, y aparece la mujer mujer, Lorenza, que es la que finalmente engaña al marido" [Woman is seen in all her different phases: she appears in old age in the figure of Ortigosa, the woman who helps commit the transgression; she appears as an adolescent in the figure of Cristinica, who is urging the married woman to commit adultery, and she appears as the true woman, Lorenza, the one who finally deceives her husband] ("Los géneros teatrales," 116, trans. mine). It can be deduced from the title of the interlude that being old is somewhat more important than being jealous, as this last word is the adjective modifying the noun *viejo.* On the other hand, jealousy is the noun and "extremeño" the adjective in the title of the exemplary novel, so in the novelistic work the *celos* of Carrizales are more important than his origin.

2. The different meanings of the word *celoso* studied in the exemplary novel can be perfectly applied to this adjective in the interlude: "Historically, according to the 1726 *Diccionario de Autoridades,* '[Celoso se] aplicaba también al demasiadamente cuidadoso, y vigilante de lo que de algún modo le pertenece, sin permitir la menor cosa en su contra [*Celoso* was also applied to the person who was too careful or vigilant of his belongings, someone who never allowed anything to harm them].' This inclusive sense of celoso, closer in meaning to its English cognate "zealous" than to "jealous," is intrinsic to Carrizales's character independent of romantic circumstances: '*de su natural condición* era el más celoso hombre del mundo [Because of his natural condition, he was the most jealous/zealous man in the world]' " (Armon, "Paper Key," 98 trans. mine).

3. "Carrizales . . . has traded silver for a wife, yet he fails to capitalize on either the one or the other . . ." (ibid., 107). All quotes hereafter cited in text are from Miguel Cervantes Saavedra's *Eight Interludes.*

4. About the legendary character of King David, Huarte de San Juan affirms: "Haber vivido sano en todo el discurso de su vida parece que se puede probar. Porque, en su historia, de sólo una enfermedad se hace mención, y ésta era disposición natural de los que viven muchos años: que, por habérsele resuelto el calor natural, no podía calentar en la cama, para cuyo remedio acostaban con él una doncella hermosa que le diera calor. Y, con esto, vivió tantos años, que dice el Texto . . . murió David en su buena vejez, lleno de días, de riquezas y de gloria" [It seems that one can prove that he was healthy during his whole life. Because in the story of his life, there is only one illness mentioned, and this illness is natural for people who have lived many years. Having lost his natural heat, he couldn't get warm in the bed. To remedy this, they sent a beautiful young girl to bed with him to warm him up. And in this way, he lived many years, as the Sacred text says . . . David died at a very old age, his days full of riches and glory] (*Examen,* 592–93, trans. mine).

5. Amezcua Gómez states that in the Golden Age *comedias* women in the street have a very specific role: "Si vemos a una mujer en la calle, es porque, o está deshonrada y carece de varón que pueda pugnar por restituirle el honor, o porque viaja encubierta a reunirse con quien será su esposo" [If we see a woman in the street, it is because she is either dishonored

and lacks a man to restore her honor or because she is traveling in disguise to meet the man who will be her husband] ("Los géneros teatrales," 7, trans. mine). Ortigosa's ability to walk freely in the street makes her a special woman, able to alter the established order, as she has features that are usually attributed to men (street), and because of her age, she does not have to worry very much about her honor. Thus, she has control of the space of the street and can walk about freely. She is also a woman, so she dominates the space of the house, and as a neighbor, she has the right to enter Lorenza's house without the restrictions that a male character would have.

6. Concerning the last age of the human existence, there are different and original ideas in Juan Huarte de San Juan's *Examen de ingenios para las ciencias:* "La última edad del hombre es la vejez; en la cual está el cuerpo frío y seco, y con mil enfermedades y flaco: todas las potencias perdidas, sin poder hacer lo que antes solían . . . Pero con todo eso, cuenta Aristóteles seis vicios que tienen los viejos por razón de la frialdad que el hombre tiene en esta edad . . . Lo primero son cobardes . . . Lo segundo son avarientos, y guardan el dinero más de lo que es menester; porque estando ya en los postreros tercios de la vida y que la razón les había de dictar que con poca hacienda podrían pasar, entonces les crece más la codicia, como si estuvieran en la niñez y considerando que les restaba cinco edades por pasar y que era bien guardar con que comprar de comer. Lo tercero son sospechosos . . . esto les nace de haber visto por experiencia tantas maldades de los hombres, y acordándose de los vicios y pecados que ellos propios cometieron en su mocedad; y, así viven siempre con recato, sabiendo que hay poco que fiar de los hombres. Lo cuarto son de mala esperanza y jamás piensan que los negocios han de suceder bien; y de dos o tres fines que pueden tener, siempre eligen el peor y a aquél están esperando. Lo quinto son desvergonzados . . . Lo sexto son incrédulos: jamás piensan que les dicen verdad, trayendo a la memoria los embustes y engaños de los hombres y lo que han visto en el mundo en el largo discurso de su vida" [The last of man's ages is old age, when the body is cold, dry and thin, having thousands of sicknesses: with all powers lost, without being able to do what it was normal before. Aristotle mentions six vices that old people have because of the natural coldness of that age. First of all, they are cowardly. Second, they are mean and tend to accumulate more money than they really need. Being in the third stage of their lives, reasonably they should get used to spending less, but it is just the opposite. They get more and more greedy, as if they were in their childhood, thinking that they still need to accumulate food in order to live the remaining five stages of their lives. Third, they are suspicious because they have had so many experiences with men's evil ways and tend to remember the vices and sins that they committed when young; thus, they are always cautious, showing that they cannot trust men. Fourth, they are pessimistic and never believe things can work out fine; out of two or three possibilities they always choose the worst. Fifth, they are shameless. Sixth, they are incredulous: they never think that they are told the truth, bringing into memory men's lies, deceptions and all the things they have seen during their long existence] (270–71, trans. mine).

7. Juan Huarte de San Juan, a humanist doctor, recommended looking at the behavior of the subjects of study in order to diagnose human maladies: "Los médicos de ninguna señal se aprovechan tanto para conocer y entender si un hombre está sano o enfermo como mirarle a las obras que hace. Si estas son buenas y sanas, es cierto que tiene salud; y si lesas y dañadas, infaliblemente está enfermo [Doctors should pay special attention to a specific sign in order to find out if a man is healthy or sick, and this is the pure observation of the things he does. If these are good and beneficial, he is certainly healthy; if they are low and harmful, there is no doubt that he is sick] (*Examen*, 174, trans. mine).

8. Amezcua Gómez considers that the tradition of associating women with the house was established around the times of publication of *The Jealous Old Man*. In this sense, the attitude of the husbands would not be very different from the behavior of the old man of the interlude. However, the difference between the main character of the interlude and similar characters of the *comedias* has to do with the reflective attitude about his own behavior and personality and the rationalization of his imbalance in Cañizares. On the other hand, traditionally, honor *blinds* husbands of the comedia and leads them irremediably to tragic solutions when honor is lost: "Desde *Los comendadores de Córdoba* de Lope de Vega, se sitúa esta oposición topológica casa/descampado en el centro de las preocupaciones espaciales de los dramaturgos: se reúne a los personajes femeninos dentro de la casa 'la mujer en su casa y con la pierna quebrada,' que dice el refrán en tanto que los varones circulan libremente en la calle, en el camino, en el mar. El marido guarda así, echando llave a la puerta, a la mujer, y con ella, el tesoro de su honor, la limpieza de su opinión" [Since the publication of Lope de Vega's *Los comendadores de Córdoba*, the spatial opposition between home vs. open country is established; for most of the comedia writers, this division of the dramatic space turns into an obsession. They usually start gathering all female characters inside the house, as in the saying 'women at home and with a broken leg.' In the meantime, male characters walk around freely in the open spaces: roads, sea, etc. Husbands keep with them and watch over the key of their house, locking away their wives. This way they can keep the treasure of their honor safe by avoiding gossip] ("El espacio simbólico," 10, trans. mine). In the exemplary novel by Cervantes with similar plot, *The Jealous Man of Extremadura*, the role of the house has been extensively studied, and critics conclude that there are two different strengths associated with the main character of the novel. Both, we can affirm, correspond to similar characteristics of Cañizares's association with his house: "La casa viene a representar el producto de la manifestación de dos fuerzas contrastadas que aparecen en el personaje de Felipo Carrizales. Una de ellas emerge de una necesidad social que se vale del matrimonio como forma cronológica de organizar una vida y que, para este personaje, implicaría el logro de su deseo: la posibilidad de tener un hijo heredero. La segunda manifiesta una característica psicológica muy personal e individual, los celos extremos, cuya intensidad obliga al rechazo de la secuencia temporal soltero /casado /hijo heredero impuesta por la cultura en que vive" [Felipo Carrizales's home represents the consequences of the manifestation of two contrasted forces that gather in this character. One of them is the product of social need that is based on considering marriage as a chronological way of organizing human life. In the particular case of this character, it would imply the realization of his main wish: the possibility of having a son who would inherit his fortune. The other one is the manifestation of a very special and individual psychological characteristic, his extreme jealousy. It is so powerful that it will condition him to reject the temporal sequence of being single, then married, and finally having an inheritor, which is mandated by the society in which he lives] (Avilés, "Fortaleza," 76, trans. mine).

9. Cristina would be the one who will describe graphically the decadence of the old man at a point in the play, saying that she does not know "which makes him more impotent, his hernia or his jealousy" (Cervantes, *Eight Interludes*, 134).

10. *Examen de ingenios para las ciencias* dictates that adolescence is always associated with moderation: "El adolescencia es la segunda edad del hombre; y cuéntase desde catorce años hasta veinte y cinco. La cual, según la opinión de los médicos, no es caliente, fría, húmida ni seca, sino en medio de estas calidades, templada. Con esta temperatura, están los instrumentos del cuerpo como el ánima los ha menester para todo género de virtud, especialmente para la

prudencia . . . las virtudes . . . de la adolescencia van hechas ya con discreción y prudencia, y así entiende el adolescente lo que hace y a qué propósito, y conociendo el fin, dispone los medios para conseguirlo" [Adolescence is the second age of men; and it lasts between the fourteenth to the twentieth year. Doctors think that this age is neither hot nor cold, neither humid nor dry, but it is in the middle of all these qualities: it is warm. This special temperature makes the instruments of the body as the soul needs them for any kind of virtue, especially for prudence. The virtues of adolescence are built with wit and prudence, so that an adolescent understands what he does and with what purpose; once he knows about the purpose of his actions, he will do all that is necessary to accomplish his goals] (Huarte, "Los géneros teatrales," 266–67, trans. mine).

11. Armon observes that Carrizales also "keeps his 'treasure' in stock and out of circulation" ("Paper Key," 103).

12. Vendramin, a Venetian ambassador, recalled the following Spanish saying about the silver from the Indies: "it has just the effect on them that rain does on the roof of a house—that it quickly runs off" (Casey, *Early Modern Spain*, 68). Also, in a treatise on the new economy, in 1569 Tomás de Mercado wrote that: "In Spain, the very source and fount of escudos and crowns, scarcely a handful can be scraped together, whereas if you go to Genoa, Rome, Antwerp or Venice you will see in the streets of the bankers and money-changers, without exaggeration, as many piles of coins minted in Seville, as there are piles of melons in San Salvador or in the Arenal" (ibid., 68).

13. Juan Bautista Avalle-Arce compares the house of Carrizales in *The Jealous Man of Extremadura* with an "island in the city of the Guadalquivir" ("El celoso," 199). James D. Fernández elaborates in his study of the exemplary novel an association between Carrizales and an indiano governor of his insula "inhabited by a racially diverse group of natives" ("Bonds of Patrimony," 974). He points out the lack of interest from Carrizales in "educating or indoctrinating his subjects, in having them internalize his voice of authority and thus police themselves" (975). In the interlude, though, the control exercised by Cañizares becomes a comic attitude right from the beginning of the play. The inhabitants of the house rebel against the authority of Spaniards not wishing to be oppressed to the old man, although the attitude of Cañizares toward them is still similar to the one of Cañizares, in the sense that he tries to apply his law with the authority of a husband, owner of his house with a very territorial attitude to impose his will over the other inhabitants of his house.

14. The origin of the conflict in the Cervantine interlude of *The Jealous Old Man* is the topic of the unhappy married woman. In this case, it is aggravated by the traditional difference of ages between an old man and his much younger wife, something that constitutes a clear unfairness against the wife. The marriage contract is questioned when it is signed under coercion or abuse, as happens in this play, something that is discussed also in *The Divorce Court Judge*. Cañizares's marriage is questionable because one of the valid criteria for divorce is access to marriage through a previous deceitful action by one of the members, in this case Cañizares's taking advantage of the niña Lorenza's ignorance and obligating her to marriage while consciously aware that her existence will be unhappy. On the other hand, a reflection about the background of the interlude would make us think that this play, as in *The Divorce Court Judge*, questions the validity of the conservative pact of marriage that excludes the many of the exceptions to the rule. However, the publication of both interludes (*The Jealous Old Man* and *The Divorce Court Judge*) seems to state that every generalization is pernicious because the impossible logic works out in a relative way.

15. Duality in other Cervantine works like *La española inglesa* or different chapters of the *Quijote* are studied in the chapter about Grisóstomo and Marcela in *Nuevos deslindes cervantinos* de Avalle-Arce. Ambiguity has been thoroughly studied in both the interlude (Wardropper, "Ambiguity," 24–25) and the exemplary novel (Lipmann, "Revision," 114–15, 119).

16. The allusion to the audience in this play in this quotation is a metatheatrical resource that validates the receptors of the interlude as judges of what just happened because they have had a holistic vision of the facts that none of the other characters have had, especially the old man.

17. In *The Jealous Man of Extremadura* we can note a negative association of the previous life of Carrizales within the Indeas. In this case, it seems to be some kind of a curse. As in the interlude, in the novel the old man also seems marked in someway by his previous existence. A very extensive explanation is offered in the narrative, corresponding to the possibilities of including more information in this genre: "[Carrizales] Having depleted his patrimony in his wanderings through Spain, Italy and Flanders, he seeks a second fortune in the New World. But this new wealth carries a tainted aura, for the Indies are the refuge of Spain's pariahs: 'las Indias, refugio y amparo de los desesperados de España, iglesia de los alzados, salvoconducto de los homicidas, pala y cubierta de los jugadores a quien llaman *ciertos* los peritos en el arte, añagaza general de mujeres libres, engaño común de muchos y remedio particular de pocos' " [The Indies, refuge and shelter of the desperate from Spain, the church of criminals, a safe haven for murderers, gamblers, swindlers and loose women, deceit for may and remedy for few] (99). From this particularly vehement description of the New World company Carrizales will be forced to keep, we can understand something of his uneasy association with money. If his early behavior is a reflection of his need to distance himself from his family and other affectionate ties, the desire to acquire money is perceived to be illegitimate and fraught with danger. As Peter Dunn has observed, "Carrizales' self-transformation from *hidalgo* to indiano, or New World entrepreneur, constitutes a class betrayal of his family" (Weber, "Tragic Reparation," 39).

18. This interpretation will complement the one considering Leonora from *The Jealous Old Man* as wealth that Carrizales does not know how to handle: "Leonora, as *El celoso extremeño*, may be read as an allegory of containment in which Leonora represents wealth unprofitably hoarded rather than invested in international trade. From this perspective, the newlywed's house, characterized in the novella as a harem and a convent, and compared more recently to a colonial ínsula, becomes a bank or vault into which Carrizales deposits Leonora" (Armon, "Paper Key," 101).

Works Cited

Altman, Ida. *Transatlantic Ties in the Spanish Empire*. Stanford, Calif.: Stanford University Press, 2000.

Amezcua Gómez, José. "El espacio simbólico: El caso del teatro español del Siglo de Oro." In *Cuaderno 9*, 2–13, Mexico City: Universidad Autónoma Metropolitana-Iztapalapa. 1988.

Armon, Shirfa. "The Paper Key: Money as Text in Cervantes's *El celoso extremeño* and José de Camerino's *El pícaro amante. Cervantes* 18.1 (1998): 96–144.

Avalle-Arce, Juan Bautista. " 'El celoso extremeño,' de Cervantes." In *Homenaje a María Barrenechea,* edited by Lía Schwarz Lerner and Isaías Lerner. Madrid: Castalia, 1984, 199205.

————. *Nuevos deslindes cervantinos*, Barcelona: Ariel, 1975.

Avilés, Luis F. "Fortaleza tan guardada: Casa, alegoría y melancolía en *El Celoso extremeño.*" *Cervantes: Bulletin of the Cervantes Society of America* 18.1 (1998): 71–95.

Casey, James. *Early Modern Spain*. London: Routledge, 1999.

Cervantes Saavedra, Miguel. *Eight Interludes*. Translated by Dawn Smith. London: Everyman, 1996.

Elliott, J. H. *Spain and Its World 1500–1700*. New Haven: Yale University Press, 1989.

Fernández, James D. "The Bonds of Patrimony: Cervantes and the New World." *PMLA* 109, 5 (1994): 969–81.

Huarte de San Juan, Juan. *Examen de Ingenios para las ciencias*. Madrid: Cátedra, 1989.

Huerta Calvo, Javier. "Los géneros teatrales menores en el Siglo de Oro: status y prospectiva de la investigación." *El teatro menor en España a partir del siglo XVI*. Edited by Luciano García Lorenzo. Madrid: CSIC, 1983, 23–62.

Lipmann, Stephen H. "Revision and Exemplarity in Cervantes` *El celoso extremeño.*" *Bulletin of the Cervantes Society of America* 6.2 (1986): 113–21.

Lynch, John. *The Hispanic World in Crisis and Change*, 1598–1700. Oxford: Blackwell, 1992.

Percas de Ponseti, Helena. "El misterio escondido en *El celoso extremeño.*" *Bulletin of the Cervantes Society of America* 14.2 (1994): 137–53.

Sánchez-Albornoz, Nicolás. "The First Transatlantic Transfer: Spanish Migration to the New World, 1493-1810." In *Europeans on the Move. Studies on European Migration, 1500–1800*. Oxford: Clarendon, 1994, 26–36.

Wardropper, Bruce W. "Ambiguity in *El viejo celoso.*" *Cervantes* 1.1-2 (1981): 19–27.

Weber, Alison. "Tragic Reparation in Cervantes's *The Jealous Man of Extremadura.*" *Bulletin of the Cervantes Society of America* 4.1 (1984): 35–51.

Lipmann, Stephen H. "Revision and Exemplarity in Cervantes` *El celoso extremeño.*" *Bulletin of the Cervantes Society of America* 6.2 (1986): 113–21.

Lynch, John. *The Hispanic World in Crisis and Change*, 1598-1700. Oxford: Blackwell, 1992.

Percas de Ponseti, Helena. "El misterio escondido en *El celoso extremeño.*" *Bulletin of the Cervantes Society of America* 14.2 (1994): 137–53.

Sánchez-Albornoz, Nicolás. "The First Transatlantic Transfer: Spanish Migration to the New World, 1493-1810." In *Europeans on the Move. Studies on European Migration, 1500–1800*, 26-36. Oxford: Clarendon, 1994.

Wardropper, Bruce W. "Ambiguity in *El viejo celoso.*" *Cervantes* 1.1–2 (1981): 19–27.

Weber, Alison. "Tragic Reparation in Cervantes's *The Jealous Man of Extremadura.*"

Don Dinero Encounters Don Juan: The Transatlantic Trading of Money and Desire in Tirso de Molina's *La villana de Vallecas*

Julio Vélez-Sainz

THE SEVILLIAN *CASA DE LA CONTRATACIÓN* (HOUSE OF CONTRACTS) WAS A mandatory sojourn for every merchant who traveled from America to the Peninsula hoping to trade his goods. In Nicolás Monardes's *Diálogo del Hierro y de sus grandezas,* one finds a lively description of its many characters, its overpowering atmosphere, and the hectic activity of its patio. The behavior of the traders was somewhat erratic: some dealers talked to themselves or looked down at the ground; seamen and soldiers awaited their pay; a few smugglers hastily showed their certificates, and gold traders argued with the scriveners. As Monardes sums up: "Había gran grita de muchos, satisfaciendo partidas, que se mataban sobre ello; los señores jueces estaban en acuerdo, y mucha gente esperándolos, de modo que yo solo estaba para mirar, y todos los demás para negociar, que ha sido para mí, que sin pasión los miraba, una comedia con muchos entremeses" [There was great yelling over inventories, as though they were killing each other over the inventories; the judges agreed and many people were waiting for them, I was only there to observe everything and the rest to negotiate, which was my detached viewpoint a play with much comic relief] (f. 127v cf. Tirso de Molina 296). Monardes's account reconstructs the chaotic and carnivalesque character of the casa de la contratación (House of Contracts), its convoluted structure, and its bureaucratization certainly resembled a comedia with many interludes. Given that the exchange and declaration of goods was, in fact, so similar to drama, it is not surprising that many Early Modern playwrights introduced references to trading and money in their works. In this essay, I will trace the path of Amer-

ican gold, silver, and jewels in the imaginary geography of a variety of comedias. I will particularly focus, however, on one of Tirso's lesser known plays:
La villana de Vallecas (c. 1621). Since Tirso depicts the mishaps of a *caballero
indiano* who travels to Madrid to get married, describing thus the movement
of wealth in Golden Age Spain, I argue for a reading of the indiano as a vari-
ant on Quevedo's satire "Don Dinero," whose protagonist is also, strictly
speaking, an indiano, and whose trajectory depicts the flow of capital in the
early Modern world.[1] In his travels, Tirso's Don Dinero encounters yet another famous character from the period, Don Juan, in a conflation of money
and craving.

DON DINERO
MAKES THE WORLD GO AROUND

Contesting the idealistic vision of the Renaissance put forward by cultural
historians such as Giorgio de Santillana or Jacob Burckhardt,[2] most recent
studies of the time period underscore the visibility of materialism in the shap-
ing of the Renaissance. Historians such as Lisa Jardine, revising dominant
concepts with a materialist analysis, emphasize how culture functioned as a
commodity. This vision has influenced Early Modern Spanish literary scholars, particularly *cervantistas*: Carroll Johnson has analyzed the material basis
of *Quijote* and a few *Novelas ejemplares*, and Barbara Fuchs has dwelt on *Las
dos Doncellas* and how "the intimate thefts of their marriage plot function [. . .]
as a synecdoche for the much larger circulation of gold out of Spain and to
Italy in the period" (*Empire Unmanned*, 290).[3] Henry Kamen has expanded
on this notion and defined empire as a "business" of exchange "brought into
existence by the collaboration of powerful provincial élites and enterprising
traders who operated across nations rather than within one nation alone. It
was the first globalized economy" (*Empire*, 287). This historical context is key
to understanding both Quevedo's ballad and Tirso's *La villana de Vallecas*.
However, they both deal with a trope in Western literature, so an analysis of
these texts with their "cultural memory" is also appropriate.[4]

    The theme of money, be it the celebration of prodigality or the satirical
criticizing of excessive spending, is a commonplace of Western culture from
Horace's third ode to Scarface's *Push it to the Limit*.[5] In Spanish literature,
one can easily find examples in Juan Ruiz's "Los excesos del dinero y la
bebida" (*The Evils of Money and Drink*) in his *Libro de buen amor* (*Book of
Good Love*).

En resumen lo digo, entiéndelo mejor,
el dinero es del mundo el gran agitador,
hace señor al siervo y siervo hace al señor,
toda cosa del siglo se hace por su amor.

(stanza 510; 133)

[All in all, I advise you to take advantage of it, for where there is money,
mountains are moved. It turns the servant into the master, the master into
the servant and all things everywhere obey its call. (Ruiz, 290)][6]

Fernando de Rojas's *Celestina* similarly extols the power of money: "Todo
lo puede el dinero: las peñas quebranta, los ríos pasa en seco" [Money can
do anything. It splitteth hard rocks. It passeth over rivers dry-foot (102,
Mabbe translation, 26). The *Celestina* expounds a harsh critique of money
spending.

A significant number of Golden Age works deal with greed as a literary
motif. They develop the Horatian commonplace but add a transatlantic perspective to the equation. The West Indies are constantly seen as a source of
riches and wealth to be exploited and from which capital flows to the center
of the empire to enrich it. At the same time, serious thought on the negative
flow of extraneous capital into the metropolis is also common. Money is
sometimes considered pernicious and even venomous.

In several Golden Age plays we find references to the power of money and
America as the locus where wealth is produced. Lope de Vega Carpio's *El sembrar en buena tierra* (1618) presents a character who spends so much that not
even indian gold would be enough to pay off his debt: "Dios no crió / oro en
las Indias [. . .] / para pagar lo que deues" [God did not create / enough Gold
in the Indies [. . .] / to pay off your debt] (425–27). Lidoro in Calderón's *Fortunas de Andromeda y Perseo* (1683) compares gold to somebody's greed: "si yà
no à codicia necia / de presumir que podia / enriquecer su sobervia / con el
oro de otras Indias" [His unwitty greed / made him presume that he could /
better his snobbism / with some other Indies Gold] (998–1001). Even Tirso's
La villana de Vallecas insists on the motif: "Las Indias que oro derraman" [The
Indies pour out gold] (83). Many treatise writers and political thinkers of the
Golden Age argued against the accumulation of money. Pedro de Valencia
stated that labor and agriculture were the basis of imperial economy and rejected gold, silver, and money for their poisonous qualities. So did Miguel
Caxa de Leruela in his *Restauración de la abundancia de España*. Luis de Góngora criticized his contemporaries' avarice in his *Soledades* where greed becomes the vessel that navigates searching for new mines to plunder:

Piloto hoy la Codicia, no de errantes
árboles, mas de selvas inconstantes,
al padre de las aguas Océano,
de cuya monarquía
el Sol, que cada día
nace en sus ondas, y en sus ondas muere,
los términos saber todos no quiere,
dejó primero de su espuma cano
sin admitir segundo
en inculcar sus límites al mundo.

(92)

[Today Greed is the Pilot, not of errant ships but of inconstant jungles who taught the limits of the Ocean to the father of the waters, whose limits not even the sun, who rises and dies everyday in the Ocean's waves, does not want to acknowledge nor even admit a second to inculcate the limits of the world.]

For Góngora, the globe is clearly marked by greed, which defeats both the sun and the ocean in showing the world its limits. The advances of cartography thus are useful only for mercantile purposes. Gold itself is depicted as Midas's "metales homicidas" (homicidal metals), an image that is also utilized in Tirso's drama. Greed was the real force behind the discoveries of the early-modern period and was very widely criticized by moralists and playwrights. For instance, in *Amar, servir, y esperar* (1635), Lope de Vega Carpio has his protagonist Pedro de Medina moved to the West Indies to "a la codicia del dorado cebo" [because of greed of the golden bait] (644). Lope reinforces his critique in *De cosario a cosario* (1624):

mas plata y oro,
y mas perlas ay en ella,
y mayor codicia arguyen
Indias del sol y de estrellas.

(361–64)

[There is more gold, silver, pearls and greed in the Indies than that in the Sun and the Stars.]

Already in exile, Tirso criticizes the greedy conquistadors in *La lealtad contra la embidia* (1631), the third part of the Pizarro trilogy in which three soldiers, Chacón, Peñafiel, and Granero attempt to steal gold from the Incas "Como la codicia esfuerza" [just like greed tells us] (579) only to see how

Chacón is captured by demons and almost dismembered by them due to his greed. This is the literary and spiritual framework of Quevedo's famous ballad and Tirso's *La villana de Vallecas*.

In his *Tesoro*, Sebastián de Covarrubias explains that "dinero" could also be "hombre adinerado, el que tiene mucha moneda" [a wealthy person, a person with cash] (473a). Quevedo's "Poderoso caballero es Don Dinero" (*Poesía Original*, 660) is based upon the metaphor of capital, specifically gold, as a real person, a certain *Don Dinero* who travels around the Early Modern world.[7] Aptly labeled the knight of the tongs (*caballero de la tenaza*) due to his stinginess with money, Quevedo attempts to describe profusely the life and deeds of Don Dinero who is:

> Nace de las Indias honrado,
> Donde el mundo le acompaña;
> viene a morir en España
> y es en Génova enterrado.
>   (vv. 11–14)

[Born and honored in the West Indies / where the world accompanies him / he then moves to Spain to die / and finds his tomb in Genoa.]

In his satire, Quevedo traces the movement of capital in the Spanish Empire. The Atlantic route of trade was the "principal lifeline of the empire" (Kamen, *Empire*, 290) and gold did, in fact, start its life in the American mines only to be "killed" in Spain. The Crown squandered it to support its multiple wars and pay debts owed to Genoese banks. Quevedo skillfully depicts a map of the limits of the Empire, and all the geographical points he mentions lie inside it. Quevedo emphasizes that *Don Dinero* is a "Don," a member of the nobility. His portrayal of this nobleman, however, departs from the traditional representation of the hidalgo in the Early Modern period. Most satires and attacks on the aristocracy underscored the poverty of the lower nobility. The *escudero* in *El Lazarillo de Tormes* lives off his page's mercy; Cervantes's hidalgo Alonso Quijano is hardly able to maintain his expenses; Quevedo himself echoes this critique, almost a commonplace, in many of his satirical poems. "Don Dinero," however, is honored above the rest as his *venas* (both mineral and bodily veins) are gilded. Gold makes all blood the same and "hace iguales / al duque y al ganadero" [is even able to equalize / the duke and the shepherd]. The abundance of capital is understood as a social motor, and thus Quevedo can be said to describe the evolution from a feudal society based on the power of land to a capitalistic (at least pre-industrially capitalistic) model where power lies in the flow of money, and in whomever controls it.[8] *Don Dinero* challenges the norms and structure of the ancien régime and offers a new way to climb the social ladder. Money is a powerful gentleman (*poderoso caballero*), which does indeed make the world go around.

The stock character of the indiano also embodies the flow of cash in the Empire. A significant number of plays by Lope de Vega delve into this character and he offers a variety of representations of the indiano. The indiano can be either cheap (as in *Pobreza no es vileza* [304]) or generous (as in *El testigo contra si* [269]) but he is constantly identified with money. In *De cosario a cosario* (1624) Lope presents a character as "Indiano y rico en efeto" (v. 705). Lope's *El amante agradecido* (1618) attempts to define the character type. The protagonist disguises himself as an indiano and gives us a detailed summary of the characteristics of this figure. He wears a big collar, a coat, and a golden chain that display his wealth and honor; he smells of grey amber and is a gallant, seductive character. If *Don Dinero* adorns those who accompany him, this indiano is quite literally Don Dinero. In fact, it could be argued that this Indiano and Tirso's Don Pedro de Mendoza were inspired on Quevedo's "Don Dinero" since the poem was one of the most popular songs of the time: it was published in the influential *Flores de poetas ilustres* (1603), and was sung in the streets (Jauralde, *Quevedo,* 141).

Like Lope's *La villana de Getafe* and his *La villana de la Sagra,* Tirso's *La villana de Vallecas* belongs to the group of Golden Age dramas whose protagonist is a village girl. All of these works deal with several commonplaces of the *comedia nacional* including ladies in disguise, honor code breeches, convoluted plots and, significantly, the condemnation of greed. In *La villana de Vallecas,* Doña Violante loses her virginity to the treacherous Don Gabriel de Herrera, who pretends to be Don Pedro de Mendoza. The damsel decides to restore her honor. After writing a letter to her brother Don Vicente about her case, she disguises herself in male attire and moves to Madrid accompanied by Vicente's servant Aguado. Meanwhile, the real Don Pedro de Mendoza, an indiano nobleman, travels to Madrid to marry Doña Serafín. On his way, he and his servant Agudo encounter Don Gabriel and the gracioso Cornejo. Agudo neglects to watch his master's suitcase and because of this, Don Gabriel accidentally takes the wrong suitcase with him the following morning. Don Gabriel steals the *indiano's* identity and marries Doña Serafín himself. In Madrid, he is showered with attention by Serafín's family and is adopted as the true Don Pedro. The latter, meanwhile, is dismayed to find out that he has lost all his marvelous possessions including several written documents that certify his identity. He travels to Madrid and tries to convince his prospective in-laws to welcome him by trusting his word. None of them, however, believe his story. At this point, Doña Violante appears dressed as a village girl who sells bread and meets Serafín's brother Don Juan, who falls madly in love with her. The real Don Pedro is thrown in jail for a crime committed by Don Gabriel in Flanders and also for dishonoring Doña Violante who, disguised as an indiana, has convinced Doña Serafín's brother (Don Juan) that Don Pedro (Don Gabriel) has sworn to marry her. She changes costumes, once again disguising herself as a villana and asks Don Juan and his family to attend her wedding to a farmer. The indiano Don Pedro is also told to attend the wedding. At the wedding in Vallecas, Violante reveals her true identity and forces Don Gabriel to keep his word. Serafín marries the real Don Pedro, while Don Vicente and even Doña Serafín's brother, the despised Don Juan, are content with the wedding.

The plot of *La villana* includes many of Tirso's most characteristic tropes: cross-dressing, identity confusion among several characters, and passion as a motor for plot action. However, Tirso clearly converts honor and greed into the driving forces behind the actions of the upper-class characters. The indiano Don Pedro is the individual whose material possessions are most often described. Tirso devotes three scenes to counting Don Pedro's assets. In the first one, Pedro's encounter with the deceiver Don Gabriel, the indiano introduces himself as a criollo

> de Mejico, que es nombre
> Que dan las Indias al que en ella[s] nace;
> A su virey [*sic*] serví de gentil-hombre,
> Que a bien nacidos honra y satisface;
> La hacienda heredo a un padre y el renombre.
> (52)

[a Mexican creole, which is / how the Western Indies name their natives; I have served the Viceroy, who honors and cherishes the well-bred, as a gentleman. I have inherited my father's renown and belongings.]

Here, he briefly mentions his wealth along with his honor but does not go into detail. At a later point, however, the contents of his suitcase are revealed. In it Don Gabriel finds "joyas y dinero, / Que deben de valer cinco mil pesos, [. . .] cartas, libranzas y procesos" [jewels and money / that must be worth five thousand *pesos* [. . .] letters, records, checks] (55). The *maleta* is also described as a beehive of gold: "En fin, la maleta está / hecha una colmena [. . .] Y da panales de el oro que amas" [In sum, the suitcase is / like a beehive / [. . .] whose cells of gold you love] (84). In fact, according to Cornejo and Gabriel's counting, he has three bars of gold of a thousand ducats each; several jewels, a strip of diamonds, seven pearl necklaces, emeralds, a turtle's shell, an egg-sized nugget, nacre, and ivory.

In the third instance in which Don Pedro's wealth is enumerated, Tirso again describes Don Dinero's path to Madrid. When Don Pedro goes to doña Serafín's family to make clear he is the real Don Pedro, he goes on to describe the route of his own wealth. Don Pedro claims exaggeratedly that the value of his gold bars is thirty thousand pesos. Don Pedro prefers Sanlucar de Barrameda, that is, the port of Cádiz to Seville. Indeed he points out that he did not stop in the Casa de la Contratación (House of Contracts) as was mandated:

> No quisieron deseos de Castilla
> Detenerse en Sevilla registrando
> De su contratación tantos haberes,
> Ni hablar sus codiciosos mercaderes;
> Antes, por ver que entonces ocupados
> Andaban en registros y cobranzas,
> Para otro tiempo dilaté cuidados.
>
> (53)

[My desires to be in Castile / did not permit me to show in Seville to register / my belongings in its *contratación* / nor to talk to its greedy merchants. / When I saw that they were busy with registries and payments / I decided to put off the business for some other time.]

That is, Don Pedro avoids stopping to declare the value of his goods and instead smuggles his money into the country. Far from being a possible criticism of Don Pedro, I believe Tirso might be reflecting on the empire's flow of cash, which, indeed was related to contraband. As Henry Kamen puts it: "Smuggling became necessary in order to survive [. . .] The unofficial trade was in reality the dominant and therefore the official trade" (*Empire*, 472). Don Gómez reinforces the idea later when he also explains how long it takes to get money flowing in the country:

> Primero que en registros de la plata
> Negocie con papeles y averias
> Con la Contratación que en eso trata,
> Es fuerza consumir algunos dias
> Obligando ministros y oficiales,
> Confusos entre tantas mercancías.
>
> (Tirso, *La villana*, 94)

[It is customary that, prior to registering silver / one must negotiate papers and trades / with the *contratación*, which is devoted to it, / thus wasting a few days / obliging servants and ministers / who are confused among these goods.]

Commerce is a slow and tiresome activity. The entrance of cash into the country is in actuality not as rapid as Quevedo depicts it, but rather it is a complicated process which requires energy and time. The Casa de la Contratación was declared the main customs point by the Catholic monarchs in 1503, as one could see in the *Recopilación de las leyes de las Indias libro nono* (*Compilation of the Laws Concerning the Indies. Book 9*) for the "navegación, trato y comercio de nuestras Indias, Islas de Tierrafirme del mar Occeano" [navigation, trading and commerce of the Spanish Indies, isles and mainland of the "Ocean sea"] (f. lii v.). It also served as a judicial court for cases concerning trading. Tirso and Nicolás Monardes point out that the Casa de la Contratación does not forward negotiations, but it rather impedes them. Tirso portrays negatively the Casa in a harsh social criticism of the excessive bureaucratizing of the empire and even offers a solution. Since the sluggishness of the Casa forced merchants to bootleg their goods, contraband was the key to solve cash-flow problems for small merchants and indianos, represented in Don Pedro. It is clear that Tirso reflects a profound concern with money in his comedia. However, Tirso's play is in the end a comedy and deals more with desire than with material needs. I would like to argue, finally, that in Tirso's comedia (as well as in Quevedo's ballad) even the language of love reflects material exchanges among the characters.

THE CASE OF THE FAKE INDIANO:
DON DINERO AS DON JUAN

Since Don Juan is one of the most easily recognizable characters of Western culture, a brief summary of this figure seems in order. While the seducer is an eternal archetype in folklore, the conception of its early modern version (Don Juan) dates from Spain's Golden Age. The seventeenth-century authors Andrés de Claramonte and Tirso de Molina vie as Don Juan's fathers. Claramonte composed *Tan largo me lo fiais* around 1634–35, a play of deceit and desire where Don Juan is seen as a seducer. Tirso's own Don Juan is much more complex. Some time before *La villana de Vallecas*, Tirso wrote *El burlador de Sevilla* (1616, pub. 1627–29) where he utilizes Don Juan as an example of immoral behavior amongst the young nobility, a topic that Tirso tackles through a number of different characters throughout several plays. Tirso sets the plot in the fourteenth century, but the characters dress and behave anachronistically like seventeenth-century people. Don Juan flees Naples at night, after trying to seduce the Duchess Isabella, to find himself stranded by a storm on the Spanish coast. A young fisherwoman, Tisbea, shelters him and is seduced by Don Juan's charms. Don Juan rushes to Seville, where the news of his Neapolitan adventure has already preceded him. In Seville, he disguises himself in order to seduce Doña Ana. Her father, the Commander Don Gonzalo d'Ulloa, comes to her aid and dies under the sword of Don Juan. Don Juan retires to the country and after seducing Aminta, a peasant woman, meets his final punishment under the hand of the Golem-like figure of Don Gonzalo's statue who invites Don Juan for supper. Don Juan accepts the invitation where awaits a macabre feast during which the statue offers him its hand. Refusing his repentance, which comes too late, the Golem drags Don Juan into the fires of Hell. Being a post-Tridentine friar, it is not surprising that Tirso tinges his plot with several theological references and supports eternal punishment for hedonistic tendencies. After Tirso's character, Don Juan has had several famous avatars. Besides many others, one can mention the following.[9] Molière was the first to see Don Juan as sort of a spirit of the age and thus made his *Dom Juan ou le Festin de pierre* (1665) a representation of Spain's essence. Opposed to Tirso's theologically based character, Molière converted Don Juan into a rebel. In the late eighteenth century and early nineteenth century, a significant change occurred: Don Juan became a burlesque character. Mozart converted Don Juan into one of the icons of Western civilization in his *Don Giovanni,* (1787). Female desire plays a really important role in *Don Giovanni* for Donna Anna, Donna Elvira, and Zerlina are desiring subjects rather than objects of desire; the ultimate womanizer is turned into an object of desire in Mozart's burlesque.[10] In 1821, Lord Byron also saw the antihero in Don Juan and penned his *Don Juan* as a semipicaresque romance whose main character is seen as a crooked mirror for the women that he seduces and the societies he visits. The character returned to Spain in José Zorrilla's *Don Juan Tenorio* (1844), who transformed him into a sublime romantic hero working against the established order.

Although the romantics aggrandized enormously Don Juan's individualism, it is especially significant that throughout the centuries Don Juan has constantly been seen as a rebel against the system and the community, being punished in the Golden Age or hailed in later times. As Anthony Cascardi has argued, in *El burlador de Sevilla* Don Juan "unleash[es] free flows of desire

that disrupt the established order" (171). Don Juan thus serves as a destabilizing force since his travels, his arrogance, his charm, and his wealth allow him
not to abide by any rule. These characteristics permit the conflation of Don
Juan and Don Dinero in the minds of the Golden Age. As I previously mentioned, the obsession of Western culture with money could be traced to
Horace's *Odes* III.16. This poem describes Jupiter's seduction of Danäe:

> fore enim tutum iter et patens
> conuerso in pretium deo.
> aurum per medio ire satellites
> et perrumpere amat saxa potentius
> ictu fulmineo: concidit auguris
> Argivi domus ob lucrum
> Demersa exitio.
>   (*Opera* III.XVI.7–13)

[open once Jupiter had turned himself into money. / Gold loves to go
through the midst of / bodyguards and to break through stones more / pow-
erfully than a thunderbolt; because of money / the house of the Argive seer
fell, / overwhelmed by destruction.]

Jupiter's metamorphosis into golden rain to possess Danäe becomes, for
Horace, a symbol to analyze the role of money in overcoming all barriers
posed against the lover-seducer. The power of money and the power of desire
are thus equated, for both are able to subdue societal limits. Don Juan's seducing powers allow him to escape the strictures of the Early Modern power
structure: he is thus able to seduce duchesses and peasants alike as well as tick
off the bases of the ancien régime: honor and lineage. In the same fashion,
Don Dinero equates the noble and the layman, capital provides wealth and
power to the disowned. Desire and wealth, symbolically represented in the
figures of Don Juan and Don Dinero share societal functions for pre-modern
societies.

In their classic *Anti-Oedipus*, Gilles Deleuze and Félix Guattari have described how precapitalist societies restricted their economic development in
the hope of preventing the accumulation of capital, which might ultimately
destroy their basis (176). In a sense, this is the reason why *La Celestina* and *El
burlador de Sevilla* criticize money. Moreover, Hippocratic tradition held that
love was the equivalent of avarice. In the *Libro de los buenos proverbios,* one
finds: "El amor es cobdiçia que se faze en el coraçon y yuntasse en el mentiras
de la cobdiçia, y quanto mas fuere la cobdiçia fuerte, mas crece el cuydado y

la porfia y la quexa y el mucho velar" [Love is greed made in the heart where it joins with greedy lies, and the more greed grows, greater the pain and suffering and complaints and subterfuge grow] (147). The anonymous translation of Hunain's work is probably based on the commonplace confusion of *cupiditas* and *cobdicia*, which ultimately links money and desire. In his *Etymologiarum*, Isidore of Seville finds a common etymology for these two words "Cupidus a capiendo multum, id est accipiendo, vocatus" [*Cupidus* derives from 'to accumulate,' that is, 'to grab'] (809). Covarrubias also underscores this connection: "Codiciar. *Quasi* cupdiciar, de *cupiditas* se dixo cupdicia y codicia, y de alli codiciar, codicioso, etc" [to want, almost to codiciate, of *cupiditas* we derive cupdicia and codicia, and hence greed, greedy, etc.] (331b).

Don Dinero thus resembles Don Juan's archetype: the seducer who breaks away from the norms to satisfy his desire, destabilizing society in the process. They are both motivated by greed and desire. Quevedo's *Don Dinero* is, after all, a satirical love ballad "él es mi amante y mi amado" [gold is my lover and beloved], where Quevedo outlines the connection between the typical Hippocratic description of lovesickness "de contino anda amarillo" [he is costantly tinged with gold] and a witty reference to the color of gold: "Amarillo." Lamentations of love are equated with lamentations of money. Finally, like Tirso's Don Juan, Quevedo's Don Dinero is able to break away from the old structures: "[Don Dinero] da y quita el decoro / y quebranta cualquier fuero" [(Money) gives and takes *decorum* / and breeches every right].

Tirso's *La villana de Vallecas* also illustrates the intertwining of desire and money. At the beginning of the play, Don Vicente laments doña Violante's indiscretions with Don Gabriel:

> ¡Sin honra doña Violante!
> Tras la hacienda que he perdido,
> La joya más importante
> Pierdo también: ¡el honor
> Que de mi padre heredé!
> ¡El patrimonio mejor,
> que en Valencia espejo fue
> de la nobleza y valor!
>
> (11)

[Doña Violante without honor! / Along with losing my belongings I have lost / the most important jewel: / the honor I received from my father! / That great patrimony / that was in Valencia a model of nobility and value!]

In his complaint, Don Vicente equates his sister's deflowering to the loss of their patrimony. Tirso is presumably following the medieval tradition of viewing marriage as a form of bartering. This equation is common in preindustrial societies. As Claude Lévi-Strauss argues in *The Elementary Structures of Kinship*, "marriage is the archetype of exchange" (483). Doña Violante's virginity is thus seen as a jewel, a marketable good. Don Vicente, known for his taste in games and debauchery, complains that a gambler has tricked him and stripped him of his fortune and inheritance. His sister's symbolic value resides in her honor which is compared to a possession: a jewel. The seducer, Don Gabriel, has stolen her market value.

Tirso underscores Don Pedro's dowry and inheritance before Pedro starts his journeys to marry Serafín. Serafín's main possession is symbolic, for her honor is constantly compared to a marketable good. Her reputation follows the path of the ships that journeyed westward from the Peninsula to the Indies to obtain gold. Serafín and Don Pedro's love letters are indeed sent with the ships: "Siendo estafetas una y otra armada" [being one or the other battleship our postal couriers] (*La villana,* 52). Here rumor and gossip are the channels of communication between the lovers, and Don Pedro is amazed to find out that Serafín's fame has arrived "Limpia a Mejico, y a prueba / De las lenguas" [pristine to Mexico, and also / slanderer-proof] (25). Doña Serafín's has a high market value.

Tirso's reflections on the power of money involve the commonplace theatrical device of the exchanging of personalities. Don Pedro de Mendoza encounters Don Gabriel, a Don Juan figure. The latter, after trading suitcases, goods and beloveds, pretends to be the former. Don Gabriel steals name, capital, fiancé and good fortune from Don Pedro, who claims that "Sin duda / la fortuna se me muda / después que el nombre he mudado" [Without a doubt / my Fortune changed / after I switched my name] (261). Don Pedro, an indiano Don Dinero, and Don Gabriel, a Don Juan, exchange personalities and trades and are thus equated. While Don Gabriel is greedy for Don Pedro's possessions (including his marriage), Don Pedro desires to marry Serafín for her virtue. Arguably, Tirso follows the Horatian motive and the medieval tradition and uses his characters to represent *cobdicia* (greed) and *cupiditas* (desire). In Golden Age terms, we could say that Don Dinero meets Don Juan. Tirso also adds the transatlantic component to the equation of money and love and thus outlines Don Pedro and Don Gabriel's exchangeability by geographical references. Don Pedro comes from the western Indies and journeys eastward to Sanlúcar, then to Cuenca and finally to Arganda. He does not stop in Seville and does not certify his possessions. Don Gabriel de Herrera is born in Granada, goes to war in Flanders, and escapes from battle to Valencia and then moves westward to Arganda. They both meet at a central point in Spain's geography. Don Gabriel becomes both a rich indiano (Don Dinero) and a Don Juan figure who disrupts the social order for the love of money. Tirso clearly explains that "Bravo tentador / Es el oro, del amor!" [Gold is a great tempter of love] (88).

In the end, Doña Violante solves the riddle of the loss of her dowry/honor by invoking the power of trading herself. She exchanges her peasant costume for that of an indiana. Doña Violante pretends to be Doña Inés and tells Doña Serafín's brother, Don Juan, a story in which she has been wooed by Don Pedro after his promising to marry her. With her new mask, Violante is obviously reflecting her own story with the seducer Don Gabriel and is capable of reprimanding Don Gabriel for his misbehavior. Violante's language also reflects the play's equation of love and money. Don Pedro/Don Gabriel owes her: "Porque el ingrato deudor / Tarde paga y presto olvida" [Since the ungrateful debtor / pays late and easily forgets] (213). In her narrative doña Violante/Doña Inés equates Tirso's previous couples. She treats Don Pedro (Don Dinero) as a Don Juan seducer, and in this way restores social order. If the exchange of personalities between Don Pedro and Don Gabriel threatened to depreciate her own exchange with Don Gabriel, her trading the personalities of Don Gabriel and Don Pedro puts everything back in place. In Tirso's play, Don Juan and Don Dinero are interchangeable only insofar as the real creditor appears to claim her right to repossess her wealth.

In sum, Tirso's *La villana de Vallecas*, an under-studied but valuable work, underscores the material world underlying the supposedly idealistic *comedia nacional*. Tirso's characters are driven by their will to possess both money and love, which become almost indistinguishable. This reading is grounded both in the historical context of the comedia and in a traditional topos that equates desire and money, for they both serve to destabilize society alike. Seduction, represented in the Don Juan figure, attacks the pillars of Spain's rigid estate system based on honor and lineage. The wealth that is extracted from the Indies, refracted into the Don Dinero character, equalizes the noble and rich third estate merchants. Finally, personifications of Don Dinero and Don Juan, two of the most influential characters of Spanish literature (both of the Golden Age and later times), are, in fact, intertwined in Tirso's work. Don Juan encounters Don Dinero in an exchange of wealth and love.

NOTES

1. It should be clarified that I am using the term *indiano* throughout this piece as an adjective with the Golden Age sense of somebody born of Spanish descent in the Americas, and not as a noun meaning somebody who travels to America and returns to Castile with acquired wealth.

2. De Santillana defines the Renaissance as "The age of the unearthing of great texts, of the introduction of Greek, of brave hopes and memorable formulations of the dignity of man. It is also the age of the printing press and the discovery of America. It culminates in those decades between 1500 and 1520, which brought forth perhaps the greatest density of significant production that history can remember" (*Age of Adventure,* 17). Jacob Burckhardt states that with Neoplatonism "one of the most precious fruits of the knowledge of the world and of man here comes to maturity, on whose account alone the Italian Renaissance must be called the leader of the modern ages" (*Civilization,* 410).

3. The concept of the West Indies in Cervantes's work has been addressed from a different viewpoint in a groundbreaking essay by James Fernández, which studies the many mentions of America in *El celoso extremeño* to reveal how the discourses of race and gender, the concerns of colonialism and humanism, are ultimately intertwined.

4. My notion of the term "cultural memory" as well as the limits of the new historicist tool to conflate text and context without giving attention to previous literary history is heavily indebted to David Quint's *Epic and Empire* (15).

5. As John G. Cawelti points out in his study of the recreations of the Al Capone-like hero in post-30s film: "in most of the fictional versions of Capone—Little Caesar and Scarface, for instance—the tragic protagonist was literally killed. Thus the gangster hero became a kind of tragic scapegoat for the corruption and violence that surrounded his rise. . . . The Capone hero was blatantly lower-class and despite his rapid rise to wealth and power, he stayed that way" ("New Mythology," 333). Tony Montana's ultimate downfall is a harsh moral criticism of fast cash.

6. Although I reproduce Jill R. Webster's canonical translation of the *Libro de buen amor,* I would like to offer an alternative translation that underscores the intertwining of money and desire underlying Juan Ruiz's paragraph: "All in all, I advise you to take advantage of it, money is the great shaker of the world. It turns the servant into the master, the master into the servant and all things everywhere obey its call of love." Unless otherwise noted, all translations are mine.

7. The ballad is typically studied along with "Vuela, pensamiento, y diles / a los ojos que más quiero / que hay dinero" [Fly, thought, and tell / the eyes I adore: / there is money] (Quevedo, *Poesía Original,* 659). Pablo Jauralde Pou has convincingly argued that Quevedo patterned this last ballad after Góngora's *letrilla* "Vuela, pensamiento, y diles / a los ojos que más quiero / que eres mío" [Fly, thought, and tell the eyes I adore: / you are mine] [(Quevedo, 901). In his edition of Góngora's *Letrillas,* Robert Jammes argues that Quevedo copied not Góngora but Alonso de Ledesma who composed a ballad with the same chorus (67).

8. José Antonio Maravall has explained that "Quevedo no rechaza el medro económico. Condena, claro está, la riqueza conseguida con medios ilícitos, mas no la que se alcanza honestamente. Y aún a esta, eso es cierto, le pone un límite" [Quevedo does not reject economic development. He condemns wealth obtained by illicit means, but not wealth honestly earned. But it is true that he puts a limit on the latter] ("Pensamiento," 113).

9. Let it be noted that Doña Serafín's brother, Don Juan, has nothing to do with Don Juan as an archetype of the seducer. In Tirso's *Villana,* the only character who behaves in a don-juanesque fashion is Don Gabriel de Herrera who tries to seduce Doña Violante.

10. For a good summary of the Don Juan figure, see Christian Biet's essay (*Don Juan*) on the thousand and three versions of the Don Juan as well as Pierre Brunel's *Dictionnaire.* James Mandrell has analyzed the figure from a historical and psychological standpoint in his *Don Juan and the Point of Honor.*

11. It is fascinating to consider what a real-life Don Juan, Giacomo Casanova, who attended the Prague premier of *Don Giovanni* and, much like Don Juan, kept record of his numerous erotic conquests, might have made of these womens' desires.

WORKS CITED

Burckhardt, Jacob. *The Civilization of the Renaissance in Italy.* Edited by Hajo Holborn. New York: Modern Library, 1952.

Biet, Christian. *Don Juan, Mille et trois récits d'un mythe.* Paris: Gallimard, 1998.

Brunel, Pierre. *Dictionnaire de Don Juan.* Paris: Robert Laffont, 1999.

Calderón de la Barca, Pedro. *Las fortunas de Andromeda y Perseo. Sexta parte de Comedias de . . . Don Pedro Calderon de la Barca . . . que corregidas por sus originales pvblica Don Juan de Vera Tassis y Villarroel.* Madrid: Francisco Sanz, 1683. Digital edition TESO, http://teso.chadwyck.com.

Cawelti. John G. "*The New Mythology of Crime.*" *Boundary* 23, No. 2 (Winter 1975): 324–57.

Caxa de Leruela, Miguel. *Restauración de la abundancia de España.* Edited by Jean Paul Le Flem. [Madrid: 1631]. Madrid: Instituto de Estudios Fiscales, 1975.

Covarrubias Orozco, Sebastián de. *Tesoro de la Lengua Castellana.* Salamanca: Anaya, 1986.

Deleuze, Gilles and Félix Guattari. *Anti-Oedipus: Capitalism and Schizophrenia.* Translated by Hurley, Seem, and Lane. Minneapolis: University of Minnesota Press, 1983.

de Santillana, Giorgio de. *The Age of Adventure.* New York: Mentor, 1956.

Fernández, James. "The Bonds of Patrimony: Cervantes and the New World." *PMLA: Publications of the Modern Language Association of America* 109, No. 5 (1994): 969–81.

Fuchs, Barbara. "*Empire Unmanned: Gender Trouble and Genoese Gold in Cervantes's 'The Two Damsels'* " *PMLA: Publications of the Modern Language Association of America* 116, No. 2 (2001): 285–99.

Góngora, Luis de, *Letrillas.* Edited by Robert Jammes. Madrid: Castalia, 1980.

———. *Soledades.* Edited by John Beverley. Madrid: Cátedra, 1980.

Horati. [Horace] *Opera.* Edited by Edward Wickham. Oxford: Clarendon, 1901.

Isidore of Seville. *Etymologiarum. Etimologías. Edición Bilingüe.* Edited by Manuel Díaz y Díaz. Madrid: Editorial Católica, 1972.

Jardine, Lisa. *Worldly Goods: A New History of the Renaissance.* London: Macmillan, 1996.

Jauralde Pou, Pablo. *Francisco de Quevedo (1580-1645).* Madrid: Castalia, 1999.

Johnson, Carroll B. *Cervantes and the Material World.* Chicago: University of Illinois Press, 2000.

Kamen, Henry. *Empire: How Spain Became a World Power, 1492-1763*. New York: Harper-Collins, 2003.

Lévi-Strauss, Claude. *The Elementary Structures of Kinship*. Translated by Rodney Needham. Boston: Beacon, 1969.

Libro de los buenos proverbios: A Critical Edition. Edited by Harlan Sturm. Lexington: University Press of Kentucky, 1970.

Mandrell, James B. *Don Juan and the Point of Honor: Seduction, Patriarchal Society, and Literary Tradition*. University Park: University of Pennsylvania State Press, 1992.

Maravall, José Antonio. "Sobre el pensamiento social y político de Quevedo (Una revisión)". In *Academia Literaria Renacentista. Homenaje a Quevedo*. Edited by Víctor García de la Concha, 69-131. Salamanca: Universidad de Salamanca Press, 1982.

Molina, Luis de. *Tratado sobre los prstamos y la usura*. Edited by Francisco Gómez Camacho. Madrid: Instituto de Cooperación Iberoamericana [Instituto de Estudios Fiscales], 1989.

Monardes, Nicolás. *Diálogo del hierro y de sus grandezas*. Edited by Modesto Bargalló y Francisco Guerra. México: Compañía Fundidora de Fierro y Acero de Monterrey, 1961.

Quevedo, Francisco de. *Poesía original completa*. Edited by José Manuel Blecua. Madrid: Planeta, 1981.

Quint, David. *Epic and Empire: Politics and Generic Form from Virgil to Milton*. Princeton, N.J.: Princeton University Press, 1993.

Recopilación de leyes de las Indias by Consejo de Indias. Archivo Digital de la Legislación del Perú (ADLP)]. *http://www.leyes.congreso.gob.pe/LeyIndiaP.htm*.

Rojas, Fernando de. *La Celestina: Tragicomedia de Calisto y Melibea*. Edited by Francisco Lobera, Guillermo Serés, Palona Díaz-Mas, Carlos Mota, Íñigo Ruiz Arzalluz and Francisco Rico. Barcelona: Crítica, 2000.

―――. *Celestina or the Tragi-Comedy of Calisto and Melibea*. Translated by James Mabbe and Eric Bentley. New York: Applause, 1992.

Ruiz, Juan. "The Evils of Money and Drink." Translated by Jill R. Webster. In *Medieval Iberia: Readings from Christian, Muslim, and Jewish Sources*. Edited by Olivia Remie Constable, 288-91. Philadelphia: University of Pennsylvania Press, 1999.

―――. *Libro de buen amor*. Edited by Alberto Blecua. Madrid: Cátedra, 1992.

Tirso de Molina. *El burlador de Sevilla*. Edited by Mercedes Sánchez Sánches. Madrid: Castalia, 1997.

―――. *La villana de la Sagra. El colmenero divino*. Edited by Berta Pallares. Madrid: Castalia, 1999.

―――. *La lealtad contra la envidia. Doze comedias nuevas de Tirso de Molina*. Valencia: Pedro Mey, 1631. Digital edition TESO. http://teso.chadwyck.com/.

―――. *La villana de Vallecas*. Edited by Adolfo Bonilla y San Martín. Madrid: Ruiz Hermanos Editores, 1916.

Vega Carpio, Lope Félix. *El amante agradecido*. Decima parte de las comedias de Lope de Vega Carpio . . . sacadas de svs originales. Dirigidas por el mismo al Excelentissimo señor Marques de Santacruz. Madrid: Alonso Martín de Balboa, 1618. Digital edition TESO. http://teso.chadwyck.com/.

————. *Amar, servir, y esperar. Decima parte de las comedias de Lope de Vega Carpio . . . sacadas de svs originales. Dirigidas por el mismo al Excelentissimo señor Marques de Santacruz.* Madrid: Alonso Martín de Balboa, 1618. Digital edition TESO. http://teso.chadwyck.com/.

————. *De cosario a cosario. Parte decinveve y la meior parte de las comedias de Lope de Vega Carpio . . . Dirigidas a diversas personas.* Madrid: Iuan Gonçalez., 1624. Digital edition TESO. http://teso.chadwyck.com/.

————. *Pobreza no es vileza. Parte veinte de las comedias de Lope de Vega Carpio . . . dividida en dos partes.* Madrid : Alonso Martin, 1625. Digital edition TESO. http://teso.chadwyck.com/.

————. *El sembrar en buena tierra. Decima parte de las comedias de Lope de Vega Carpio . . . sacadas de svs originales. Dirigidas por el mismo al Excelentissimo señor Marques de Santacruz.* Madrid: Alonso Martin de Balboa, 1618. Digital edition TESO. http://teso.chadwyck.com/.

————. *El testigo contra si.* El Fenix de España Lope de Vega Carpio . . . Sexta parte de svs comedias. Dirigidas a Don Pedro Docon y Trillo. Madrid: Alonso Martín, 1615. Digital edition TESO. http://teso.chadwyck.com/.

Contributors

Mindy E. Badía earned a PhD from Indiana University, Bloomington with a major in Hispanic Literature and a minor in French Literature. She was an assistant professor at the University of Arkansas (Fayetteville, Arkansas) from 1996–2000 and has taught at Indiana University Southeast since 2000, where she is now an associate professor. Her principal research interest is early modern Spanish drama, especially contemporary performance of the Comedia. She has published articles on plays (and performances of plays) by Lope de Vega, Calderón de la Barca, Tirso de Molina, and Juan Ruiz de Alarcón. She is a member of the Association Internacional de Teatro Español y Novohispano de los Siglos de Oro (AITENSO) and the Association for Hispanic Classical Theater (AHCT), and since 2000 has served as an elected member of the AHCT's board of directors.

Yolanda Gamboa (PhD, Purdue University) has taught at the University of South Africa (UNISA) and is currently Assistant Professor of Spanish literature at Florida Atlantic University in Boca Raton, Florida. Her publications have appeared in *Hispanic Review*, *The University of South Africa Press*, and *RLA*. In her manuscript in progress, "Mapas, cuerpos y estado moderno en la narrativa de María de Zayas" [Maps, Bodies, and the Modern State in the Narrative of Maria de Zayas], she explores the work of Maria de Zayas by delving into the cultural and material world of seventeenth-century Spain. She combines her interest in early modernity with literary translation as a form of criticism and contribution to the canon. One such example is her recent critical translation of *The World as a Work of Art: A Western Story* (Bucknell University Press, 2005).

Christopher D. Gascón is an Assistant Professor of Spanish at the State University of New York College at Cortland. His work includes a book-length study, *The Woman Saint in the Spanish Golden Age Drama* (Bucknell University Press, 2006), and articles and reviews that have appeared in the *Bulletin of the Comediantes* and *Comedia Performance*. A member of the Board of Direc- . tors of the Association for Hispanic Classical Theater, he is engaged in the promotion and study of contemporary stagings of Spanish Golden Age drama. His research includes analyses of post-September 11 performances of the *comedia*.

Bonnie L. Gasior is an Assistant Professor of Spanish at California State University, Long Beach. Her research, which centers on gender issues in sixteenth- and seventeenth-century Spain and Spanish America, includes articles and reviews with: *Romance Languages Annual, Cuaderno Internacional de Estudios Hispánicos y Lingüística, Asociación Internacional de literatura femenina hispánica, Jornadas Metropolitanas, Charles University Press* (Prague), *ASECS, Comedia Performance,* and *Journal of Research in International Education*. She is currently working on a book-length study, funded in part by Spain's Ministry of Culture and the College of Liberal Arts at CSULB, on manifestations of female monstosity in select dramatic works of the Early Modern period.

Michael J. Horswell is an associate professor of Spanish and Latin American literature at Florida Atlantic University. He is the author of the book *Decolonizing the Sodomite: Queer Tropes of Sexuality in Colonial Andean Culture* (2005) as well as articles and book chapters on issues of gender and sexuality in Latin American literature. He is currently working on a new project exploring hybridity theory in transatlantic studies.

Eric J. Kartchner is Associate Professor of Spanish at Colorado State University-Pueblo. He has published *Unhappily Ever After: Deceptive Idealism in Cervantes's Marriage Tales* (2005). His work has also appeared in the *Bulletin of the Comediantes, Yearbook of Comparative and General Literature, Cincinnati Romance Review, RLA,* and other journals, as well as in scholarly editions.

Bradley J. Nelson is currently Associate Professor and Chair of Classics, Modern Languages, and Linguistics at Concordia University in Montreal. His work has appeared in the *Bulletin of the Comediantes, Cervantes, Gestos,* and several volumes of the series *Hispanic Issues*. He has recently completed a manuscript on emblematic and allegorical modes of discourse in Early Modern Spain entitled *The Persistence of Presence: Emblem and Ritual in Early Modern Spain*.

Vicente Pérez de León is Assistant Professor of Hispanic Studies at Oberlin College. He has published *Tablas destempladas. Los entremeses de Cervantes a examen* (2005). His work has also appeared in scholarly journals such as *Hispania*, the *Bulletin of the Comediantes,* and *Hispanófila.* His research interests include Golden Age short drama and early modern journalism and medicine.

Julio Vélez-Sainz is Assistant Professor at the University of Massachusetts at Amherst. His work has centered on medieval and Golden Age Spanish literature. His anthology of Quevedo's works was published in Editorial Eneida in 2005 and his study of Golden Age poetry was published in Editorial Visor in the same year. He has also published articles on writers such as Cervantes, Quevedo, Sor Juana, Álvaro de Luna, and Góngora among others in journals such as *Cervantes,* the *Bulletin of the Comediantes, Hispanófila, La Corónica,* the *Dictionary of Literary Biography,* and Editorial Castalia. His current research deals with fifteenth-century Spanish defenses of women and the poetic quarrel between Quevedo and Góngora.

Index